# BASIC SPANISH GRAMMAR

# BASIC
# SPANISH
# GRAMMAR

ANA C. JARVIS
San Bernardino Valley College

RAQUEL LEBREDO
California Baptist College

FRANCISCO MENA
California State University, Chico

D. C. HEATH AND COMPANY
Lexington, Massachusetts    Toronto

Cover: Pablo Picasso, *The Reader*, Collection of the
Art Institute of Chicago.

All photographs by Peter Menzel.

Published simultaneously in Canada.

Printed in the United States of America.

International Standard Book Number: 0-669-03086-4

Library of Congress Catalog Card Number: 79-89554

# Preface

*Basic Spanish Grammar* is a guide to the essential points of Spanish grammar for students whose professions require a working knowledge of Spanish. It presents concise, simple explanations of the structures that are indispensable for communication. Each grammatical concept is illustrated by means of brief conversational exchanges. This method first exposes students to a specific point of grammar, and then demonstrates its correct usage in a natural, everyday situation.

This textbook is the nucleus of a complete Spanish program, which contains various workbooks and tapes specifically designed for different professions: Business and Finance, Law Enforcement, Medicine, Teaching, and Social Services.

Each workbook presents specific vocabulary needed for a given profession. Each lesson in the workbooks parallels the same lesson in the basic text. This means that the student will simultaneously be exposed to a grammatical structure explained in the principal text and to the practical application of that structure in the corresponding workbook.

In addition to the workbooks for professionals, the program includes a workbook designed for practical communication. Every effort has been made in this workbook to develop realistic, practical dialogues and situational exercises that emphasize normal daily communication.

Students studying Spanish for professional reasons have specific needs and limited study time. Aware of the unique situation of these students, we have endeavored to present the material in a way that facilitates its use for individualized instruction.

*Basic Spanish Grammar* includes:

1. A preliminary lesson that consists of words and expressions useful to persons in every walk of life (i.e., personal data, greetings and farewells, etc.).

2. Twenty lessons, each containing:
   - Grammatical structures
   - Conversational exchanges illustrating each grammatical point
   - Exercises to practice and reinforce each concept
   - A study of cognates
   - New vocabulary introduced in the lesson. Every effort has been made to include high-frequency words and expressions.
3. A self-testing section after every five lessons. Answer keys are provided in the appendix.
4. The following appendices:
   - Rules governing Spanish pronunciation
   - Verb paradigms
   - Glossary of useful grammatical terms.
   - List of careers and occupations
   - Answer key for self-testing sections
5. An end vocabulary including:
   - Spanish-English vocabulary
   - English-Spanish vocabulary
6. Index

## Workbooks

Lesson formats are generally as follows:

1. Dialogues presenting situations characteristic of each specific profession. For example, "At the Doctor's Office" and "In the Emergency Room" are two such dialogues in the workbook for medical personnel.
2. Study of cognates
3. Pertinent vocabulary
4. Dialogue recall practice
5. Grammatical structure exercises
6. Question-answer exercise
7. Dialogue completion
8. Situational exercise
9. Class activity

Vocabulary reviews are presented after every five lessons. An end vocabulary includes both a Spanish-English vocabulary and an English-Spanish vocabulary.

## Tape Programs

A tape program consisting of four cassettes (approximately four hours duration) accompanies each workbook. The program for communication consists of six cassettes of approximately six hours duration. This material provides additional practice in listening-comprehension.

Several textbooks have been written for use in Spanish courses geared to the different professions. *Basic Spanish Grammar*, with its workbooks and cassettes is the first *complete* program that teaches communication skills through the correct use of vocabulary pertinent to a given profession in its appropriate grammatical structure.

We would like to express our appreciation to Professors Milton Azevedo, University of California, Berkeley, and T. Bruce Fryer, University of South Carolina, for their constructive criticism. Special thanks are due the members of the editorial staff of D. C. Heath and Company for their many valuable suggestions, which have substantially enhanced the quality of the manuscript.

A.C.J.

R.L.

F.M.

# Contents

## PRELIMINARY LESSON

| | |
|---|---|
| 1. Personal data | 2 |
| 2. Greetings and farewells | 3 |
| 3. Days of the week | 5 |
| 4. Cardinal numbers (0–31) | 6 |
| 5. Months and seasons of the year | 6 |

## LESSON 1

| | |
|---|---|
| 1. Subject pronouns | 10 |
| 2. Present indicative of regular -ar verbs | 11 |
| 3. Interrogative sentences | 12 |
| 4. Negative sentences | 13 |
| 5. Gender | 14 |
| 6. Cardinal numbers (31–200) | 15 |

## LESSON 2

| | |
|---|---|
| 1. Plural forms | 18 |
| 2. The definite article | 18 |
| 3. Position of adjectives | 19 |
| 4. Forms of adjectives | 19 |
| 5. Agreement of articles, adjectives, and nouns | 20 |

6. Present indicative of **-er** and **-ir** verbs          20
7. The personal **a**                                      21

### LESSON 3

1. Possession with **de**                                  26
2. Possessive adjectives                                   26
3. The indefinite article                                  27
4. Present indicative of **ser**                           28
5. The irregular verbs **ir, dar,** and **estar**          29

### LESSON 4

1. The verbs **ser** and **estar** (summary of uses)       32
2. Contractions                                            33
3. The comparison of adjectives and adverbs                34
4. The irregular comparison of adjectives and
   adverbs                                                 36
5. The irregular verbs **tener** and **venir**             37
6. Cardinal numbers (200–1000)                             38

### LESSON 5

1. Expressions with **tener**                              42
2. Telling time                                            43
3. Stem-changing verbs (**e** > **ie**)                    44
4. **Ir a** + infinitive                                   45
5. The uses of **hay**                                     46

TEST YOURSELF: LESSONS 1–5          48

### LESSON 6

1. Some uses of the definite article                       58
2. Stem-changing verbs (**o** > **ue**)                    59
3. Affirmative and negative expressions                    60
4. Ordinal numbers and their uses                          61
5. Uses of **tener que** and **hay que**                   62

## LESSON 7

1. Stem-changing verbs (**e** > **i**) 66
2. More about irregular verbs 67
3. The impersonal **se** 68
4. Direct object pronouns 69
5. **Saber** vs. **Conocer** 71
6. Formation of adverbs 72

## LESSON 8

1. Demonstrative adjectives 76
2. Demonstrative pronouns 77
3. Present progressive 78
4. Indirect object pronouns 79
5. Direct and indirect object pronouns used together 81
6. **Pedir** vs. **Preguntar** 82

## LESSON 9

1. Possessive pronouns 86
2. Reflexive constructions 88
3. The command forms (**Ud.** and **Uds.**) 90
4. Uses of object pronouns with the command forms 92

## LESSON 10

1. Preterit of regular verbs 98
2. Preterit of **ser, ir,** and **dar** 99
3. The expression **acabar de** 100
4. The absolute superlative 100
5. Weather expressions 101

TEST YOURSELF: LESSONS 6–10     104

## LESSON 11

| | |
|---|---|
| 1. Time expressions with **hacer** and **llevar** | 112 |
| 2. Irregular preterits | 113 |
| 3. **¿De quién. . .?** for "whose?" | 114 |
| 4. The imperfect tense | 115 |

## LESSON 12

| | |
|---|---|
| 1. The past progressive | 120 |
| 2. Preterit vs. imperfect | 120 |
| 3. **En** and **a** for "at" | 122 |
| 4. Changes in meaning with imperfect and preterit of **conocer, saber, querer,** and **poder** | 123 |

## LESSON 13

| | |
|---|---|
| 1. More about irregular preterits | 128 |
| 2. Uses of **por** and **para** | 129 |
| 3. Special construction with **gustar, doler,** and **hacer falta** | 130 |
| 4. Pronouns as object of a preposition | 132 |

## LESSON 14

| | |
|---|---|
| 1. **Qué** and **cuál** for "what" | 136 |
| 2. **Hace** meaning "ago" | 137 |
| 3. Uses of **hacía . . . que** | 137 |
| 4. More uses of the definite article | 138 |
| 5. Past participles | 139 |

## LESSON 15

| | |
|---|---|
| 1. The present perfect tense | 142 |
| 2. The past perfect tense (pluperfect) | 143 |
| 3. Past participles used as adjectives | 144 |
| 4. Diminutive suffixes | 144 |
| TEST YOURSELF: LESSONS 11–15 | 147 |

## LESSON 16

1. The future tense 156
2. The conditional tense 158
3. The present subjunctive 160
   a. Use of the present subjunctive 160
   b. Formation of the present subjunctive 161
   c. Subjunctive forms of stem-changing verbs 162
   d. Verbs that are irregular in the subjunctive 162

## LESSON 17

1. The subjunctive in indirect or implied commands 166
2. The subjunctive to express emotion 167
3. The subjunctive with impersonal expressions 168

## LESSON 18

1. The subjunctive to express doubt and unreality 172
2. The familiar command (tú form) 175
   a. The affirmative command 175
   b. The negative command 176

## LESSON 19

1. The subjunctive after conjunctions implying uncertainty or unfulfillment 180
2. The present perfect subjunctive 181
3. Uses of the present perfect subjunctive 182

## LESSON 20

1. The imperfect subjunctive 186
2. Uses of the imperfect subjunctive 186
3. "If" clauses 188

TEST YOURSELF: LESSONS 15–20 190

### APPENDICES

A. Pronunciation                             199
B. Verbs                                     213
C. Glossary of Grammatical Terms             231
D. Careers and Occupations                   233
E. Answer Key to Self-testing Sections       235

### VOCABULARY

Spanish-English                              247
English-Spanish                              255

### INDEX

                                             263

# BASIC SPANISH GRAMMAR

# Preliminary Lesson

# 1. PERSONAL DATA

| | |
|---|---|
| ¿Nombre y apellido? | *Name and surname?* |
| María Valdés. | *María Valdés.* |
| ¿Estado civil? | *Marital status?* |
| Casada. | *Married.* |
| ¿Apellido de soltera? | *Maiden name?* |
| Rivas. | *Rivas.* |
| ¿Nacionalidad? | *Nationality?* |
| Argentina. | *Argentinian.* |
| ¿Lugar de nacimiento? | *Place of birth?* |
| Buenos Aires. | *Buenos Aires.* |
| ¿Edad? | *Age?* |
| Veinte años. | *Twenty (years old).* |
| ¿Ocupación? | *Occupation?* |
| Estudiante. | *Student.* |
| ¿Dirección? | *Address?* |
| Calle Magnolia,[1] número veinte. | *Number twenty, Magnolia Street.* |
| ¿Ciudad? | *City?* |
| Riverside. | *Riverside.* |

## VOCABULARY: PERSONAL DATA

| | | | |
|---|---|---|---|
| los años | years | divorciado | divorced (*masculine*) |
| el apellido | surname | | |
| el apellido de soltera | maiden name | la edad | age |
| | | el estado civil | marital status |
| la calle | street | la fecha de nacimiento | date of birth |
| casada | married (*feminine*) | | |
| | | femenino | feminine |
| casado | married (*masculine*) | el lugar de nacimiento | place of birth |
| la ciudad | city | | |
| la dirección, el domicilio | address | el lugar donde trabaja | place of work |
| | | masculino | masculine |
| divorciada | divorced (*feminine*) | la naciona-lidad | nationality |

[1] In Spanish, the name of the street is placed before the number.

| | | | |
|---|---|---|---|
| el nombre | name | la ocupación | occupation[1] |
| norteamericana | North American (*feminine*) | separada | separated (*feminine*) |
| norteamericano | North American (*masculine*) | separado | separated (*masculine*) |
| el número | number | el sexo | sex |
| el número de la licencia para conducir | driver's license number | soltera | single (*feminine*) |
| | | soltero | single (*masculine*) |
| | | el teléfono | telephone |
| | | la viuda | widow |
| el número de seguro social | social security number | el viudo | widower |
| | | y | and |

## Exercise

Ask the person next to you the following questions:

1. ¿Nombre y apellido?
2. ¿Estado civil?
3. ¿Apellido de soltera? (If you are talking to a married woman.)
4. ¿Nacionalidad?
5. ¿Lugar de nacimiento?
6. ¿Ocupación?
7. ¿Dirección? (¿Domicilio?)
8. ¿Ciudad?

## 2. GREETINGS AND FAREWELLS

**Buenos días, doctor Rivas. ¿Cómo está usted?**
*Good morning, Doctor Rivas. How are you?*

**Muy bien, gracias. ¿Y usted?**
*Very well, thank you. And you?*

**Bien, gracias. Hasta luego. Adiós.**
*Fine, thank you. See you later. Good-bye.*

**Mucho gusto, profesor Vera.**
*A pleasure to meet you, Professor Vera.*

**El gusto es mío, señorita Reyes.**
*The pleasure is mine, Miss Reyes.*

[1] For a list of occupations, see Appendix.

| | |
|---|---|
| Buenas tardes, señora. | *Good afternoon, madam.* |
| Buenas tardes, señor. | *Good afternoon, sir.* |
| Pase y tome asiento, por favor. | *Come in and sit down, please.* |
| Gracias. | *Thank you.* |
| | |
| Buenas noches, señorita. | *Good evening, miss.* |
| ¿Cómo está usted? | *How are you?* |
| No muy bien, doctor. | *Not very well, doctor.* |
| Lo siento. Hasta mañana. | *I'm sorry. I'll see you tomorrow.* |
| | |
| Muchas gracias, señora. | *Thank you very much, madam.* |
| De nada, señor. Adiós. | *You're welcome, sir. Good-bye.* |

## VOCABULARY

### GREETINGS AND FAREWELLS

| | |
|---|---|
| Adiós. | Good-bye. |
| Buenas noches. | Good evening. (Good night.) |
| Buenas tardes. | Good afternoon. |
| Buenos días. | Good morning. (Good day.) |
| ¿Cómo está usted? | How are you? |
| El gusto es mío. | The pleasure is mine. |
| Hasta luego. | I'll see you later. |
| Hasta mañana. | I'll see you tomorrow. |
| Mucho gusto. | How do you do? (*lit.,* much pleasure) |

### FORMAL TITLES

| | |
|---|---|
| doctor (*abbrev.* **Dr.**) | doctor |
| profesor | professor |
| señor (*abbrev.* **Sr.**) | Mr., sir, gentleman |
| señora (*abbrev.* **Sra.**) | Mrs., madam, lady |
| señorita (*abbrev.* **Srta.**) | Miss, young lady |

### USEFUL EXPRESSIONS

| | |
|---|---|
| bien | well, fine |
| De nada. | You're welcome. |
| Lo siento. | I'm sorry. |
| Muchas gracias. | Thank you very much. |
| Muy bien, ¿y usted? | Very well, and you? |
| no | no, not |
| Pase. | Come in. |
| por favor | please |
| Tome asiento. | Sit down. *or* Take a seat. |

**Exercises**

A. Memorize all the above dialogues, and act them out with another student.

B. What would you say in the following situations?

1. You meet Mr. García in the morning and ask him how he is.
2. You thank Miss Vera for a favor and tell her you will see her tomorrow.
3. You greet Mrs. Nieto (afternoon) and ask her to come in and sit down.
4. Professor Maria Rivas says *"mucho gusto"* to you.
5. Someone thanks you for a favor.
6. Mr. Ortiz says he is not feeling well.

## 3. DAYS OF THE WEEK

| | |
|---|---|
| **¿Qué día es hoy?** | *What day is it today?* |
| **Hoy es lunes.** | *Today is Monday.* |
| | |
| **Hoy es martes, ¿no?** | *Today is Tuesday, isn't it?* |
| **No, hoy es miércoles.** | *No, today is Wednesday.* |
| | |
| **¿Qué día es hoy?** | *What day is it today?* |
| **¿Jueves?** | *Thursday?* |
| **No, hoy es viernes.** | *No, today is Friday.* |
| | |
| **Hoy es . . . sábado . . . ¡no!** | *Today is . . . Saturday* |
| **domingo . . .** | *. . . no! Sunday . . .* |
| **Sí, hoy es domingo.** | *Yes, today is Sunday.* |

The days of the week are:

| | | | |
|---|---|---|---|
| **lunes** | Monday | **viernes** | Friday |
| **martes** | Tuesday | **sábado** | Saturday |
| **miércoles** | Wednesday | **domingo** | Sunday |
| **jueves** | Thursday | | |

ATENCIÓN: The days of the week are not capitalized in Spanish.

**Exercise**

Respond, following the model:

*Modelo:* Hoy es lunes, ¿no?
      **No, hoy es domingo.**

1. Hoy es miércoles, ¿no?
2. Hoy es domingo, ¿no?
3. Hoy es viernes, ¿no?
4. Hoy es martes, ¿no?
5. Hoy es sábado, ¿no?
6. Hoy es jueves, ¿no?

## 4. CARDINAL NUMBERS (0–31)

| | | | |
|---|---|---|---|
| 0 | cero | 11 | once |
| 1 | uno | 12 | doce |
| 2 | dos | 13 | trece |
| 3 | tres | 14 | catorce |
| 4 | cuatro | 15 | quince |
| 5 | cinco | 16 | diez y seis (dieciséis) |
| 6 | seis | 17 | diez y siete (diecisiete) |
| 7 | siete | 18 | diez y ocho (dieciocho) |
| 8 | ocho | 19 | diez y nueve (diecinueve) |
| 9 | nueve | 20 | veinte |
| 10 | diez | 21 | veinte y uno (veintiuno) |

| | |
|---|---|
| 22 | veinte y dos (veintidós) |
| 23 | veinte y tres (veintitrés) |
| 24 | veinte y cuatro (veinticuatro) |
| 25 | veinte y cinco (veinticinco) |
| 26 | veinte y seis (veintiséis) |
| 27 | veinte y siete (veintisiete) |
| 28 | veinte y ocho (veintiocho) |
| 29 | veinte y nueve (veintinueve) |
| 30 | treinta |
| 31 | treinta y uno |

**Exercise**

Read the following numbers aloud:

0, 23, 18, 7, 9, 13, 30, 11, 5, 15, 4, 20, 12, 10, 14, 31, 16, 1, 8, 17, 25, 19, 3, 22, 6, 12, 29

## 5. MONTHS AND SEASONS OF THE YEAR

| | |
|---|---|
| ¿Qué fecha es hoy? | What's the date today? |
| Hoy es el quince de enero. | Today is January the fifteenth. |
| | |
| ¿Qué fecha es hoy? | What's the date today? |
| Hoy es el primero de septiembre. | Today is September the first. |

The months of the year are:

| | | | |
|---|---|---|---|
| **enero** | January | **julio** | July |
| **febrero** | February | **agosto** | August |
| **marzo** | March | **septiembre** | September |
| **abril** | April | **octubre** | October |
| **mayo** | May | **noviembre** | November |
| **junio** | June | **diciembre** | December |

ATENCIÓN: The names of the months are not capitalized in Spanish.

The seasons are:

**primavera**  spring      **verano**   summer
**otoño**      fall        **invierno** winter

● To ask for the date, say:

   **¿Qué fecha es hoy?**  *What's the date today?*

● When telling the date, always begin with the expression **Hoy es el . . .:**

   **Hoy es el** veinte de mayo.

● Start with the number followed by the preposition **de** (*of*), and then the month:

   **quince de mayo**        *May 15th*
   **diez de septiembre**    *September 10th*
   **doce de octubre**       *October 12th*

● The ordinal number **primero** (*first*) is used when referring to the first day of the month:

   **primero de febrero**  *February first*

## Exercises

   A. Give the Spanish equivalent of the following dates:

   1. The 4th of July          7. March 21st
   2. The 31st of October      8. April 1st
   3. The 1st of January       9. June 20th
   4. May 5th                 10. September 9th
   5. February 12th           11. August 13th
   6. December 25th           12. November 11th


   B. Say in which season the following months fall:

   1. febrero     5. octubre
   2. agosto      6. julio
   3. mayo        7. abril
   4. enero       8. noviembre

PERSONAL INFORMATION

Provide the information requested.

| Apellido y nombres | Fecha de nacimiento | | |
|---|---|---|---|
| ..................................................... | DÍA | MES[1] | AÑO |
| Dirección | | | |
| ..................................................... | | | |
| Teléfono | | | |
| ..................................................... | | | |

Estado civil                    Sexo                    Edad

1. _____ soltero         Masculino _____      _____

2. _____ casado         Femenino _____

3. _____ divorciado

4. _____ viudo

5. _____ separado

Nacionalidad .........................................................................

Ocupación ............................................................................

Lugar donde trabaja ............................................................

Número de seguro social ...................................................

Número de la licencia para conducir ...............................

[1] **mes:** month

Lesson 1

## 1. SUBJECT PRONOUNS

| | Singular | | Plural | |
|---|---|---|---|---|
| yo | *I* | | nosotros | *we (masculine)* |
| | | | nosotras | *we (feminine)* |
| tú | *you (familiar)* | | | |
| usted[1] | *you (formal)* | | ustedes[2] | *you* |
| él | *he* | | ellos | *they (masculine)* |
| ella | *she* | | ellas | *they (feminine)* |

● The masculine plural form may refer to the masculine gender alone or to both genders together:

Juan y Roberto: **ellos**      *John and Robert: **they***
Juan y María: **ellos**        *John and Mary: **they***

ATENCIÓN: Use the **tú** form as the equivalent of *you* when addressing a close friend, a relative, or a child. Use the **usted** form in *all* other instances.

### Exercise

Give the personal pronoun you would use for the following:

*Modelo:* You refer to Mr. Smith as . . .
     **I refer to Mr. Smith as *él*.**

1. You point to yourself and say . . .
2. You refer to Mrs. Smith as . . .
3. You are talking to a little boy and you call him . . .
4. You are talking to a woman you just met and you call her . . .
5. Your mother refers to herself and her sister as . . .
6. Your father refers to himself and his sister as . . .
7. You are talking to a few people and you call them . . .
8. You refer to Mr. Smith and his daughter as . . .
9. You refer to Mrs. Smith and her daughter as . . .
10. You refer to Mr. and Mrs. Smith as . . .

[1] Abbreviated **Ud.**
[2] Abbreviated **Uds.**

## 2. PRESENT INDICATIVE OF REGULAR -**ar** VERBS

Regular verbs ending in -**ar** are conjugated like **hablar**.

| | | | **hablar** (to speak) |
|---|---|---|---|
| | | | *Singular* |
| | *Stem* | *Ending* | |
| yo | habl- | **o** | Yo **hablo** español. |
| tú | habl- | **as** | Tú **hablas** español. |
| Ud. | habl- | **a** | Ud. **habla** español. |
| él | habl- | **a** | Juan **habla** español. Él **habla** español. |
| ella | habl- | **a** | Ana **habla** español. Ella **habla** español. |
| | | | *Plural* |
| nosotros | habl- | **amos** | Nosotros **hablamos** español. |
| Uds. | habl- | **an** | Uds. **hablan** español. |
| ellos | habl- | **an** | Ellos **hablan** español. |
| ellas | habl- | **an** | Ellas **hablan** español. |

- The infinitive of all Spanish verbs consists of a stem (such as **habl-**) and an ending (such as -**ar**). When looking up a verb in the dictionary you will always find it listed under the infinitive. The infinitive endings for the three verb conjugations are -**ar**, -**er**, and -**ir**.

- The stem does not change. The endings change with the subjects.

- The Spanish present tense is equivalent to three English forms:

Yo **hablo** español.   { *I **speak** Spanish.* / *I **do speak** Spanish.* / *I **am speaking** Spanish.* }

- Since the verb endings indicate who the speaker is, the subject pronouns are frequently omitted:

| | |
|---|---|
| **Hablas** inglés, ¿no? | *You speak English, don't you?* |
| Sí, **hablo** inglés. | *Yes, I speak English.* |

However, they may be used for emphasis or clarification:

| | |
|---|---|
| **Uds.** hablan inglés, ¿no? | *You speak English, don't you?* |
| **Yo** hablo inglés. **Él** habla español. | *I speak English. **He** speaks Spanish.* |

● Some other common verbs that follow the same pattern are: **trabajar** (*to work*), **necesitar** (*to need*), and **estudiar** (*to study*):

María y Juan **trabajan** en Los Ángeles, ¿no?      *María and Juan work in Los Angeles, don't they?*
Sí, ellos **trabajan** en Los Ángeles.      *Yes, they work in Los Angeles.*

Ud. **necesita** dinero, ¿no?      *You need money, don't you?*
Sí, **necesito** dinero.      *Yes, I need money.*

Uds. **estudian** español, ¿no?      *You study Spanish, don't you?*
Sí, **estudiamos** español.      *Yes, we study Spanish.*

### Exercises

A. Item substitution: Conjugate the verbs according to the new subject:

1. Yo **estudio** español.  (nosotros, Ud., tú, ellos, él, Uds.)
2. Ella **trabaja** en San Diego.  (yo, nosotras, tú, Ud., ellos)
3. Tú **necesitas** dinero.  (ellos, nosotros, Ud., yo, ella)

B. Complete the following sentences with the present indicative of **hablar, necesitar, trabajar,** and **estudiar,** as needed. Use each verb twice.

1. María y yo _____ en Los Ángeles.
2. José _____ dinero.
3. Tú _____ inglés, ¿no?
4. Marta y Anita _____ dinero.
5. Ud. _____ inglés, ¿no?
6. Yo _____ en Harvard.
7. María _____ en Buenos Aires.
8. Uds. _____ en Chile, ¿no?

## 3. INTERROGATIVE SENTENCES

In Spanish there are several ways to ask a question to elicit a *yes/no* answer:

1. ¿**Ustedes** necesitan dinero? ⎫
2. ¿Necesitan **ustedes** dinero? ⎬ Sí, nosotros necesitamos dinero.
3. ¿Necesitan dinero **ustedes**? ⎭

These three questions ask for the same information and have the same meaning. Example 1 is a declarative sentence that is made interrogative by a change in intonation:

Ustedes necesitan dinero.      ¿Ustedes necesitan dinero?

Example 2 is an interrogative sentence formed by placing the subject (**ustedes**) after the verb. Example 3 is the most common interrogative form. The subject (**ustedes**) has been placed at the end of the sentence. Notice that Spanish uses two question marks, one at the end of the sentence and an inverted one at the beginning.

## Exercise

Change the following sentences to interrogatives, according to the model:

*Modelo:* **Elena** trabaja en Buenos Aires.
   **¿Trabaja *Elena* en Buenos Aires?**
   **¿Trabaja en Buenos Aires *Elena?***

1. Juan y María necesitan dinero.
2. Ella estudia inglés.
3. Uds. hablan español.
4. Pedro necesita estudiar.
5. Tú trabajas en California.

## 4. NEGATIVE SENTENCES

To make a sentence negative, simply place the word **no** in front of the verb:

| | |
|---|---|
| Ella   habla inglés. | *She speaks English.* |
| Ella **no** habla inglés. | *She doesn't speak English.* |
| Yo   trabajo en California. | *I work in California.* |
| Yo **no** trabajo en California. | *I don't work in California.* |

If the answer to a question is negative, the word **no** will appear twice: at the beginning of the sentence, as in English, and in front of the verb:

| | |
|---|---|
| ¿Necesitas dinero? | *Do you need money?* |
| **No**, (yo) **no** necesito dinero. | *No, I don't need money.* |

ATENCIÓN: The subject pronoun need not appear in the answer.

## Exercise

Make the following sentences negative:

1. Pedro y yo hablamos inglés.
2. Tú necesitas dinero.
3. Nosotros necesitamos trabajar.
4. María trabaja en California.
5. Ud. estudia español.

## 5. GENDER

In Spanish all nouns, including those denoting nonliving things, are either masculine or feminine:

| *masculine* | *feminine* |
|---|---|
| señor | señora |
| teléfono | banana |

Some practical rules to determine gender of Spanish nouns:

1. Most words ending in -**a** are feminine; most words ending in -**o** are masculine:

| *masculine* | *feminine* |
|---|---|
| teléfon**o** | sill**a** (*chair*) |
| diner**o** | cas**a** (*house*) |
| libr**o** (*book*) | mes**a** (*table*) |

ATENCIÓN: There are exceptions to these rules. Two important exceptions are: día (*day*), which is masculine, and mano (*hand*), which is feminine.

2. Nouns ending in -**sión**, -**ción**, -**tad**, and -**dad** are feminine:

| | |
|---|---|
| televi**sión** | ciu**dad** |
| lec**ción** | liber**tad** |

ATENCIÓN: Although the following words end in -**a**, they are masculine:

| | |
|---|---|
| sistema | programa |
| telegrama | problema |
| idioma | |

3. The gender of other nouns must be learned. For example: **español** (*Spanish language*) is masculine, while **calle** (*street*) is feminine.

### Exercise

Tell whether the following nouns are feminine or masculine:

| | | |
|---|---|---|
| 1. número | 5. día | 9. libro |
| 2. problema | 6. dinero | 10. mano |
| 3. calle | 7. nacionalidad | 11. ciudad |
| 4. dirección | 8. silla | 12. libertad |

## 6. CARDINAL NUMBERS (31–200)

| | | | |
|---|---|---|---|
| 31 | treinta y uno | 80 | ochenta |
| 32 | treinta y dos . . . | 90 | noventa |
| 40 | cuarenta | 100 | cien[1] |
| 50 | cincuenta | 101 | ciento uno . . . |
| 60 | sesenta | 150 | ciento cincuenta . . . |
| 70 | setenta | 200 | doscientos |

### Exercise

Read the following numbers aloud:

| | | | | | | | |
|---|---|---|---|---|---|---|---|
| 33 | 48 | 57 | 69 | 74 | 80 | 91 | 100 |
| 123 | 200 | 197 | 136 | 115 | 175 | 169 | 185 |

---

## STUDY OF COGNATES

Remember the following rules about cognates:[2]

1. Some words are exact cognates; only the pronunciation is different:

    **singular** *singular*   **plural** *plural*
    **mineral** *mineral*   **banana** *banana*

2. Some cognates are almost the same, except for a written accent mark, a final vowel, or a single consonant:

    televisión *television*   problema *problem*
    Roberto *Robert*   telegrama *telegram*
    programa *program*   profesor *professor*
    sexo *sex*

3. Most nouns ending in -**tion** in English end in -**ción** in Spanish:

    atención *attention*

4. English nouns ending in -**ty** end in -**tad** or -**dad** in Spanish:

    libertad *liberty*
    ciudad *city*

5. There are other easily recognizable cognates for which no rule can be given:

    **lección** *lesson*   **sistema** *system*   **teléfono** *telephone*

---

[1] **Cien** is used before nouns and the numerals **mil** and **millones. Ciento** is used before numerals under 200.

[2] Verbs will not be treated as cognates.

## NEW VOCABULARY

| Nouns | | Verbs | |
|---|---|---|---|
| la casa | house | estudiar | to study |
| el dinero | money | hablar | to speak |
| el español | Spanish | necesitar | to need |
| | (*language*) | trabajar | to work |
| el idioma | language | | |
| el inglés | English | Other words and expressions | |
| | (*language*) | sí | yes |
| el libro | book | en | in |
| la mano | hand | | |
| la mesa | table | | |
| la silla | chair | | |

Lesson 2

## 1. PLURAL FORMS

Spanish nouns are made plural by adding an **-s** to words ending in a vowel and an **-es** to words ending in a consonant. Nouns ending in **-z** change the **z** to **c** and add **-es**:

| | |
|---|---|
| teléfon**o** | teléfon**os** |
| mesa | mes**as** |
| profeso**r** | profesor**es** |
| lápi**z** (*pencil*) | lápi**ces** |

ATENCIÓN: When an accent mark falls on the *last* syllable of a word, it is omitted in the plural form:

lecci**ón**        lecci**ones**

### Exercise

Give the plural of the following nouns:

1. silla
2. libro
3. lápiz
4. apellido
5. universidad

6. telegrama
7. ciudad
8. lección
9. ocupación
10. señor

## 2. THE DEFINITE ARTICLE

Spanish has four forms equivalent to the English definite article *the:*

| | Singular | Plural |
|---|---|---|
| *Masculine* | el | los |
| *Feminine* | la | las |

| | |
|---|---|
| el profesor | la profesora |
| los profesores | las profesoras |
| el mineral | la banana |
| los minerales | las bananas |

ATENCIÓN: Try to learn the accompanying definite article when you learn each noun. This will help you to remember its gender.

**Exercise**

Give the definite articles for the following nouns:

1. universidades
2. lápices
3. profesor
4. doctor
5. señora

6. señores
7. día
8. televisión
9. silla
10. profesoras

11. dinero
12. profesores
13. banana
14. telegrama

## 3. POSITION OF ADJECTIVES

A. In Spanish descriptive adjectives (such as adjectives of color, size, etc.) generally follow the noun:

el libro **rojo**      *the **red** book*
la casa **grande**     *the **big** house*

B. Adjectives denoting nationality always follow the noun:

el profesor **norteamericano**      *the **North American** professor*

C. Other kinds of adjectives (possessive, demonstrative, numerals, etc.) precede the noun, as in English:

**cinco** lápices      ***five** pencils*

**Exercise**

Give the Spanish equivalent:

1. the red pencil
2. the big city
3. the American doctor

4. fifteen chairs
5. the big table

## 4. FORMS OF ADJECTIVES

Adjectives whose masculine ends in **-o** have four forms, ending in **-o, -a, -os, -as.** Most other adjectives have only two forms, a singular and a plural. Like nouns, adjectives are made plural by adding **-s, -es,** or by changing **-z** to **c** and adding **-es.**

| *Singular* | | *Plural* | |
|---|---|---|---|
| *Masculine* | *Feminine* | *Masculine* | *Feminine* |
| negro (*black*) | negra | negros | negras |
| inteligente | inteligente | inteligentes | inteligentes |
| feliz (*happy*) | feliz | felices | felices |
| verde (*green*) | verde | verdes | verdes |

Adjectives of nationality ending in a consonant are made feminine by adding **-a** to the masculine singular form:

español     española

## 5. AGREEMENT OF ARTICLES, ADJECTIVES, AND NOUNS

In Spanish the article, the noun, and the adjective agree in number and gender:

| | |
|---|---|
| **la** silla blanca | *the white chair* |
| **el** libro blanco | *the white book* |
| **las** sillas blancas | *the white chairs* |
| **los** libros blancos | *the white books* |

### Exercise

Make the adjectives agree with the nouns in the list and add the corresponding definite article:

1. _____ mesa     negra
   _____ libro     _____
   _____ sillas    _____
   _____ lápices   _____

2. _____ señor     español
   _____ señores   _____
   _____ señoras   _____
   _____ señora    _____

3. _____ profesor    inteligente
   _____ profesores  _____
   _____ profesora   _____
   _____ profesoras  _____

4. _____ señorita   feliz
   _____ señor      _____
   _____ señoritas  _____
   _____ señores    _____

## 6. PRESENT INDICATIVE OF -er AND -ir VERBS

Regular verbs ending in **-er** are conjugated like **comer**.
Regular verbs ending in **-ir** are conjugated like **vivir**.

| comer (*to eat*) | | vivir (*to live*) | |
|---|---|---|---|
| yo | com- **o** | yo | viv- **o** |
| tú | com- **es** | tú | viv- **es** |
| Ud.⎱ él ⎰ ella⎰ | com- **e** | Ud.⎱ él ⎰ ella⎰ | viv- **e** |
| nosotros | com- **emos** | nosotros | viv- **imos** |
| Uds.⎱ ellos⎰ ellas⎰ | com- **en** | Uds.⎱ ellos⎰ ellas⎰ | viv- **en** |

Some other common verbs that follow the same patterns are: **beber** (*to drink*), **aprender** (*to learn*), **leer** (*to read*), **comprender** (*to understand*), **escribir** (*to write*), **abrir** (*to open*), **recibir** (*to receive*), and **decidir** (*to decide*).

| | |
|---|---|
| ¿Tú **bebes** café o té? | *Do you drink coffee or tea?* |
| **Bebo** café. | *I drink coffee.* |
| ¿**Comen** Uds. temprano? | *Do you eat early?* |
| No, **comemos** tarde. | *No, we eat late.* |
| ¿Dónde **vive** Ud.? | *Where do you live?* |
| **Vivo** en la calle Unión. | *I live on Union Street.* |
| ¿**Escribe** el profesor en español? | *Does the professor write in Spanish?* |
| Sí, **escribe** en español. | *Yes, he writes in Spanish.* |

**Exercises**

A. Item substitution:

1. Yo no **como** temprano. (nosotros, el profesor, tú, Uds., ella)
2. Ud. no **comprende** la lección. (tú y yo, ellas, yo, Ana, Uds.)
3. Eva **escribe** en español. (yo, José y Luis, nosotros, Ud., él)
4. Tú **decides** estudiar inglés. (nosotras, Uds., él, yo, Juan)

B. Complete the following sentences with the present indicative form of **beber, leer, comprender, comer, escribir, vivir, abrir, recibir, decidir,** and **aprender,** as needed. Use each verb only once.

1. Yo _____ té o café.
2. Carmen y Elena no _____ la lección.
3. Marta y yo _____ en la calle Universidad.
4. ¿Dónde _____ tú? ¿En el restaurante?
5. Uds. _____ en español.
6. Ella _____ dinero.
7. El profesor _____ los libros.
8. Rosa _____ aprender español.
9. Ud. _____ el libro.
10. Yo no _____ inglés.

## 7. THE PERSONAL **a**

In Spanish, as in English, a verb has a subject and may have one or more objects. The function of the object is to complete the idea expressed by the verb.

In English, a direct object is one that cannot be separated from the verb by a preposition: *She killed **the burglar**. He sees **the nurse**.* In the preceding sentences, *the burglar* and *the nurse* are direct objects.

In Spanish, the preposition **a** must be used before a direct object referring to a definite person. This preposition is called the personal **a**. The personal **a** is *not* used when the direct object is not a person.

| | |
|---|---|
| ¿A quién espera Ud.? | *Whom are you waiting for?* |
| Espero **a** la profesora. | *I'm waiting for the professor.* |
| | |
| ¿Qué esperas? | *What are you waiting for?* |
| Espero el ómnibus. | *I'm waiting for the bus.* |
| | |
| ¿Visitan Uds. **a** Rafael? | *Do you visit Rafael?* |
| No, visitamos **a** Pedro. | *No, we visit Pedro.* |
| | |
| ¿Visitan los estudiantes el museo o el teatro? | *Are the students visiting the museum or the theatre?* |
| Visitan el museo. | *They are visiting the museum.* |

## Exercise

Give the Spanish equivalent:

1. We are waiting for the professor. (*fem.*)
2. What are the students visiting? The theatre?
3. They are waiting for the bus.
4. Who visits Mary?
5. We are waiting for Carmen and Paco.

## STUDY OF COGNATES

1. The following words are the same in Spanish and English, except for a written accent mark, final vowel, or single consonant:

   | | |
   |---|---|
   | **el restaurante** | restaurant |
   | **inteligente** | intelligent |

2. The following words are approximate cognates:

   | | |
   |---|---|
   | **el museo** | museum |
   | **el, la estudiante** | student |
   | **el teatro** | theater |

## NEW VOCABULARY

### Nouns

| | |
|---|---|
| **el café** | coffee |
| **el lápiz** | pencil |
| **el té** | tea |
| **el ómnibus** | bus |

### Verbs

| | |
|---|---|
| **abrir** | to open |
| **aprender** | to learn |
| **beber** | to drink |
| **comer** | to eat |
| **comprender** | to understand |
| **decidir** | to decide |
| **escribir** | to write |
| **esperar** | to wait for |
| **leer** | to read |
| **recibir** | to receive |
| **visitar** | to visit |
| **vivir** | to live |

### Adjectives

| | |
|---|---|
| **blanco(a)** | white |
| **español(a)** | Spanish |
| **feliz** | happy |
| **grande** | big |
| **negro(a)** | black |
| **rojo(a)** | red |
| **verde** | green |

### Other words and expressions

| | |
|---|---|
| **¿dónde?** | where? |
| **o** | or |
| **¿qué?** | what? |
| **¿quién?** | who? |
| **tarde** | late |
| **temprano** | early |

Lesson 3

# 1. POSSESSION WITH **de**

Possession is expressed in Spanish by the preposition **de** + *noun*. This is equivalent to the English construction *noun + apostrophe + s:*

El libro **de Ricardo**          *Richard's book*

Study the possessive constructions in the following examples:

¿Necesita Ud. el libro **de**          *Do you need Richard's book?*
  **Ricardo?**
No, necesito el libro **de la**          *No, I need the professor's book.*
  **profesora.**

ATENCIÓN: The apostrophe is never used in Spanish to express possession. There is no Spanish construction similar to *Richard's book.*

# 2. POSSESSIVE ADJECTIVES

| Forms of the Possessive Adjectives | | |
|---|---|---|
| *Singular* | *Plural* | |
| mi | mis | *my* |
| tu | tus | *your* (*familiar*) |
| su | sus | $\left\{\begin{array}{l} his \\ her \\ its \\ your \\ their \end{array}\right.$ |
| nuestro(a) | nuestros(as) | *our* |

A. Possessive adjectives agree in number with the nouns they modify:

¿Necesita Ud. **mi libro?**          *Do you need my book?*
No, no necesito **su libro.**          *No, I don't need your book.*

¿Necesita Ud. **mis libros?**          *Do you need my books?*
No, no necesito **sus libros.**          *No, I don't need your books.*

B. **Nuestro** is the only possessive adjective that has the feminine endings **-a, -as.** The others use the same endings for both the masculine and feminine genders:

¿Con quién habla Ud.?          *With whom are you speaking?*
Hablo con nuestras amigas.          *I am speaking with our*
          *friends.*

ATENCIÓN: These forms of the possessive adjectives precede the nouns they introduce and are never stressed.

C. Since both **su** and **sus** may have different meanings, the form **de él** (**de ella, de ellos, de ellas, de Ud., de Uds.**) may be substituted to avoid confusion:

| | |
|---|---|
| ¿Con quién hablan Uds.? | *With whom are you talking?* |
| Hablamos con **su** amigo. | *We are talking with **his** (or: **her, your, their**) friend.* |
| Hablamos con el amigo **de Ud.** | *We are talking with **your** friend.* |
| ¿Estudia con **mi** libro? | *Are you studying with **my** book?* |
| No, estudio con el libro **de ella.** | *No, I'm studying with **her** book.* |

### Exercise

Give the following possessive adjectives in Spanish:

1. (my) _____ amigos
2. (his) _____ libro / _____ libro _____ _____.
3. (our) _____ casa /
4. (her) _____ idioma / _____ idioma _____ _____.
5. (your—**Ud.**) _____ dinero / _____ dinero _____ _____.
6. (my) _____ mano
7. (our) _____ mesas
8. (your—**tú**) _____ silla
9. (your—**Uds.**) _____ lápices / _____ lápices _____ _____.
10. (their—*fem.*) _____ lección / _____ lecciones _____ _____.

## 3. THE INDEFINITE ARTICLE

The indefinite article is the Spanish equivalent of *a*, *an*, and *some*.

| | *Masculine* | *Feminine* |
|---|---|---|
| *Singular* | un | una |
| *Plural* | unos | unas |

| | |
|---|---|
| ¿Escribimos con **una** pluma o con **un** lápiz? | *Do we write with a pen or a pencil?* |
| Escribimos con **un** lápiz. | *We write with a pencil.* |
| ¿Qué lee Ud. ahora? | *What are you reading now?* |
| Leo **unas** lecciones de español. | *I am reading some Spanish lessons.* |

ATENCIÓN: Spanish uses the preposition **de** + *noun* as the equivalent of the English use of two nouns, when the first one functions as an adjective:

*history*          *lesson* = lección **de historia**
noun as adjective    noun

### Exercise

Give the Spanish equivalent:

1. a pen
2. a friend (*masc.*)
3. some days
4. some chairs
5. a problem
6. a house

## 4. PRESENT INDICATIVE OF ser

| | | |
|---|---|---|
| yo | soy | *I am* |
| tú | eres | *you are (familiar)* |
| Ud. | | *you are (formal)* |
| él | es | *he is* |
| ella | | *she is* |
| | | |
| nosotros | somos | *we are* |
| Uds. | | *you are (formal)* |
| ellos | son | *they are (masculine)* |
| ellas | | *they are (feminine)* |

A. **Ser** is used to indicate characteristics of things and persons:

¿**Son altos** los hijos de Juan?
Sí, ellos **son altos.**

*Are Juan's sons tall?*
*Yes, they are tall.*

¿**Es difícil** tu lección de español?
No, mi lección no **es difícil.**

*Is your Spanish lesson difficult?*
*No, my lesson is not difficult.*

B. **Ser** is used with the preposition **de** to indicate origin and possession:

¿**De** dónde **es** Ud.?
Yo **soy de** Buenos Aires.

*Where are you from?*
*I am from Buenos Aires.*

¿**Son** tus copias?
No, **son** las copias **de** María.

*Are they your copies?*
*No, they are Maria's copies.*

**Exercise**

Complete the following sentences with the present indicative of **ser:**

1. María _____ alta.
2. Nosotros _____ los hijos de la señora Carreras.
3. Yo _____ de Buenos Aires.
4. Tú no _____ feliz.
5. ¿_____ Uds. de México?
6. La lección de historia _____ difícil.
7. Ud. _____ inteligente.
8. ¿_____ las copias de Ana?

## 5. THE IRREGULAR VERBS **ir, dar,** AND **estar**

|         | **ir** (*to go*) | **dar** (*to give*) | **estar** (*to be*) |
|---------|--------|----------|---------|
| yo      | voy    | doy      | estoy   |
| tú      | vas    | das      | estás   |
| Ud.<br>él<br>ella | vá | da | está |
| nosotros | vamos | damos   | estamos |
| Uds.<br>ellos<br>ellas | van | dan | están |

| | |
|---|---|
| ¿A dónde **va** Ud.? | *Where are you going?* |
| **Voy** a la biblioteca. | *I'm going to the library.* |
| ¿**Dan** Uds. dinero? | *Do you give money?* |
| Sí, **damos** dinero. | *Yes, we give money.* |
| ¿Dónde **está** Elena? | *Where is Helen?* |
| Ella **está** en el hotel. | *She is at the hotel.* |

**Exercise**

Complete the following sentences with the present indicative of **ir, dar,** and **estar,** as needed:

1. Él _____ su nombre y dirección.
2. Yo _____ a la biblioteca.
3. ¿Dónde _____ mis libros?
4. Ud. _____ a Los Ángeles con los hijos de él.
5. Ellos _____ dinero.

6. Uds. _____ en México.
7. Yo no _____ mi número de teléfono.
8. Nosotras _____ a la casa de María.
9. ¿_____ Ud. en el hotel?
10. Yo _____ en el hospital.

---

## STUDY OF COGNATES

1. Exact cognates:

   **el hospital**   hospital
   **el hotel**      hotel

2. Spanish words ending in **-ia** or **-io,** instead of English *-y:*

   **la copia**      copy

3. Approximate cognates:

   **Brasil**    Brazil
   **difícil**   difficult

---

## NEW VOCABULARY

| NOUNS | | ADJECTIVES | |
|---|---|---|---|
| **el amigo** | friend | **alto(a)** | tall |
| **la biblioteca** | library | | |
| **el hijo** | son | OTHER WORDS AND EXPRESSIONS | |
| **la pluma** | pen | **a** | to |
| | | **¿con quién?** | with whom? |
| VERBS | | **de** | of |
| **dar** | to give | **lección de historia** | history lesson |
| **estar** | to be | | |
| **ir** | to go | | |
| **ser** | to be | | |

Lesson 4

# 1. THE VERBS ser AND estar (SUMMARY OF USES)

The verbs ser and estar (both meaning *to be*) are used to indicate the following:

| ser | estar |
|---|---|
| 1. Possession | 1. Current condition |
| 2. Profession | 2. Location |
| 3. Nationality | |
| 4. Origin | |
| 5. Basic characteristics | |
| 6. Marital status | |
| 7. Expressions of time and dates | |
| 8. Material that things are made of | |

El auto es de Pedro, ¿no?
No, es de Juan.

*The auto is Peter's, isn't it?*
*No, it's John's.*

¿Cuál es la profesión de José?
José es ingeniero.

*What is Joseph's profession?*
*Joseph is an engineer.*

Elena es muy inteligente.
Ella es de Argentina,
    ¿no?
Sí, es argentina.

*Helen is very intelligent.*
*She's from Argentina, isn't*
    *she?*
*Yes, she's an Argentinian.*

¿Es Ud. casada?
No, soy soltera.

*Are you married?*
*No, I am single.*

¿Qué día es hoy?
Hoy es martes.

*What day is today?*
*Today is Tuesday.*

¿Es la botella de plástico?
No, es de vidrio.

*Is the bottle made of plastic?*
*No, it is made of glass.*

¿Cómo está Ud.?
Estoy bien, gracias.

*How are you?*
*I am fine, thanks.*

¿Dónde está su hijo?
Está en el hospital. Está
    enfermo.

*Where is your son?*
*He is in the hospital. He is*
    *sick.*

**Exercise**

Complete the following sentences using the correct form of **ser** or **estar,** as needed:

1. ¿Dónde _____ los profesores?
2. ¿De qué color _____ los autos?
3. ¿Cómo _____ Ud.? ¿Bien?
4. Mi esposo _____ ingeniero y mis hijos _____ profesores.
5. Ella _____ en Lima.
6. El libro que _____ en la mesa _____ de Pedro.
7. Ellos _____ de Venezuela.
8. Ella _____ muy inteligente. ¿Cuál _____ su profesión?
9. ¿_____ Ud. enferma?
10. Hoy _____ jueves.
11. La botella no _____ de vidrio. _____ de plástico.
12. Yo _____ viudo.

## 2. CONTRACTIONS

There are only two contractions in Spanish:

The preposition **de** (*of, from*) plus the article **el** are contracted to form **del:**

Leen los libros **de** + **el** profesor.    Leen los libros **del** profesor.

The preposition **a** (*to, toward*) plus the article **el** are contracted to form **al.**

Esperamos **a** + **el** profesor.    Esperamos **al** profesor.

ATENCIÓN: None of the other combinations of preposition and definite article (**de la, de los, de las, a la, a los, a las**) is contracted.

¿Esperan Uds. **al** profesor de español?

*Are you waiting for the Spanish professor?*

No, esperamos **a la** profesora de inglés.

*No, we are waiting for the English professor.*

¿**A** quién visitan Uds. cuando van a San Diego?

*Whom do you visit when you go to San Diego?*

Visitamos **al** señor García y **a los** señores Torres.

*We visit Mr. Garcia and Mr. and Mrs. Torres.*

| | |
|---|---|
| El dinero es **del** profesor, ¿no? | *The money is the professor's, isn't it?* |
| No, el dinero es **de los** estudiantes. | *No, the money is the students'.* |

### Exercise

Complete the sentences using one of the following: **de la, de las, del, de los, a la, a las, al, a los:**

1. Necesito los libros _____ estudiantes.
2. Hablamos _____ doctor Gómez.
3. La casa es _____ señora Pérez.
4. Esperamos _____ señor García y _____ señorita Díaz.
5. ¿Cuándo vamos _____ hospital?
6. Recibimos dinero _____ universidad.
7. ¿Visitas _____ esposas _____ doctores?
8. El presidente recibe _____ profesores.

## 3. THE COMPARISON OF ADJECTIVES AND ADVERBS

A. In Spanish, the comparative of most adjectives and adverbs is formed by placing **más** (*more*) or **menos** (*less*) before the adjective or the adverb and **que** after:

| | | | | | |
|---|---|---|---|---|---|
| **más** | | | adjective | | |
| | + | | *or* | + | **que** |
| **menos** | | | adverb | | |

In this construction, **que** is the equivalent of the English *than.*

| | |
|---|---|
| Jorge es muy alto, ¿no? | *George is very tall, isn't he?* |
| Sí, pero yo soy **más** alta **que** él. | *Yes, but I am taller than he.* |
| ¿Quién llega **más** tarde? ¿Tú o ella? | *Who arrives later? You or she?* |
| Ella llega **más** tarde **que** yo. | *She arrives later than I.* |

B. In an equal comparison **tan . . . como** is used:

| | | | | | |
|---|---|---|---|---|---|
| | | | adjective | | |
| **tan** | + | | *or* | + | **como** |
| | | | adverb | | |

**Tan . . . como** is the equivalent of the English *as . . . as:*

| | |
|---|---|
| ¿Está Ud. **tan** cansada **como** ellos? | *Are you as tired as they?* |
| No, yo estoy menos cansada que ellos. | *No, I am less tired than they.* |

C. The superlative construction is similar to the comparative. It is formed by placing the definite article before the person or thing being compared:

| | | | | | | |
|---|---|---|---|---|---|---|
| definite article | + | [noun] | + | **más** | + | adjective |

| | |
|---|---|
| ¿Quién es **la** chica **más** bonita **de** la clase? | *Who is the prettiest girl in the class?* |
| Elena es **la** chica **más** bonita **de** la clase. | *Helen is the prettiest girl in the class.* |

ATENCIÓN:  1. The Spanish equivalent of the English *in* after a superlative is **de.**
2. In many instances, the noun may not be expressed in a superlative.

| | |
|---|---|
| Elena es **la más** bonita **de** la clase. | *Helen is the prettiest (one) in the class.* |

## Exercise

Complete the following sentences with the Spanish equivalent of the words in parentheses:

1. Rosa es _____ (prettier than) Marcia.
2. Él llega _____ (as early as) ella.
3. Mis estudiantes son _____ (less intelligent than) Uds.
4. Mi hijo es _____ (as tall as) yo.
5. Él llega _____ (later than) Uds.
6. Es _____ (the most difficult lesson in the) libro.
7. José es _____ (the least intelligent boy in) la clase.
8. Ud. está _____ (less tired than) Rafael.

# 4.  THE IRREGULAR COMPARISON OF ADJECTIVES AND ADVERBS

The following adjectives and adverbs have irregular comparative forms in Spanish:

| Irregular Comparison of Adjectives and Adverbs | | | | |
|---|---|---|---|---|
| | | | | *Comparative Forms* |
| *Adjectives* | **mucho** | much (many) | **más** | more, most |
| | **poco** | little (few) | **menos** | less, fewer |
| | **bueno** | good | **mejor** | better, best |
| | **malo** | bad | **peor** | worse, worst |
| | **grande** | large | **mayor** | older, oldest |
| | **pequeño** | small | **menor** | younger, youngest |
| *Adverbs* | **mucho** | much | **más** | more, most |
| | **poco** | little | **menos** | less, least |
| | **bien** | well | **mejor** | better, best |
| | **mal** | badly | **peor** | worse, worst |

ATENCIÓN:  When the adjectives **grande** and **pequeño** refer to size, the regular form is used: **más grande** (*bigger*) and **más pequeño** (*smaller*).

| | |
|---|---|
| ¿Quién estudia **más**? ¿Ud. o Marta? | *Who studies more? You or Martha?* |
| Yo estudio **mucho,** pero Marta estudia **más.** | *I study a great deal, but Martha studies more.* |
| ¿Quién es **mayor**? ¿Ud. o Elsa? | *Who is older? You or Elsa?* |
| Yo soy **mayor** que Elsa. | *I am older than Elsa.* |
| ¿Quién habla **mejor** el español, Ud. o su esposo? | *Who speaks Spanish better, you or your husband?* |
| Yo hablo el español **mejor** que mi esposo. | *I speak Spanish better than my husband.* |
| La casa de Elena es **más grande** que la casa de José, ¿no? | *Helen's house is bigger than Joseph's house, isn't it?* |
| Sí, la casa de Elena es **más grande** que la casa de José. | *Yes, Helen's house is bigger than Joseph's house.* |

### Exercise

Give the Spanish equivalent:

1. I read many books, but he reads more.
2. Cuba is bigger than Puerto Rico.
3. My son is older than your daughter.
4. My professors are better than Robert's professors.
5. He speaks English worse than I.
6. My professor is younger than you.
7. My house is smaller than Mary's house.
8. I write well, but you write better.
9. You drink little coffee, but I drink less.
10. My book is bad, but your book is very good.

## 5. THE IRREGULAR VERBS **tener** AND **venir**

| tener (*to have*) | | venir (*to come*) | |
|---|---|---|---|
| yo | tengo | yo | vengo |
| tú | tienes | tú | vienes |
| Ud.⎫ | | Ud.⎫ | |
| él ⎬ | tiene | él ⎬ | viene |
| ella⎭ | | ella⎭ | |
| nosotros | tenemos | nosotros | venimos |
| Uds.⎫ | | Uds.⎫ | |
| ellos⎬ | tienen | ellos⎬ | vienen |
| ellas⎭ | | ellas⎭ | |

| | |
|---|---|
| ¿Con quién **viene** Ud.? ¿Con su hijo? | *With whom are you coming? With your son?* |
| No, **vengo** sola. | *No, I am coming alone.* |
| ¿Cuántos estudiantes **tiene** Ud.? | *How many students do you have?* |
| **Tengo** treinta estudiantes. | *I have thirty students.* |

ATENCIÓN: The personal **a** is not used with the verb **tener.**

### Exercise

Complete the following sentences with the present indicative of **tener** or **venir,** as needed:

1. Yo _____ tres hijos.
2. ¿Con quién _____ Uds. a la clase?

3. ¿_____ él tarde o temprano?
4. Ellos no _____ la dirección de Pedro, pero nosotros _____ su
   número de teléfono.
5. ¿Cuándo _____ ellos?
6. ¿Cuántas botellas _____ tú?
7. Yo _____ sola, pero Marisa _____ con Carlos.
8. ¿Cuántos estudiantes _____ Ud. en la clase?
9. ¿Cuál es el mejor profesor que Uds. _____?
10. Él _____ una casa muy grande.

## 6. CARDINAL NUMBERS (200-1000)

| | | | |
|---|---|---|---|
| 200 | doscientos | 600 | seiscientos |
| 272 | doscientos setenta y dos | 700 | setecientos |
| 300 | trescientos | 800 | ochocientos |
| 400 | cuatrocientos | 900 | novecientos |
| 500 | quinientos | 1000 | mil |

### Exercise

Read the following numbers aloud:

| | | | | | |
|---|---|---|---|---|---|
| 896 | 380 | 519 | 937 | 222 | 765 |
| 451 | 978 | 643 | 504 | 715 | 1000 |

## STUDY OF COGNATES

1. Exact cognates:

   **el auto**      auto, automobile
   **el color**     color

2. The following words are the same in Spanish and English, except
   for a written accent mark, a final vowel, or a single consonant:

   **el plástico**      plastic
   **el presidente**    president
   **la clase**         class
   **la profesión**     profession

3. Approximate cognates:

   **el ingeniero**     engineer

NEW VOCABULARY

### Nouns

| | |
|---|---|
| **la botella** | bottle |
| **la chica** | girl |
| **el chico** | boy |
| **el vidrio** | glass |

### Verbs

| | |
|---|---|
| **llegar** | to arrive |
| **tener** | to have |
| **venir** | to come |

### Adjectives

| | |
|---|---|
| **bonito**(a) | pretty |
| **bueno**(a) | good |

| | |
|---|---|
| **cansado**(a) | tired |
| **enfermo**(a) | sick |
| **solo**(a) | alone |

### Other words and expressions

| | |
|---|---|
| **¿a quién?** | to whom? |
| **con** | with |
| **¿cuál?** | which?, what? |
| **¿cuándo?** | when? |
| **¿cuántos**(as)? | how many? |
| **muy** | very |
| **pero** | but |

Lesson 5

## 1. EXPRESSIONS WITH **tener**

Many useful idiomatic expressions are formed with the verb **tener:**

| | |
|---|---|
| **tener frío** | to be cold |
| **tener hambre** | to be hungry |
| **tener sed** | to be thirsty |
| **tener calor** | to be hot |
| **tener sueño** | to be sleepy |
| **tener prisa** | to be in a hurry |
| **tener miedo** | to be afraid |
| **tener razón** | to be right |
| **tener . . . años (de edad)** | to be . . . years old |

ATENCIÓN: The equivalent of *I am very hungry*, for example, is **Tengo mucha hambre** (literally, *I have much hunger*).

| | |
|---|---|
| **¿Tienes hambre,** Carlos? | *Are you hungry, Charles?* |
| No, pero **tengo** mucha **sed.** | *No, but I am very thirsty.* |
| ¿Cuántos **años tiene** su hija? | *How old is your daughter?* |
| Mi hija **tiene** seis **años.** | *My daughter is six years old.* |
| Deseo hablar con el instructor, por favor. | *I wish to speak with the instructor, please.* |
| Ahora no. Lo siento. Él **tiene** mucha **prisa.** | *Not now. I'm sorry. He is in a big hurry.* |
| **Tiene razón.** Es tarde. | *You're right. It's late.* |

### Exercises

A. Answer the following questions, first in the affirmative and then in the negative:

1. ¿Tiene Ud. hambre?
2. ¿Tienen Uds. miedo?
3. ¿Tienes sueño?
4. ¿Tiene mucha sed el profesor (la profesora)?
5. ¿Tú tienes diez años?
6. ¿Tengo razón yo?
7. ¿Tienen Uds. prisa?
8. ¿Tiene calor?
9. ¿Tienen Uds. frío?

B. Give the Spanish equivalent:

1. Charles is not hungry, but he is very thirsty.
2. Are you sleepy, Madam?

3. My daughter is not afraid.
4. You are right, Miss Vera. The instructor is in a hurry.
5. I am twenty-seven years old.
6. I am not hot. I am cold.

## 2. TELLING TIME

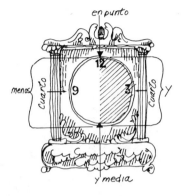

A. Remember the following points when telling time in Spanish:

1. Say the hour first, then the minutes:

Son las cuatro y diez.  *It is ten after four.*
(literally, *four and ten*)

2. The equivalent of *past* and *after* is **y**:

Son las doce **y** cinco.  *It's five after twelve.*

3. The equivalent of *to* and *till* is **menos:**

Son las ocho **menos** veinte.  *It's twenty to eight.*

4. The singular **es** is only used with **una** (*one*):

**Es** la una y media.  *It's one-thirty.*

5. The definite article is always used before the hour:

Son **las** nueve y cuarto.  *It's a quarter after nine.*

6. The equivalent of *at* + time is **a** + **la(s)** + time:

Mi clase es **a la una y media.**  *My class is at one-thirty.*
Su clase es **a las tres.**        *His class is at three.*

B. The difference between **de la** and **por la,** when used with time.

1. When a specific time is mentioned, **de la** (**mañana, tarde, noche**) should be used:

Mi clase de inglés es a las seis **de la** tarde. *My English class is at six in the evening.*

2. When a specific time is *not* mentioned, **por la (mañana, tarde, noche)** should be used:

> Nosotros trabajamos **por la** mañana. *We work in the morning.*

### Exercises

A. ¿Qué hora es?

B. Give the Spanish equivalent:
1. We are coming at two-thirty in the afternoon.
2. He is going to the library in the morning.
3. They don't work in the evening.
4. It's three (o'clock) in the morning!
5. I am arriving at nine o'clock in the evening.

## 3. STEM-CHANGING VERBS (e > ie)

Certain verbs undergo a change in the stem in the present indicative. When the **e** is the last stem vowel and it is stressed, it changes to **ie**.

| **preferir** (*to prefer*) | |
| --- | --- |
| yo prefiero | nosotros preferimos |
| tú prefieres | |
| Ud. ⎱<br>él ⎬ prefiere<br>ella ⎰ | Uds. ⎱<br>ellos ⎬ prefieren<br>ellas ⎰ |

- Notice that the stem vowel is not stressed in the verb forms corresponding to **nosotros,** and therefore the **e** does not change to **ie**.
- Stem-changing verbs have regular endings like other **-ar, -er,** and **-ir** verbs.

ATENCIÓN: Some other verbs that undergo the same change are: **cerrar** (*to close*), **perder** (*to lose*), **comenzar** (*to begin*), **querer** (*to want*), **entender** (*to understand*), and **empezar** (*to start*).

| | |
|---|---|
| **¿Quieres** ir al cine? | *Do you want to go to the movies?* |
| No, no **quiero** ir al cine. **Prefiero** ir al concierto. | *No, I don't want to go to the movies. I prefer going to the concert.* |
| ¿A qué hora **cierran** Uds.? **Cerramos** a las nueve. | *What time do you close? We close at nine.* |
| ¿Cuándo **comienzan** las clases? **Comienzan** en septiembre. | *When do classes start? They start in September.* |
| Pedro **entiende** el francés y el alemán, ¿no? | *Pedro understands French and German, doesn't he?* |
| **Entiende** el francés, pero no **entiende** el alemán. | *He understands French, but he doesn't understand German.* |

### Exercise

A. Practice the conjugations of each of the verbs used in the above example sentences.

B. Complete the following sentences with the present indicative of **preferir, cerrar, empezar, comenzar, querer, perder,** and **entender,** as needed. Use each verb once.

1. Nosotros no _____ estudiar alemán; _____ estudiar francés.
2. El concierto _____ a las ocho de la noche.
3. Yo no _____ la lección.
4. ¿Por qué _____ (tú) el libro?
5. Las clases _____ en marzo.
6. Roberto _____ su dinero en Las Vegas.

## 4. ir a + INFINITIVE

The construction **ir a** + *infinitive* is used to express future time. It is equivalent to the English expression *to be going to*. The formula is:

| **ir** | + | **a** | + | infinitive | |
|---|---|---|---|---|---|
| **Yo voy** | | **a** | | **viajar** | **solo.** |
| *I'm going* | | *to* | | *travel* | *alone.* |

| | |
|---|---|
| ¿Qué **vas a comprar?** | *What are you going to buy?* |
| **Voy a comprar** una camisa y una blusa. | *I'm going to buy a shirt and a blouse.* |
| ¿Con quién **van a ir** Uds. a la reunión? | *With whom are you going (to go) to the meeting?* |
| **Vamos a ir** con la hermana de Enrique y el hermano de Juan. | *We are going (to go) with Henry's sister and John's brother.* |
| ¿A qué hora **va a empezar** la clase? | *What time is the class going to start?* |
| **Va a empezar** a las siete. | *It's going to start at seven.* |

### Exercises

A. Item Substitution:

1. Tú **vas** a perder el dinero. (nosotros, mi hermana, yo, Ud., ellos)
2. El inspector **va** a hablar con ella. (yo, Uds., nosotras, tú)
3. Nosotros **vamos** a comenzar la lección. (ellas, Luis, yo, Uds.)

B. Answer the following questions, first in the affirmative, then in the negative:

1. ¿Va a cerrar Ud. el libro?
2. ¿Van a ir Uds. al cine solos?
3. ¿Vas a comprar una camisa?
4. ¿La reunión va a comenzar a las siete?
5. ¿Van a hablar en español los profesores?
6. ¿Su profesor va a dar su nombre y apellido?

## 5. THE USES OF **hay**

The form **hay** means *there is, there are*. It has no subject, and must not be confused with **es** (*it is*) and **son** (*they are*).

| | |
|---|---|
| ¿**Hay** pescado en el refrigerador? | *Is there (any) fish in the refrigerator?* |
| No, no **hay** pescado. | *No, there isn't (any) fish.* |
| ¿**Hay** vuelos para Lima hoy? | *Are there flights to Lima today?* |
| Sí, **hay** un vuelo a las ocho de la noche. | *Yes, there is one flight at eight P.M.* |

**Exercise**

Answer the following questions:

1. ¿Cuántos estudiantes hay en la clase?
2. ¿Hay pescado en su refrigerador?
3. Hay un vuelo para Bogotá esta noche. ¿Quiere ir?
4. Hoy es domingo. ¿Hay clase?
5. ¿Cuántos teatros hay en su ciudad?
6. ¿Hay niños en la clase?

---

## STUDY OF COGNATES

1. Exact cognates:

   | | |
   |---|---|
   | **el inspector** | inspector |
   | **el instructor** | instructor |

2. Approximate cognates:

   | | |
   |---|---|
   | **la blusa** | blouse |
   | **el concierto** | concert |
   | **el refrigerador** | refrigerator |

---

## NEW VOCABULARY

NOUNS

| | |
|---|---|
| **el alemán** | German (language) |
| **la camisa** | shirt |
| **el cine** | movie (theater) |
| **el francés** | French (language) |
| **la hermana** | sister |
| **el hermano** | brother |
| **la hija** | daughter |
| **la mañana** | morning |
| **la noche** | (late) evening, night |
| **el pescado** | fish |
| **la reunión** | meeting |
| **la tarde** | afternoon |
| **el vuelo** | flight |

VERBS

| | |
|---|---|
| **cerrar (e > ie)** | to close |
| **comenzar (e > ie)** | to begin |
| **comprar** | to buy |
| **desear** | to wish |
| **empezar (e > ie)** | to begin |
| **entender (e > ie)** | to understand |
| **perder (e > ie)** | to lose |
| **preferir (e > ie)** | to prefer |
| **querer (e > ie)** | to want |

OTHER WORDS AND EXPRESSIONS

| | |
|---|---|
| **para** | to |

# Test Yourself: Lessons 1-5

A. Subject pronouns

Give the plural of the following:

1. yo (*masc.*)    4. ella
2. él              5. yo (*fem.*)
3. usted

B. Present indicative of **-ar** verbs

Item substitution. Make the necessary changes:

1. Yo hablo español.
2. Nosotros _____.
3. _____ inglés.
4. Tú _____.
5. _____ trabajas en Lima.
6. Ellos _____.
7. Ud. _____.
8. _____ estudia _____.
9. Yo _____.
10. _____ necesito dinero.
11. Él _____.
12. Nosotros _____.

C. Interrogative sentences / Negative sentences

Make the following sentences interrogative, then negative:

1. Elena trabaja en Buenos Aires.
2. Uds. hablan inglés.
3. Tú necesitas dinero.
4. Juan y María estudian español.
5. Usted trabaja en Los Ángeles.

D. Gender

Divide the following words into two columns: masculine and feminine:

programa, telegrama, televisión, señor, teléfono, señora, banana, libro, día, mano, silla, casa, sistema, mesa, dinero, problema, idioma, libertad, lección, ciudad, calle, número, nacionalidad, tema.

E. Cardinal numbers (0-200)

Give the answers to the following problems: (+: más; −: menos)

1. cuarenta + veinte y seis =
2. treinta − diez y siete =
3. doscientos − ciento nueve =
4. ochenta − siete =
5. catorce + cinco =
6. cincuenta + cien =

## LESSON 2

A. Plural forms / Agreement of adjectives and nouns / Definite articles

Make the following plural:

1. la casa verde
2. el lápiz negro
3. el profesor inteligente
4. la silla grande
5. el libro blanco
6. la señorita feliz

B. Present indicative of **-er** and **-ir** verbs

Give the Spanish equivalent:

1. Where do you live, Mrs. Vera?
2. They drink coffee. I drink tea.
3. We read the lessons.
4. He decides to study English.
5. Do you (*tú*) understand?
6. You (*Uds.*) eat early.
7. She writes in Spanish.
8. We open the books.
9. I'm learning Spanish.
10. They don't receive the money.

C. The personal **a**

Read the following sentences. Use the personal **a** when needed:

1. ¿Esperan Uds. _____ el ómnibus?
2. Nosotros no visitamos _____ la señora Pérez.
3. Ellos visitan _____ los museos.
4. Rosa espera _____ Carlos.
5. Los estudiantes visitan _____ los profesores.

## LESSON 3

A. Possession with **de**

Arrange the following in complete sentences, according to the model:

*Modelo:* Yo / necesitar / señorita Peña / libro
   **Yo necesito el libro de la señorita Peña.**

1. Nosotros / recibir / Carlos / dinero
2. Ella / leer / la profesora / lección
3. Los / estudiantes / visitar / Enrique / esposa
4. ¿Tú / esperar / Teresa / profesora?
5. Ud. / no necesitar / María / silla

B. Possessive adjectives

Use the possessive adjective that corresponds to each subject. Follow the model:

*Modelo:* **Yo** necesito _____ libro.
   **Yo necesito mi libro.**
1. **Tú** necesitas _____ mesa.
2. **Ella** necesita _____ lápices. (Los lápices _____ _____)
3. **Nosotros** necesitamos _____ dinero.
4. **Ud.** necesita _____ pluma. (La pluma _____ _____)
5. **Yo** necesito _____ sillas.
6. **Tú** necesitas a _____ amigos.
7. **Nosotros** necesitamos _____ casas.
8. **Él** necesita _____ teléfono. (El teléfono _____ _____)

C. The indefinite article

Give the indefinite article for each of the following nouns:

1. sistema      5. calle        8. telegrama
2. mano         6. lápices      9. día
3. señoritas    7. lecciones    10. ciudad
4. señor

D. Present indicative of **ser**

Answer the following questions in the affirmative:

1. ¿Es Ud. alto(a)?       4. ¿Soy yo el (la) profesor(a)?
2. ¿Eres de California?   5. ¿Es difícil tu lección de español?
3. ¿Son Uds. felices?     6. ¿Son ellos de México?

E. The irregular verbs **ir, dar,** and **estar**

Item substitution. Change the verbs according to each new subject. Make all other necessary changes.

1. Yo **doy mi** número de teléfono. (ellos, nosotros, tú, Uds., ella)
2. Ud. **está** en **su** casa. (yo, ellos, nosotros, ella, tú, Uds.)
3. Ella **va** a **sus** clases. (nosotros, Ud., tú, yo, ellos)

## LESSON 4

A. The verbs **ser** and **estar**

Write sentences using the following pairs of items and **ser** or **estar,** as needed. Follow the model:

*Modelo:* Mi esposo / profesor
     **Mi esposo es profesor.**

1. La botella / plástica
2. La señorita López / enferma
3. Las casas / de Jorge
4. Los estudiantes / mexicanos
5. El profesor / en el hospital
6. Yo / de Arizona
7. Nosotros / bien
8. María / alta
9. Gustavo y yo / casados
10. Mañana / sábado
11. Yo / en la calle Universidad
12. El hijo de la señora Nieto / ingeniero

B. Contractions

Give the Spanish equivalent:

1. We are waiting for Mr. Peña.
2. She is visiting Mr. Linares and Mrs. Viera.
3. The money is Mr. Diaz's.
4. He goes to the hospital.
5. We need Dr. Mena's phone number.

C. The comparative of adjectives and adverbs

Answer the following questions in the negative:

1. ¿Es Ud. tan alto(a) como el profesor (la profesora)?
2. ¿Llega el profesor más tarde que los estudiantes?
3. ¿Es Ud. el (la) estudiante menos inteligente de la clase?

4. ¿Es Ud. la persona más feliz de la clase?
5. ¿Es Ud. el (la) peor estudiante?
6. ¿Son Uds. mayores que sus amigos?
7. ¿Soy yo el (la) mejor de la clase?
8. ¿La casa de su amigo es más grande que su casa?

D. The irregular verbs **tener** and **venir**

Item substitution. Change the verb according to each new subject. Make all other necessary changes.

1. **Yo** vengo con **mi** hijo. (nosotros, tú, ellos, Ud., Uds., él)
2. **Nosotros** tenemos **nuestros** libros. (yo, ella, tú, Uds., Ud.)

E. Cardinal numbers (200-1000)

Give the answers to the following problems:

1. setecientos − doscientos =
2. cien + novecientos =
3. trescientos + doscientos cincuenta =
4. mil − ochocientos =
5. cuatrocientos + quinientos =
6. seiscientos − ciento cincuenta =

# LESSON 5

A. Expressions with **tener**

Tell what is happening in each of the pictures. Follow the model:

*Modelo:*

Ella . . . .
**Ella tiene hambre.**

1. Carlos . . . .

2. Él . . . .

3. Yo . . . .

4. Ellas . . . .

5. ¿Ud. . . . ?

6. Tú . . . .

7. Nélida . . . .

B. Telling time

Answer the following questions:

1. ¿A qué hora es su clase de español?
2. ¿A qué hora comen Uds.?
3. ¿A qué hora va Ud. a la universidad?
4. ¿Estudia Ud. por la mañana, por la tarde o por la noche?
5. ¿A qué hora llega el profesor a clase?

C. Stem-changing verbs (**e** > **ie**)

Answer the following questions:

1. ¿Prefieren Uds. estudiar francés o alemán?
2. ¿Quieres ir al cine hoy?
3. ¿A qué hora empieza la clase de español?
4. ¿Entienden Uds. las lecciones?
5. ¿Pierden Uds. mucho dinero en Las Vegas?
6. ¿A qué hora cierran la biblioteca?
7. ¿A qué hora comienza su programa de televisión favorito?

D. **Ir a** plus infinitive

Complete the following sentences using **ir a** plus the infinitive of the verb given in parentheses. Follow the model:

*Modelo:* Yo _____ por la tarde.  (*study*)
     **Yo voy a estudiar** por la tarde.

1. Nosotros _____ pescado hoy.  (*eat*)
2. Él _____ una camisa.  (*buy*)
3. ¿A qué hora _____ la reunión?  (*start*)
4. Tú no _____ a tu hermano.  (*visit*)
5. Mi hija _____ en el vuelo de las ocho de la noche.  (*arrive*)
6. Yo _____ sola.  (*come*)
7. Nosotros _____ mucho dinero.  (*need*)
8. ¿_____ Uds. a casa de Roberto?  (*go*)

E. The uses of **hay**

Give the Spanish equivalent:

1. How many students are there?
2. There is not (any) money.
3. There are two flights to Lima.
4. There is a meeting today.
5. How many chairs are there?

Lesson 6

# 1. SOME USES OF THE DEFINITE ARTICLE

A. The definite article is used in Spanish with expressions of time, the seasons, and the days of the week:

| | |
|---|---|
| ¿Cuándo es su clase de español? | *When is your Spanish class?* |
| Tengo clase de español **los**[1] lunes, miércoles y viernes. | *I have Spanish class on Mondays, Wednesdays, and Fridays.* |

ATENCIÓN: It is omitted with the seasons and days of the week when used after the verb **ser:**

| | |
|---|---|
| ¿Es primavera ahora en Chile? | *Is it spring in Chile now?* |
| Sí, es primavera. | *Yes, it is spring.* |
| ¿Qué día de la semana es hoy? | *What day of the week is today?* |
| Hoy es domingo. | *Today is Sunday.* |

B. The definite article is included with nouns used in a general sense:

| | |
|---|---|
| ¿Qué quieren **las** mujeres y **los** hombres de hoy? | *What do today's women and men want?* |
| Quieren igualdad. | *They want equality.* |

C. The definite article is used with abstract nouns:

| | |
|---|---|
| ¿Es importante **la** libertad? | *Is freedom important?* |
| Sí, **la** libertad es importante. | *Yes, freedom is important.* |

D. The definite article is used before **próximo** (*next*) and **pasado** (*last*) with expressions of time:

| | |
|---|---|
| ¿Cuándo comienzan las clases? | *When do classes begin?* |
| Comienzan **la** semana **próxima.** | *They begin next week.* |

## Exercise

Complete the following sentences with the appropriate definite article, if one is needed:

1. Hoy es _____ jueves.
2. Vamos al hospital _____ domingos.
3. Prefiero _____ verano a _____ primavera.
4. Tengo clase de español _____ miércoles.
5. ¿Qué _____ fecha es hoy?

[1] Notice that the definite article is used here as the equivalent of *on.*

6. _____ libertad es importante.
7. Empiezo mis clases _____ próximo lunes.
8. Ahora es _____ invierno en Canadá.
9. _____ hombres y _____ mujeres quieren _____ igualdad.
10. La reunión es _____ semana próxima.

## 2. STEM-CHANGING VERBS (o > ue)

A. As you learned in Lesson 5, certain verbs undergo a change in the stem in the present indicative. When **o** is the last vowel of the stem and it is stressed, it changes to **ue**.

| volver (*to come back*) | |
|---|---|
| **vue**lvo | volvemos |
| **vue**lves | |
| **vue**lve | **vue**lven |

• Notice that the stem vowel is not stressed in the verb form corresponding to **nosotros,** and therefore the **o** does not change to **ue**.

¿Cuándo **vuelven** Uds.?     *When are you coming back?*
**Volvemos** a las siete.     *We are coming back at seven.*

• Some other common verbs that follow the same change in the stem are: the **-ar** verbs **recordar** (*to remember*) and **volar** (*to fly*), the **-er** verb **poder** (*to be able*), and the **-ir** verb **dormir** (*to sleep*).

¿**Puede** Ud. trabajar mañana?     *Are you able to work tomorrow?*
Sí. ¡Ah! No, porque ahora **recuerdo** que voy a estudiar.     *Yes. Oh! No, because now I remember that I'm going to study.*

¿Cuándo **vuela** Ud.?     *When are you flying?*
**Vuelo** la próxima semana.     *I'm flying next week.*

¿Cuándo **pueden** Uds. ir al hospital?     *When can you go to the hospital?*
**Podemos** ir mañana.     *We can go tomorrow.*

¿Cuántas horas **duerme** él?     *How many hours does he sleep?*
Él **duerme** diez horas.     *He sleeps ten hours.*

**Exercise**

Complete the following sentences with the correct form of the verb given in parentheses:

1. ¿Cuándo _____ (volver) Ud. de México?
2. Yo nunca _____ (recordar) su número de teléfono.
3. Nosotras _____ (volar) la semana que viene.
4. Ellos no _____ (poder) ir con sus hijos ahora.
5. Tú no _____ (volver) en el verano porque no _____ (poder).
6. Uds. _____ (volar) en mayo.
7. Yo _____ (poder) venir mañana.
8. ¿_____ (recordar) Ud. a la hija de Juan?
9. Nosotros _____ (dormir) mucho pero él _____ (dormir) más.
10. Nosotras no _____ (poder) estudiar hoy.

## 3. AFFIRMATIVE AND NEGATIVE EXPRESSIONS

A. Study the expressions in the following table:

| Affirmative | | Negative | |
|---|---|---|---|
| **algo** | something | **nada** | nothing |
| **alguien** | someone, anyone | **nadie** | nobody, no one |
| **alguno(a)** | | **ninguno(a)** | |
| **algún** | any, some | **ningún** | none, not any |
| **algunos(as)** | | | |
| **siempre** | always | **nunca** | |
| | | **jamás** | never |
| **también** | also, too | **tampoco** | neither |
| **o . . . o** | either . . . or | **ni . . . ni** | neither . . . nor |

| | |
|---|---|
| ¿Hay **algo** en la mesa? | *Is there anything on the table?* |
| No. No hay **nada**. | *No. There is nothing.* |
| ¿Hay **alguien** con el director? | *Is there anyone with the director?* |
| No, no hay **nadie**. | *No, there is nobody.* |
| ¿Van Uds. **siempre** a Los Ángeles? | *Do you always go to Los Angeles?* |
| No, no vamos **nunca**. | *No, we never go.* |
| ¿Quieren venir Uds. **también?** | *Do you want to come too?* |
| No, Juan no quiere ir **ni** yo tampoco. | *No, John doesn't want to go and neither do I.* |
| ¿Qué quiere Ud.? ¿El piano **o** la radio? | *What do you want? The piano or the radio?* |

No quiero **ni** el piano **ni** la
radio.

*I want neither the piano nor
the radio.*

- **Alguno** and **ninguno** drop the -o before a masculine singular noun; but **alguna** and **ninguna** keep the final -a.

¿Hay **algún** libro o **alguna**
pluma en la mesa?
No, no hay **ningún** libro ni
**ninguna** pluma.

*Is there any book or pen on the
table?*
*No, there isn't any book or
pen.*

- **Alguno(a)** may be used in the plural form, but **ninguno(a)** is used in the singular form.

¿Desea comprar **algunos**
regalos?
No, no deseo comprar **ningún**
regalo.

*Do you want to buy any
presents?*
*No, I don't want to buy any
presents.*

B.  Spanish frequently uses a double negative. In this construction, the adverb **no** is placed before the verb. The second negative word either follows the verb or appears at the end of the sentence. However, if the negative word precedes the verb, **no** is never used:

¿Habla Ud. español **siempre**?
No, yo **no** hablo español **nunca.**
Yo **nunca** hablo español.

*Do you always speak Spanish?*
*No, I never speak Spanish.*

¿Compra Ud. **algo** aquí?
No, **no** compro **nada nunca.**
**Nunca** compro **nada.**

*Do you buy anything here?*
*No, I never buy anything.*

### Exercise

Answer the following questions in the negative:

1. ¿Necesita Ud. algo?
2. ¿Hay alguien aquí?
3. ¿Estudia Ud. siempre por la noche?
4. ¿Quieres un piano o una radio?
5. ¿Va a traer Ud. algunos regalos?
6. Juan no va a la reunión. ¿Vas tú?

## 4. ORDINAL NUMBERS AND THEIR USES

| | | | |
|---|---|---|---|
| primero(a) | *first* | sexto(a) | *sixth* |
| segundo(a) | *second* | séptimo(a) | *seventh* |
| tercero(a) | *third* | octavo(a) | *eighth* |
| cuarto(a) | *fourth* | noveno(a) | *ninth* |
| quinto(a) | *fifth* | décimo(a) | *tenth* |

- The ordinal numbers **primero** and **tercero** drop the final **-o** before masculine singular nouns:

| | |
|---|---|
| ¿Qué día llegan Uds.? | *What day are you arriving?* |
| Llegamos el **primer** día del mes. | *We are arriving the first day of the month.* |

- Ordinal numbers agree in gender and number with the nouns they modify:

| | |
|---|---|
| ¿Qué oficina prefiere? | *Which office do you prefer?* |
| Prefiero **la** quinta. | *I prefer the fifth (one).* |

- Ordinal numbers are seldom used after *the tenth:*

| | |
|---|---|
| ¿En qué piso viven Uds.? | *On which floor do you live?* |
| Vivimos en el piso **doce.** | *We live on the twelfth floor.* |

- Spanish uses cardinal numbers for dates except for *the first:*

| | |
|---|---|
| ¿Qué día es hoy? | *What day is it today?* |
| Hoy es el **treinta** de abril. Mañana es el **primero** de mayo. | *Today is April 30th. Tomorrow is the first day of May.* |

### Exercise

Complete the following sentences with the correct ordinal number:

1. Él es el _____ (*first*) estudiante.
2. Yo vivo en el _____ (*fifth*) piso.
3. Ella prefiere la _____ (*second*) mesa.
4. La oficina de mi esposo está en el _____ (*third*) piso.
5. Llegamos el _____ (*first*) de mayo.
6. Vuelven en los _____ (*first*) días del mes.
7. Yo quiero la _____ (*fourth*), la _____ (*sixth*), y la _____ (*seventh*) sillas.
8. No tenemos clases ni la _____ (*ninth*) ni la _____ (*tenth*) semana.

## 5. USES OF **tener que** AND **hay que**

A. The Spanish equivalent of *to have to* is **tener que:**

| | |
|---|---|
| ¿Qué **tiene que** hacer hoy? | *What do you have to do today?* |
| **Tengo que** trabajar. | *I have to work.* |

B. The Spanish equivalent of *one must* is **hay que:**

| | |
|---|---|
| ¿Qué **hay que** hacer para tener éxito? | *What must one do to succeed?* |
| **Hay que** trabajar. | *One must work.* |

**Exercise**

Complete the following sentences with **hay que** or the correct forms of **tener que,** as needed:

1. Para tener éxito, _____ trabajar.
2. Yo _____ estudiar mucho.
3. Nosotros _____ trabajar mañana.
4. _____ llegar temprano.
5. Ud. _____ volver a las diez de la noche.
6. _____ comenzar más tarde.

---

## STUDY OF COGNATES

1. Exact cognates:

   | | |
   |---|---|
   | **el director** | director |
   | **el piano** | piano |
   | **la radio** | radio |

2. The following words are the same in Spanish and in English, except for a written accent mark or a final vowel:

   | | |
   |---|---|
   | **Canadá** | Canada |
   | **importante** | important |

3. Approximate cognates:

   | | | | |
   |---|---|---|---|
   | **la igualdad** | equality | **la oficina** | office |

---

## NEW VOCABULARY

NOUNS

| | |
|---|---|
| **el hombre** | man |
| **el mes** | month |
| **la mujer** | woman |
| **el piso** | floor (story) |
| **el regalo** | present, gift |
| **la semana** | week |

VERBS

| | |
|---|---|
| **dormir (o > ue)** | to sleep |
| **poder (o > ue)** | to be able |
| **recordar (o > ue)** | to remember |
| **volar (o > ue)** | to fly |
| **volver (o > ue)** | to come back, return |

ADJECTIVES

| | |
|---|---|
| **pasado(a)** | last |
| **próximo(a)** | next |

OTHER WORDS AND EXPRESSIONS

| | |
|---|---|
| **ahora** | now |
| **aquí** | here |
| **mañana** | tomorrow |
| **porque** | because |
| **tener éxito** | to succeed |

CORREOS Y TELEGRAFOS

Lesson 7

# 1. STEM-CHANGING VERBS (e > i)

A. Certain **-ir** verbs undergo a special change in the stem. When **e** is the last stem vowel and it is stressed, the **e** changes to **i** in the present indicative.

| servir *(to serve)* | pedir | *to ask for, to request, to order* | seguir | *to follow, to continue* |
|---|---|---|---|---|
| sirvo    servimos | pido    pedimos | | sigo    seguimos | |
| sirves | pides | | sigues | |
| sirve    sirven | pide    piden | | sigue    siguen | |

- Notice that the stem vowel is not stressed in the verb form corresponding to **nosotros**. Therefore, the **e** does not change to **i**.

- Verbs like **seguir** drop the **u** before an **a** or an **o**: **yo sigo**. For example, **conseguir** *(to obtain)*: **yo consigo; perseguir** *(to pursue, to persecute)*: **yo persigo.**

- The verb **decir** *(to say, to tell)* undergoes the same change, but in addition it is irregular in the first person singular: **yo digo.**

| | |
|---|---|
| ¿Qué **sirven** en la cafetería de la universidad? | *What do they serve in the college cafeteria?* |
| **Sirven** sopa, ensalada, carne y postre. | *They serve soup, salad, meat, and dessert.* |
| ¿Qué **pide** Enrique? | *What is Henry ordering?* |
| **Pide** un refresco. | *He's ordering a soda.* |
| ¿A quién **siguen** ustedes? | *Whom are you following?* |
| **Seguimos** a nuestra maestra. | *We are following our teacher.* |
| ¿**Dice** Ud. la verdad siempre? | *Do you always tell the truth?* |
| Sí, yo siempre **digo** la verdad. | *Yes, I always tell the truth.* |

**Exercise**

Complete the following sentences with the correct form of the verb given in parentheses:

1. Yo _____ (conseguir) el dinero.
2. Ud. _____ (servir) sopa y ensalada.
3. Ella _____ (pedir) un refresco.
4. Nosotros _____ (seguir) al maestro.
5. Uds. _____ (decir) la verdad.
6. Ud. _____ (perseguir) a los estudiantes.

7. Yo _____ (decir) la verdad siempre.
8. Uds. siempre _____ (pedir) postre.
9. Ellos no _____ (servir) carne en la cafetería.
10. ¿_____ (seguir) Ud. en la clase?

## 2. MORE ABOUT IRREGULAR VERBS

Some common verbs are irregular only in the first person singular of the present indicative. The other persons are regular:

| | | | |
|---|---|---|---|
| salir (*to go out*): | yo **salgo** | traducir (*to translate*): | yo **traduzco** |
| hacer (*to do, to make*): | yo **hago** | conocer (*to know, to be acquainted with*): | yo **conozco** |
| poner (*to put, to place*): | yo **pongo** | caber (*to fit*): | yo **quepo** |
| caer (*to fall*): | yo **caigo** | ver (*to see*): | yo **veo** |
| traer (*to bring*): | yo **traigo** | saber (*to know how, to know a fact*): | yo **sé** |
| conducir (*to conduct, to drive*): | yo **conduzco** | | |

| | |
|---|---|
| ¿**Sale** Ud. a menudo? | *Do you go out often?* |
| Sí, yo **salgo** a menudo. | *Yes, I go out often.* |
| ¿Dónde **pone** Ud. la información? | *Where do you put the information?* |
| Yo **pongo** la información en el fichero. | *I put the information in the file.* |
| ¿**Sabe** Ud. conducir? | *Do you know how to drive?* |
| Sí, yo **sé** conducir. **Conduzco** muy bien. | *Yes, I know how to drive. I drive very well.* |
| ¿**Conoce** Ud. a mi hermano? | *Do you know my brother?* |
| Sí, yo **conozco** a su hermano. | *Yes, I know your brother.* |

### Exercise

Answer the following questions, first in the affirmative, then in the negative:

1. ¿Sabe Ud. español?
2. ¿Hace Ud. algo los domingos?
3. ¿Conduce Ud. bien?
4. ¿Pone Ud. la información en el fichero?
5. ¿Sale Ud. a menudo?
6. ¿Cabe Ud. en el coche?

7. ¿Conoce Ud. la ciudad de Nueva York?
8. ¿Traduce Ud. del español al inglés?
9. ¿Trae Ud. sus libros a clase?
10. ¿Ve Ud. a sus amigos los sábados?

## 3. THE IMPERSONAL se

A. Spanish uses the reflexive object **se** before the third person of the verb (either singular or plural, depending on the subject) as the equivalent of the passive voice in English:

*The library is opened at eight.*
La biblioteca **se abre** a las ocho.

*The offices are closed at five.*
Las oficinas **se cierran** a las cinco.

Notice the use of **se** in the following impersonal constructions, announcements, and general directions:

¿A qué hora **se abre** la biblioteca?     *What time does the library open?*
**Se abre** a las ocho.     *It opens at eight.*

¿A qué hora **se cierran** las oficinas?     *What time do the offices close?*
Las oficinas **se cierran** a las cinco de la tarde.     *The offices close at 5 P.M.*

¿Aquí **se habla** inglés?     *Is English spoken here?*
No, **se habla** sólo español.     *No, only Spanish is spoken (here).*

B. **Se** is also used as the equivalent of **one, they,** or **people,** when the subject of the verb is not definite:

**No se puede** hacer eso.     *One can't do that.*

¿Cómo **se dice** *always* en español?     *How does one say "always" in Spanish?*
**Se dice** «siempre».     *One says siempre.*

### Exercise

Answer the following questions:

1. ¿A qué hora se abre la biblioteca?
2. ¿Se habla inglés en los Estados Unidos?
3. ¿Cómo se dice *address* en español?
4. ¿A qué hora se cierran los restaurantes en esta ciudad?

5. ¿Se abren las oficinas de la universidad los domingos?
6. ¿A qué hora se cierra el museo?
7. ¿Se habla español o inglés en Chile?
8. ¿Cómo se escribe su apellido?


## 4. DIRECT OBJECT PRONOUNS

The forms of the direct object pronouns are as follows:

| Subject | Direct Object | |
|---|---|---|
| yo | **me** (me) | Ella **me** visita. |
| tú | **te** (you, *familiar*) | Yo **te** sigo. |
| Ud. | {**lo** (you, *masc., formal*) | Yo **lo** conozco. (a Ud.) |
| | **la** (you, *fem., formal*) | Yo **la** conozco. (a Ud.) |
| él | **lo** (him, it) | Él **lo** ve. |
| ella | **la** (her, it) | Él **la** ve. |
| nosotros<br>nosotras | **nos** (us, *masc. and fem.*) | Tú **nos** comprendes. |
| Uds. | **los** (you, *masc., pl., formal*) | Nosotros **los** visitamos. (a Uds.) |
| | **las** (you, *fem., pl., formal*) | Nosotros **las** visitamos. (a Uds.) |
| ellos | **los** | Él **los** ve. |
| ellas | **las** | Él **las** ve. |

A. The direct object pronoun is placed *before* a conjugated verb:

Yo conozco al <u>señor Lima</u>.
Yo            **lo**        conozco.

Ella escribe <u>la carta</u>.
Ella        **la**        escribe.

Nosotros vemos a <u>nuestros amigos</u>.
Nosotros            **los**        vemos.

B. In a negative sentence the **no** must precede the object pronoun:

Yo traduzco las lecciones.
Yo            **las**        traduzco.
Yo    **no**    **las**        traduzco.

C. Whenever two verbs are used in the same clause, the pronoun is either added to the infinitive or placed before the conjugated verb:

**Te** quiero ver.
OR:   Quiero ver**te.** ⎫ *I want to see you.*

| | |
|---|---|
| ¿**Me** ves ahora? | *Do you see me now?* |
| Sí, ahora **te** veo. | *Yes, now I see you.* |
| ¿Conduce Ud. el coche? | *Do you drive the car?* |
| Sí, yo **lo** conduzco. | *Yes, I drive it.* |
| ¿Pone Ud. la información en la mesa? | *Do you put the information on the table?* |
| Sí, yo **la** pongo en la mesa. | *Yes, I put it on the table.* |
| ¿Pides las cartas? | *Are you asking for the letters?* |
| Sí, **las** pido. | *Yes, I am asking for them.* |

### Exercises

A. Replace the object in italics with the appropriate pronoun. Follow the model:

*Modelo:*  Sirvo *el café.*
        **Lo sirvo.**

1. Pedimos *los refrescos.*
2. Digo *la verdad.*
3. Ud. sirve *los postres.*
4. Él ve a *Juan.*
5. Yo conozco a *Pedro y a Enrique.*
6. Ana conduce *el coche.*
7. Ud. da *la información.*
8. Ellos ven a *Ana y a Pilar.*
9. Ud. pide *las mesas.*
10. Ellos dicen *la verdad.*

B. Answer the questions, following the model:

*Modelo:*  ¿Quieres escribir las cartas?
        **No, no quiero escribirlas.**
    OR:   **No, no las quiero escribir.**

1. ¿Vas a ver a tus amigos?
2. ¿Quieren Uds. poner la información en el fichero?
3. ¿Va a traer Marta las mesas y las sillas?
4. ¿Quiere Ud. conocer al señor Aranda?
5. ¿Va Ud. a traducir la lección al inglés?
6. ¿Quieren Uds. conducir el coche?

7. ¿Vas a traerme a la universidad?
8. ¿Voy a llevarte al cine?

C. Give the Spanish equivalent:

1. Do you know him?
2. Does he want to see her? (*both ways*)
3. The books? I am going to bring them. (*both ways*)
4. She doesn't know us.
5. Now I see you, my son.
6. You don't know me, Mr. Lima.

## 5. saber VS. conocer

Spanish has two verbs that mean *to know:* **saber** and **conocer**.

A. **Saber** means to know something by heart, to know how to do something, or to know a fact:

| | |
|---|---|
| ¿**Sabe** Ud. ya la lección de hoy? | *Do you already know today's lesson?* |
| Sí, ya la **sé**. | *Yes, I already know it.* |
| ¿**Saben** ellos nadar? | *Do they know how to swim?* |
| Sí, ellos **saben** nadar. | *Yes, they know how to swim.* |
| ¿**Sabes** que el embajador llega hoy? | *Do you know that the ambassador arrives today?* |
| Sí, ya lo **sé**. | *Yes, I (already) know (it).* |

B. **Conocer** means to be familiar or acquainted with a person, a thing, or a place:

| | |
|---|---|
| ¿**Conoce** a la hija del vecino? | *Do you know the neighbor's daughter?* |
| Sí, la **conozco**. | *Yes, I know her.* |
| ¿**Conocen** Uds. las novelas de Cervantes? | *Do you know Cervantes' novels?* |
| Sí, las **conocemos**. | *Yes, we know them.* |
| ¿**Conocen** ellos Puerto Rico? | *Do they know Puerto Rico?* |
| No, ellos no lo **conocen**. | *No, they don't know it.* |

**Exercise**

Complete the following sentences with the present indicative of **saber** and **conocer**, as needed:

1. Ellos _____ California.
2. Ud. no _____ a mi vecino.
3. ¿Tú _____ la lección de hoy?
4. Él ya _____ al embajador.
5. Yo no _____ nadar.
6. Uds. _____ las novelas de Cervantes.
7. ¿_____ Uds. qué día es hoy?
8. Yo no _____ la ciudad de Madrid.
9. Nosotras _____ inglés y español.
10. Ellas _____ a la esposa del profesor.

## 6. FORMATION OF ADVERBS

A. Most Spanish adverbs are formed by adding **-mente** (the equivalent of English *-ly*) to the adjective:

especial *special*     especial**mente** *specially, especially*
reciente *recent*     reciente**mente** *recently*

B. If the adjective ends in **-o,** change the ending to **-a** before adding **-mente:**

lento *slow*     lent**amente** *slowly*
rápido *rapid*     rápid**amente** *rapidly*

C. If two or more adverbs are used together, only the last one ends in *-mente:*

lenta y cuidadosa**mente**     *slowly and carefully*

D. If the adjective has a written accent mark, the adverb retains it:

fácil     fácil**mente**

Study the use of the adverbs in the following sentence:

Traigo estos libros **especialmente** para Ud.     *I'm bringing these books especially for you.*
Un millón de gracias.     *Thanks a million.*

El niño escribe la carta **lenta** y **cuidadosamente.**     *The child writes the letter slowly and carefully.*
¡Pero la escribe muy bien!     *But he writes it very well!*

**Exercise**

Give the Spanish equivalent:

1. She reads slowly.
2. I need to do it carefully.
3. The chair is especially for you, sir.
4. She is going to do it rapidly but carefully.
5. Recently?
6. The lesson? We can translate it easily.

## STUDY OF COGNATES

1. The following words are the same in Spanish and English, except for a written accent mark or a final vowel:

   | | |
   |---|---|
   | **la cafetería** | cafeteria |
   | **la novela** | novel |

2. Spanish words ending in **-ción**, instead of *-tion* in English:

   | | |
   |---|---|
   | **la información** | information |

3. Approximate cognates:

   | | |
   |---|---|
   | **especial** | special |
   | **reciente** | recent |

## NEW VOCABULARY

| NOUNS | | VERBS | |
|---|---|---|---|
| **la carne** | meat | **conseguir (e > i)** | to obtain |
| **la carta** | letter | **nadar** | to swim |
| **el coche** | car | **pedir (e > i)** | to request, |
| **el embajador** | ambassador | | to ask for, |
| **la ensalada** | salad | | to order |
| **el fichero** | file | **perseguir (e > i)** | to pursue, |
| **(archivo)** | | | to persecute |
| **la maestra** | teacher | **seguir (e > i)** | to follow, |
| **el maestro** | (elementary | | to continue |
| | school) | **servir (e > i)** | to serve |
| **el postre** | dessert | | |
| **el refresco** | soda, beverage | ADJECTIVES | |
| **la sopa** | soup | **cuidadoso(a)** | careful |
| **el vecino** | neighbor | **fácil** | easy |
| **la verdad** | truth | **lento(a)** | slow |
| | | **rápido(a)** | fast |

OTHER WORDS AND EXPRESSIONS

| | |
|---|---|
| **a menudo** | often |
| **siempre** | always |
| **un millón de gracias** | thanks a million |
| **ya** | already |

# Lesson 8

# 1. DEMONSTRATIVE ADJECTIVES

Demonstrative adjectives point out persons or things. They agree in gender and number with the nouns they modify or point out.

The forms of the demonstrative adjectives are as follows:

|  | Masculine | | Feminine | |
|---|---|---|---|---|
|  | Singular | Plural | Singular | Plural |
| *this, these* | este | estos | esta | estas |
| *that, those* | ese | esos | esa | esas |
| *that, those* (*at a distance*) | aquel | aquellos | aquella | aquellas |

¿Para quién son **estas** revistas?
**Estas** revistas son para Marta y **esos** cuadernos son para Jorge.

*Who are these magazines for?*
*These magazines are for Martha, and those notebooks are for George.*

¿Podermos comer hoy en **este** restaurante?
No, vamos a comer en **aquella** cafetería que está allá.

*Can we eat in this restaurant today?*
*No, we are going to eat in that cafeteria (which is) over there.*

## Exercise

Change the demonstrative adjectives according to the new nouns:

1. Este cuaderno, \_\_\_\_\_ casa, \_\_\_\_\_ revistas, \_\_\_\_\_ programas.
2. Esas ciudades, \_\_\_\_\_ biblioteca, \_\_\_\_\_ lápices, \_\_\_\_\_ idioma.
3. Aquella cafetería, \_\_\_\_\_ sillas, \_\_\_\_\_ museo, \_\_\_\_\_ números.

## 2. DEMONSTRATIVE PRONOUNS

The demonstrative pronouns are the same as the demonstrative adjectives, except that the pronouns take a written accent.

The forms of the demonstrative pronouns are as follows:

| | Masculine | | Feminine | | Neuter |
|---|---|---|---|---|---|
| | Singular | Plural | Singular | Plural | |
| this (one), these | éste | éstos | ésta | éstas | esto |
| that (one), those | ése | ésos | ésa | ésas | eso |
| that (one), those (at a distance) | aquél | aquéllos | aquélla | aquéllas | aquello |

● Each demonstrative pronoun has a neuter form. The neuter pronoun has no accent, because there are no corresponding demonstrative adjectives.

| ¿Qué corbata quiere Ud.? **¿Ésta** o **aquélla?** | Which tie do you want? This one or that one over there? |
|---|---|
| Quiero **aquélla.** | I want that one over there. |

| ¿Necesitan Uds. estos periódicos o **ésos?** | Do you need these newspapers or those ones? |
|---|---|
| No, necesitamos **aquél** que está en la mesa. | No, we need that one (which is) on the table. |

| ¿Qué crees de **esto?** | What do you think about this? |
|---|---|
| Creo que **esto** es un problema para el presidente. | I think this is a problem for the president. |

### Exercise

Complete the following sentences with the Spanish equivalent of the pronouns in parentheses:

1. Quiero este libro y _____ (that one).
2. Necesitamos esa pluma y _____ (that one over there).
3. Compramos esos lápices y _____ (these ones).
4. Recibimos este periódico y _____ (those ones).
5. ¿Estudia Ud. esta lección o _____ (that one)?
6. ¿Comienza Ud. con este programa o con _____ (that one over there)?
7. ¿Prefieren ellos estas mesas o _____ (those ones over there)?
8. ¿Va Ud. a leer este libro o _____ (those ones)?
9. Deseo aquellas botellas y _____ (these ones).
10. ¿Van Uds. a comprar esa corbata o _____ (this one)?

## 3. PRESENT PROGRESSIVE

A.  The present progressive describes an action that is in progress at the moment we are talking. It is formed with the present of **estar** and the gerund (equivalent to the English *-ing* form) of the conjugated verb.

| Gerund Endings | | |
|---|---|---|
| **hablar** | **comer** | **vivir** |
| habl- **ando** | com- **iendo** | viv- **iendo** |

B.  Some irregular gerunds:

| pedir | **pidiendo** | servir | **sirviendo** |
|---|---|---|---|
| decir | **diciendo** | leer | **leyendo**[1] |
| venir | **viniendo** | ir | **yendo** |

| | |
|---|---|
| ¿Qué **estás estudiando?** | *What are you studying?* |
| **Estoy estudiando** mi lección de historia. | *I am studying my history lesson.* |
| ¿Dónde **están viviendo** Uds. ahora? | *Where are you living now?* |
| **Estamos viviendo** en la avenida Unión. | *We are living on Union Avenue.* |
| ¿Qué lección **está leyendo** Ud.? | *Which lesson are you reading?* |
| **Estoy leyendo** la lección de química. | *I am reading the chemistry lesson.* |

### Exercise

Change the verbs into the progressive form. Follow the model:

*Modelo:*  Yo tomo café.
            **Yo estoy tomando café.**

1.  Tú lees la lección de historia.
2.  Ellos piden dinero.
3.  Nosotros decimos la verdad.
4.  ¿Come Ud. ahora en este restaurante?
5.  José sirve el café.
6.  ¿A quién esperas?
7.  Ella habla con el presidente.

[1] Notice that the **-i** of **-iendo** becomes **y** between vowels.

8. Tú trabajas mucho.
9. Yo vivo en la avenida Washington.
10. Ellos estudian química.

## 4. INDIRECT OBJECT PRONOUNS

The forms of the indirect object pronouns are as follows:

| Subject | Indirect Object | |
|---|---|---|
| yo | **me** (to)(me) | Él **me** da las revistas. |
| tú | **te** (to)(you, *familiar*) | Yo **te** doy el cuaderno. |
| Ud. | **le** (to)(you, *formal, masc.* and *fem.*) | Ella **le** compra una corbata. |
| él ⎤ ella ⎦ | **le** (to)(him, her) | Yo **le** hablo en inglés. |
| nosotros ⎤ nosotras ⎦ | **nos** (to)(us, *masc.* and *fem.*) | Ella **nos** da la lección. |
| Uds. | **les** (to)(you, *formal pl., masc.* and *fem.*) | Yo **les** digo la verdad. |
| ellos ⎤ ellas ⎦ | **les** (to)(them, *masc.* and *fem.*) | El presidente **les** da el dinero. |

A. The indirect object pronouns are the same as the direct object pronouns, except in the third person. Indirect object pronouns are usually placed *in front* of the verb:

¿Quién **les** compra a Uds. los pasajes?
*Who is buying you the tickets?*

Mi hermano **nos** compra los pasajes.
*My brother is buying us the tickets.*

¿Qué **le** pregunta Ud.?
*What are you asking him?*

**Le** pregunto su dirección.
*I'm asking him his address.*

EXCEPTIONS:

1. When an infinitive follows the conjugated verb, the indirect object pronoun is placed in front of the conjugated verb or after the infinitive:

¿Qué vas a comprar**me**?
*What are you going to buy me?*

Voy a comprar**te** un abrigo.
*I'm going to buy you a coat.*

OR:

¿Qué **me** vas a comprar?
**Te** voy a comprar un abrigo.

2. With present participles, the indirect object pronouns can be used both ways also:

| | |
|---|---|
| ¿A quién está Ud. escribié**ndole**? | *To whom are you writing?* |
| Estoy escribié**ndole** a mi esposo. | *I'm writing to my husband.* |

OR:

¿A quién **le** está Ud. escribiendo?

**Le** estoy escribiendo a mi esposo.

3. With affirmative commands, they are always placed after the verb. The affirmative formal commands (**Ud.** and **Uds.**) are discussed in Lesson 9.

.  .  .

B. With the indirect objects **le** and **les,** clarification is necessary when the sentence or the context of the conversation does not specify the gender of the person to which the pronoun refers. Spanish uses the preposition **a** + *the personal pronouns* for this purpose:

**Le** doy la información. (*to whom?*)

**Le** doy la información **a él.** (*to him*)
**Le** doy la información **a ella.** (*to her*)
**Le** doy la información **a Ud.** (*to you, formal*)

## Exercises

A. Complete the following sentences with the correct indirect object pronouns and clarify when necessary:

1. Yo _____ compro el abrigo _____, señor Vera. (*for you*)
2. _____ da un refresco. (*to me*)
3. _____ pido los cuadernos _____. (*to her*)
4. _____ está escribiendo una carta. (*to us*) (*two forms*)
5. _____ pregunto su número de teléfono _____. (*to you, form. pl.*)
6. _____ doy los pasajes, mi hija. (*to you*)
7. _____ voy a decir la verdad _____. (*to him*)
8. _____ estamos hablando en inglés _____. (*to them, fem.*) (*two forms*)

B. Give the Spanish equivalent:

1. I am giving you the tickets, Mr. Smith.
2. Are you writing to him? (*two forms*)
3. She always tells me the truth.
4. Are you going to buy us a magazine? (*two forms*)
5. I speak to them (*fem.*) in English.

## 5. DIRECT AND INDIRECT OBJECT PRONOUNS USED TOGETHER

A. When an indirect object pronoun and a direct object pronoun are used in the same sentence, the indirect object always appears first.

| | |
|---|---|
| ¿Cuándo me pagas el dinero? | *When are you paying me the money?* |
| **Te lo** pago[1] mañana. | *I'll pay (it to) you tomorrow.* |

B. With an infinitive, the pronouns can be placed either before or after:

| | |
|---|---|
| Necesito el diccionario. ¿Puedes prestár**melo?** | *I need the dictionary. Can you lend it to me?* |
| Sí, puedo prestár**telo.** | *Yes, I can lend it to you.* |

OR:

¿**Me lo** puedes prestar?
Sí, **te lo** puedo prestar.

C. If both pronouns start with **l,** the indirect object pronoun (**le** or **les**) is changed to **se.** For clarification it is sometimes necessary to add: **a él, a ella, a Ud., a Uds., a ellos, a ellas:**

| | |
|---|---|
| ¿**Le** sirves la comida **a él** o **a ella?** | *Do you serve dinner to him or to her?* |
| **Se** la sirvo **a él.** | *I serve it to him.* |

| | |
|---|---|
| ¿**Les** dan Uds. la medicina **a ellas** o **a ellos?** | *Are you giving the medicine to them(fem.) or to them(masc.)?* |
| **Se** la damos **a ellos.** | *We are giving it to them (masc.).* |

---

[1] The present indicative is frequently used in Spanish to express future.

**Exercises**

A. Change the following sentences, according to the model:

*Modelo:* Voy a comprártelo.
**Te lo voy a comprar.**

1. Quiere dárselo.
2. No va a creérmelo.
3. Va a preguntártelo.
4. Ella va a traérnoslas mañana.
5. No quiere prestármela.
6. Estoy leyéndoselos.
7. No voy a pagársela.
8. ¿Puedes traérmelas?
9. Va a dárselos.
10. Estamos diciéndoselo ahora.

B. Complete the following sentences with the appropriate direct and indirect object pronouns:

1. Yo ____ ____ traigo. (*to you, fam. / them, fem.*)
2. Ud. ____ ____ dice. (*to me / it, masc.*)
3. Vamos a traer ____ ____. (*to him / it, fem.*)
4. Uds. ____ ____ pagan. (*to us / them, masc.*)
5. Estamos leyendo ____ ____. (*to them / it, masc.*)

C. Answer the following questions, first in the affirmative, then in the negative. Substitute pronouns for the italicized nouns, according to the model:

*Modelo:* ¿Me compra Ud. *el abrigo?*
**Sí, se lo compro.**
**No, no se lo compro.**

1. ¿Va a servirme Ud. *la comida?*
2. ¿Le presta Ud. *los cuadernos* a Paco?
3. ¿Me compra Ud. *la corbata?*
4. ¿Les paga Ud. *los pasajes* a ellos?
5. ¿Está Ud. leyéndole *el periódico* a Inés?

# 6. **pedir** VS. **preguntar**

A. **Pedir** means *to ask for* in the sense of *to request:*

| | |
|---|---|
| ¿Qué te **piden** los muchachos? | *What do the boys ask you for?* |
| Me **piden** la medicina para su madre. | *They ask me for the medicine for their mother.* |

| | |
|---|---|
| ¿Vas a **pedir**le dinero a tu tío? | *Are you going to ask your uncle for money?* |
| No, voy a **pedír**selo a mi tía. Ella es más generosa. | *No, I'm going to ask my aunt (for it). She's more generous.* |

B. **Preguntar** means *to ask (a question)*:

| | |
|---|---|
| ¿Qué vas a **preguntar**le a René? | *What are you going to ask René?* |
| Voy a **preguntar**le si conoce a mi primo. | *I'm going to ask him if he knows my cousin.* |
| ¿Qué le vas a **preguntar** a Ana? | *What are you going to ask Ana?* |
| Le voy a **preguntar** qué hora es. | *I'm going to ask her what time it is.* |

**Exercise**

Complete the following sentences with the present indicative of **pedir** and **preguntar**, as needed:

1. Ellos me _____ dinero.
2. Yo le _____ qué quiere.
3. Ella le va a _____ si es el tío de Jorge.
4. Yo nunca le _____ nada. Ella no es muy generosa.
5. Le voy a _____ a Margarita si quiere ir allá.
6. ¿Qué le vas a _____ tú a Santa Claus?[1]
7. ¿Qué te _____ Carlos? ¿Dinero?
8. Yo nunca les _____ nada a mis primos, porque ellos no saben nada.

---

STUDY OF COGNATES

1. Spanish words ending in **-a** or **-o** instead of *-e* in English:

   **la medicina**    medicine

2. Spanish words ending in **-ia** or **-io** instead of *-y* in English:

   **la historia**    history

3. Spanish adjectives ending in **-oso(a)** instead of *-ous* in English:

   **generoso**(a)    generous

4. Approximate cognates:

   **la avenida**      avenue
   **el diccionario**  dictionary

---

[1] In most Latin American countries and in Spain, it is the custom to expect presents from the Three Wise Men on January 6.

NEW VOCABULARY

NOUNS

| el abrigo | coat |
| la comida | dinner, meal |
| la corbata | tie |
| el cuaderno | notebook |
| la madre | mother |
| el muchacho | boy, young man |
| el pasaje | ticket |
| el periódico | newspaper |
| la prima / el primo | cousin |
| la química | chemistry |

| la revista | magazine |
| la tía | aunt |
| el tío | uncle |

VERBS

| creer | to believe |
| pagar | to pay |
| preguntar | to ask (a question) |
| prestar | to lend |

OTHER WORDS AND EXPRESSIONS

| allá | over there |
| ¿para quién? | for whom? |

Lesson 9

# 1. POSSESSIVE PRONOUNS

| Singular | | Plural | | |
|---|---|---|---|---|
| *Masculine* | *Feminine* | *Masculine* | *Feminine* | |
| el mío | la mía | los míos | las mías | mine |
| el tuyo | la tuya | los tuyos | las tuyas | yours (*familiar*) |
| el suyo | la suya | los suyos | las suyas | $\left\{\begin{array}{l}\text{his}\\\text{hers}\\\text{yours (formal)}\end{array}\right.$ |
| el nuestro | la nuestra | los nuestros | las nuestras | ours |
| el suyo | la suya | los suyos | las suyas | $\left\{\begin{array}{l}\text{theirs}\\\text{yours (formal)}\end{array}\right.$ |

A. The possessive pronouns in Spanish agree in gender and number with the thing possessed. They are generally used with the definite article:

| | |
|---|---|
| Aquí están los zapatos de ellos. ¿Dónde están **los nuestros**? | *Here are their shoes. Where are ours?* |
| **Los nuestros** están en el dormitorio. | *Ours are in the bedroom.* |
| Tus pantalones están aquí. ¿Dónde están **los míos**? | *Your trousers are here. Where are mine?* |
| **Los tuyos** están en la tintorería. | *Yours are at the cleaners.* |
| Mi vestido está allá. ¿Dónde está el suyo? | *My dress is over there. Where is yours?* |
| El mío está en la cama. | *Mine is on the bed.* |

EXCEPTION: After the verb **ser**, the article is omitted when mere expression of ownership is indicated.

| | |
|---|---|
| ¿Es **tuya** esta maleta? | *Is this suitcase yours?* |
| Sí, esta maleta es **mía**, pero aquéllas son **tuyas**. | *Yes, this suitcase is mine, but those are yours.* |
| ¿Este talonario de cheques es **suyo**, señor Muñoz? | *Is this checkbook yours, Mr. Muñoz?* |
| Sí, es **mío**. Gracias. | *Yes, it's mine. Thank you.* |

B. Since the third-person forms of the possessive pronouns (**el suyo, la suya, los suyos, las suyas**) could be ambiguous, they may be replaced for clarification by the following:

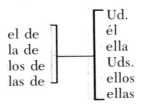

| el de | Ud. |
| la de | él |
| los de | ella |
| las de | Uds. |
| | ellos |
| | ellas |

Estos muebles son
  de Marta y Arturo,
  ¿no?
Bueno, el sofá es **de ella,** pero
  la cama y el escritorio son **de
  él.**

*These (pieces of) furniture are
  Martha's and Arthur's,
  aren't they?*
*Well, the sofa is hers, but the
  bed and the desk are his.*

## Exercises

A. Supply the correct possessive pronouns and read aloud. Follow the models:

*Modelos:*  Yo tengo una cama. Es _____.
    **Yo tengo una cama. Es mía.**

    Juan tiene un libro. Es _____. Es _____.
    **Juan tiene un libro. Es suyo. Es de él.**

1. Tú tienes un talonario de cheques. Es _____.
2. Juan tiene un escritorio. Es _____. Es _____.
3. Nosotras tenemos una maleta. Es _____.
4. Ud. tiene unos muebles. Son _____. Son _____.
5. Yo tengo un sofá. Es _____.
6. Uds. tienen dos lápices. Son _____. Son _____.
7. Yo tengo unos pantalones. Son _____.
8. Ud. tiene tres hijos. Son _____. Son _____.

B. Give the Spanish equivalent:

1. This desk is mine. Where is yours, Mr. Britos?
2. These shoes aren't ours.
3. My pants are at the cleaners. Where are yours?
4. The books are hers, but the pens are theirs.
5. My bed is here, Mrs. Ortiz. Yours is in the bedroom.

## 2. REFLEXIVE CONSTRUCTIONS

A reflexive verb is one in which the verb acts upon the subject. Most Spanish verbs can be made reflexive. The reflexive consists of the reflexive pronoun and the verb:

| Reflexive Pronouns | |
|---|---|
| me | myself, to (for) myself |
| te | yourself, to (for) yourself (**tú** form) |
| nos | ourselves, to (for) ourselves |
| se | yourself, to (for) yourself (**Ud.** form)<br>yourselves, to (for) yourselves (**Uds.** form)<br>himself, to (for) himself<br>herself, to (for) herself<br>itself, to (for) itself<br>themselves, to (for) themselves |

ATENCIÓN: Notice that except for **se**, the reflexive pronouns are the same as the direct and indirect object pronouns.

| **vestirse** (to dress oneself) | |
|---|---|
| Yo me visto | I dress myself |
| Tú te vistes | You dress yourself |
| Ud. se viste | You dress yourself |
| Él se viste | He dresses himself |
| Ella se viste | She dresses herself |
| Nosotros nos vestimos | We dress ourselves |
| Uds. se visten | You dress yourselves |
| Ellos se visten | They (*masc.*) dress themselves |
| Ellas se visten | They (*fem.*) dress themselves |

ATENCIÓN: Both the reflexive pronouns and the verb agree with the subject. The rules governing the position of the reflexive pronouns are the same as for other subject pronouns.

A. The following common verbs are frequently used in the reflexive:

| | |
|---|---|
| despertarse (e > ie) | *to wake up* |
| levantarse | *to get up* |
| vestirse (e > i) | *to get dressed* |
| desvestirse (e > i) | *to get undressed* |
| afeitarse | *to shave* |
| bañarse | *to bathe* |

sentarse (e > ie)     *to sit*
acostarse (o > ue)    *to go to bed*
preocuparse           *to worry*

B. Some verbs are *always* used with reflexive pronouns in Spanish:

acordarse (o > ue) (de)     *to remember*
quejarse (de)               *to complain*
suicidarse                  *to commit suicide*

Notice that the use of a reflexive pronoun does not necessarily imply a reflexive action.

C. Some verbs change their meaning when they are used with reflexive pronouns:

| | | | |
|---|---|---|---|
| acostar (o > ue) | *to put to bed* | acostarse | *to go to bed* |
| dormir (o > ue) | *to sleep* | dormirse | *to fall asleep* |
| levantar | *to lift, to raise* | levantarse | *to get up* |
| probar (o > ue) | *to try, to taste* | probarse | *to try on* |
| poner | *to put* | ponerse | *to put on* |

Notice the use of the reflexive in the following sentences:

¿A qué hora **se levanta** Ud., señorita López?

*What time do you get up, Miss Lopez?*

Generalmente **me levanto** a las ocho, pero no **me acuesto** hasta la medianoche.

*I generally get up at eight o'clock, but I don't go to bed until midnight.*

¿**Se acuerda** Ud. de Rosita?
Sí, **me acuerdo** de ella.

*Do you remember Rosita?*
*Yes, I remember her.*

¿Por qué no **te acuestas**, querido?

*Why don't you go to bed, dear?*

Primero voy a **acostar** a los niños.

*First I'm going to put the children to bed.*

## Exercises

A. Complete the following sentences, using the present indicative of the verbs in parentheses:

1. Elena _____ (probarse) los zapatos.
2. Él \_\_\_\_\_ (acostarse) y Ud. \_\_\_\_\_ (acostar) a los niños.
3. Juan \_\_\_\_\_ (bañarse) y Luis \_\_\_\_\_ (vestirse).
4. Tú siempre \_\_\_\_\_ (dormirse) en la clase de historia.
5. Nosotros no \_\_\_\_\_ (preocuparse) por eso.
6. Algunos alcohólicos \_\_\_\_\_ (suicidarse).
7. Debes \_\_\_\_\_ (desvestirse) antes de \_\_\_\_\_ (bañarse).
8. ¿No vas a \_\_\_\_\_ (ponerse) el abrigo, querida?

B. Answer the following questions:

1. ¿A qué hora se levanta Ud. generalmente?
2. ¿Siempre te despiertas temprano?
3. ¿Se acuerda Ud. de sus amigos?
4. ¿A qué hora se acuestan Uds.? ¿A la medianoche?
5. ¿Se queja el profesor de los estudiantes?
6. ¿Se van a poner Uds. los zapatos para salir?
7. ¿Cuántas horas duerme Ud.?
8. ¿Siempre pruebas la comida?

## 3. THE COMMAND FORMS (Ud. and Uds.)

To form the command for **Ud.** and **Uds.**,[1] add the following endings to the stem of the first person singular of the present indicative, after dropping the **-o:**

-ar verbs: **-e** (Ud.) and **-en** (Uds.)
-er verbs: **-a** (Ud.) and **-an** (Uds.)
-ir verbs: **-a** (Ud.) and **-an** (Uds.)

ATENCIÓN: Notice that the endings for the **-er** and **-ir** verbs are the same.

| Infinitive | First Person Present Ind. | Stem | Commands Ud. | Uds. |
|---|---|---|---|---|
| hablar | Yo hablo | habl- | hable | hablen |
| comer | Yo como | com- | coma | coman |
| abrir | Yo abro | abr- | abra | abran |
| cerrar | Yo cierro | cierr- | cierre | cierren |
| volver | Yo vuelvo | vuelv- | vuelva | vuelvan |
| pedir | Yo pido | pid- | pida | pidan |
| decir | Yo digo | dig- | diga | digan |

| | |
|---|---|
| ¿Con quién debo hablar? | *With whom must I speak?* |
| **Hable** con la secretaria. | *Speak with the secretary.* |
| ¿Vengo por la mañana o por la tarde? | *Shall I come in the morning or in the afternoon?* |
| **Venga** por la mañana y **traiga** sus documentos. | *Come in the morning and bring your documents.* |
| ¿Cierro la puerta? | *Shall I close the door?* |
| No, **cierre** la ventana, por favor. | *No, close the window, please.* |

[1] The **tú** form will be studied in lesson 18.

| ¿Sigo derecho o doblo a la derecha? | *Shall I continue straight ahead or shall I turn right?* |
| **Doble** a la izquierda. | *Turn left.* |

B. The command forms of the following verbs are irregular:

|  | dar | estar | ser | ir |
|---|---|---|---|---|
| Ud. | dé | esté | sea | vaya |
| Uds. | den | estén | sean | vayan |

| ¿Podemos ir solas? | *Can we go alone?* |
| No, no **vayan** solas. **Vayan** con sus padres. | *No, don't go alone. Go with your parents.* |

| ¡Le digo que quiero ver a mis hijos! | *I'm telling you I want to see my children!* |
| Un momento, señora. ¡No **sea** tan impaciente! | *One moment, madam. Don't be so impatient.* |

## Exercise

A. Answer the following questions, according to the models:

*Modelos:* ¿Hablo con el secretario? (director)
**No, hable con el director.**

¿Hablamos con el secretario? (director)
**No, hablen con el director.**

1. ¿Hago la lección número uno? (la lección número dos)
2. ¿Cerramos las ventanas? (las puertas)
3. ¿Compramos plumas? (lápices)
4. ¿Damos nuestra dirección? (mi dirección)
5. ¿Duermo aquí? (en el dormitorio)
6. ¿Estudiamos la lección cuatro? (la lección tres)
7. ¿Trabajamos hoy? (mañana)
8. ¿Vuelvo el lunes? (el martes)
9. ¿Sirvo café? (té)
10. ¿Pedimos refrescos? (sopa y postre)
11. ¿Doblo a la derecha? (a la izquierda)
12. ¿Digo que sí? (que no)
13. ¿Salimos por la tarde? (por la noche)
14. ¿Traducimos la lección ocho? (la lección seis)
15. ¿Traigo la carne? (la ensalada)
16. ¿Vamos al cine? (al teatro)

B. Give the Spanish equivalent:

1. You mustn't continue straight ahead. Turn left.
2. Don't be so impatient, ladies.
3. Wait one moment, Mr. Peña.
4. Go with the secretary.
5. Bring your documents, Miss Ruiz.

# 4. USES OF OBJECT PRONOUNS WITH THE COMMAND FORMS

A. In all direct *affirmative* commands, the object pronouns are placed *after* the verb and attached to it, thus forming only one word:

| | |
|---|---|
| ¿Dónde pongo las maletas? | *Where shall I put the suitcases?* |
| **Póngalas** en la cama. | *Put them on the bed.* |
| ¿Dónde sirvo el café? | *Where shall I serve (the) coffee?* |
| **Sírvalo** en la terraza. | *Serve it on the terrace.* |
| ¿Qué le digo? | *What shall I tell him?* |
| **Dígale** que sí. | *Tell him yes.* |
| ¿Qué les doy a las niñas? | *What shall I give the girls?* |
| **Déles** el postre. | *Give them dessert.* |
| ¿Abrimos la puerta? | *Shall we open the door?* |
| Sí, **ábranla.** | *Yes, open it.* |
| ¿Se lo digo a Ana? | *Shall I tell (it to) Ana?* |
| Sí, **dígaselo** a Ana. | *Yes, tell (it to) Ana.* |

**Exercise**

Answer the following questions, according to the models:

*Modelos:*  ¿Traigo las sillas?
   **Sí, tráigalas, por favor.**

   ¿Traemos las sillas?
   **Sí, tráiganlas, por favor.**

   ¿Le traigo el dinero?
   **Sí, tráigamelo, por favor.**

   ¿Le traemos el dinero?
   **Sí, tráiganmelo, por favor.**

1. ¿Traduzco la lección?
2. ¿Abrimos la puerta de la terraza?

3. ¿Cerramos las ventanas?
4. ¿Te servimos la sopa?
5. ¿Le decimos que sí?
6. ¿Hago el café?
7. ¿Le escribo la carta a Luis?
8. ¿Te traemos el vestido?
9. ¿Me baño?
10. ¿Nos acostamos ahora?
11. ¿Me visto?
12. ¿Nos desvestimos?
13. ¿Te traigo el té?
14. ¿Le doy el dinero a Marta?
15. ¿Le decimos tu número de teléfono a Pedro?

B. In all *negative* commands, the object pronouns are placed *in front* of the verb:

¿Nos levantamos ahora?
No, **no se levanten** todavía.

*Shall we get up now?*
*No, don't get up yet.*

Quiero traerle una corbata a Luis.
No, **no le traiga** una corbata. Tráigale una camisa.

*I want to bring Luis a tie.*
*No, don't bring him a tie. Bring him a shirt.*

Voy a traducir la lección al francés.
No, **no la traduzca** al francés. Tradúzcala al español.

*I'm going to translate the lesson into French.*
*No, don't translate it into French. Translate it into Spanish.*

¿Te traemos los vestidos?
No, **no me traigan** los vestidos. Tráiganme los abrigos.

*Shall we bring you the dresses?*
*No, don't bring me the dresses. Bring me the coats.*

¿Sirvo los refrescos?
No, **no los sirva** todavía.

*Shall I serve the sodas?*
*No, don't serve them yet.*

¿Te traemos las maletas?
No, **no me las** traigan.

*Shall we bring you the suitcases?*
*No, don't bring them to me.*

### Exercise

Respond, following the models:

*Modelos:* Voy a traer el escritorio.
**No, no lo traiga todavía.**

Vamos a traer el escritorio.
**No, no lo traigan todavía.**

Le voy a traer el escritorio.
**No, no se lo traiga todavía.**

1. Voy a comprar ese vestido.
2. Vamos a traerle la camisa a Raúl.
3. Le voy a dar un cheque.
4. Voy a acostarme.
5. Voy a desvestirme.
6. Voy a cerrar las ventanas.
7. Vamos a quejarnos.
8. Voy a levantarme.
9. Vamos a afeitarnos.
10. Le voy a dar las plumas a María.
11. Vamos a traerte el té.
12. Le voy a decir mi edad al director.
13. Le vamos a hablar.
14. Voy a ponerme los zapatos.
15. Vamos a traerte la botella.

## STUDY OF COGNATES

1. These words are the same in Spanish and English, except for written accent mark or final vowel:

   | | |
   |---|---|
   | **el sofá** | sofa |
   | **el documento** | document |
   | **el momento** | moment |

2. Spanish adverbs ending in **-mente** instead of English *-ly:*

   **generalmente**   generally

3. Spanish words ending in **-ia** or **-io** instead of English *y:*

   **la secretaria**
   **el secretario** } secretary

4. Approximate cognates:

   | | |
   |---|---|
   | **el alcohólico** | alcoholic |
   | **impaciente** | impatient |
   | **la terraza** | terrace |

NEW VOCABULARY

### Nouns

| | |
|---|---|
| **la cama** | bed |
| **el dormitorio** | bedroom |
| **el escritorio** | desk |
| **la maleta** | suitcase |
| **la medianoche** | midnight |
| **los muebles** | furniture |
| (*m.*) | (pieces of) |
| **los pantalones** | trousers, pants |
| **la puerta** | door |
| **el talonario de** | checkbook |
| **cheques** | |
| **la tintorería** | cleaner |
| **la ventana** | window |
| **el vestido** | dress |
| **los zapatos** (*m.*) | shoes |

### Verbs

| | |
|---|---|
| **deber** | must, to have to |
| **doblar** | to turn |
| **vestir(se)** | to dress, to get |
| (e > i) | dressed |

### Adjectives

**querido(a)**

### Other words and expressions

| | |
|---|---|
| **a la derecha** | to the right |
| **a la izquierda** | to the left |
| **antes de** | before |
| **seguir (e > ie)** | to continue |
| **derecho** | straight ahead |
| **tan** | so |
| **todavía** | yet |

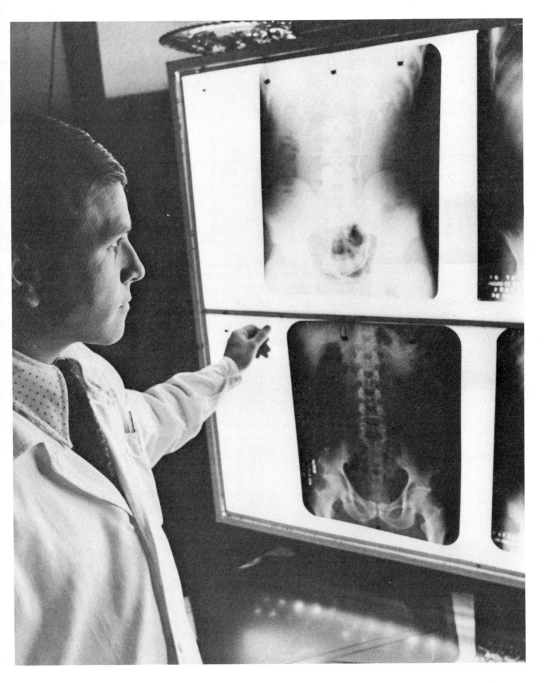

Lesson 10

# 1. PRETERIT OF REGULAR VERBS

The preterit tense is used to refer to past actions that were completed in past time.[1] The preterit of regular verbs is formed as follows:

| entrar (to enter) | comer (to eat) | escribir (to write) |
|---|---|---|
| entré | comí | escribí |
| entraste | comiste | escribiste |
| entró | comió | escribió |
| entramos | comimos | escribimos |
| entraron | comieron | escribieron |

- Notice that the endings for the -er and -ir verbs are the same.

ATENCIÓN: Spanish has no equivalent for the English *did* used as an auxiliary verb in questions and negative sentences.

| | |
|---|---|
| ¿Quién te **prestó** esa bicicleta? Me la **prestó** Carlos ayer. | *Who lent you that bicycle? Charles lent it to me yesterday.* |
| ¿A qué hora **comió** Ud. anoche? **Comí** a las ocho. | *At what time did you eat last night? I ate at eight o'clock.* |
| ¿**Abrió** Ud. las ventanas? No, no las **abrí.** | *Did you open the windows? No, I didn't open them.* |

## Exercise

Complete the sentences with the preterit of the following verbs: **esperar, estudiar, recibir, aprender, abrir, comprar, decidir, preguntar, entender, beber.** Use each verb only once.

1. ¿Dónde _____ Ud. a hablar español?
2. ¿Qué _____ Uds.? ¿Ir al hospital?
3. Yo no _____ su carta.
4. ¿Dónde _____ tú esa bicicleta.
5. Lidia y Gerardo no _____ la lección.
6. ¿_____ Ud. las puertas?
7. ¿Qué _____ Uds. acerca del examen?
8. El profesor no me _____ nada ayer.
9. Carmen y yo _____ té.
10. ¿Cuántas horas lo _____ Ud.?

[1] Spanish has two past tenses, the preterit and the imperfect. The imperfect will be studied in Lesson 11.

## 2. PRETERIT OF **ser, ir,** AND **dar**

The preterits of **ser, ir,** and **dar** are irregular. Note that **ser** and **ir** have the same preterit forms:

| **ser** (*to be*) | **ir** (*to go*) | **dar** (*to give*) |
|---|---|---|
| fui | fui | di |
| fuiste | fuiste | diste |
| fue | fue | dio |
| fuimos | fuimos | dimos |
| fueron | fueron | dieron |

| | |
|---|---|
| Ud. **fue** profesora en la universidad de Arizona, ¿no? | *You were a professor at the University of Arizona, weren't you?* |
| Sí, yo **fui** profesora de Economía. | *Yes, I was a professor of Economics.* |
| ¿Con quién **fue** Ud. a la tienda ayer? | *With whom did you go to the store yesterday?* |
| **Fui** con mis padres. | *I went with my parents.* |
| ¿Quién le **dio** la medicina al niño? | *Who gave the medicine to the boy?* |
| Se la **dio** la enfermera. | *The nurse gave it to him.* |

### Exercise

Complete the following sentences with the preterit of the verbs **ir, ser,** or **dar,** as needed:

1. Yo _____ con mis padres al hospital.
2. Ella _____ mi profesora de Economía el año pasado.
3. Nosotros no le _____ el dinero anoche.
4. ¿Le _____ a Ud. la medicina el dentista?
5. El doctor _____ al laboratorio.
6. Yo no te _____ el cuaderno.
7. Nosotros no _____ sus estudiantes.
8. ¿Le _____ Ud. la maleta a la enfermera?
9. ¿Quién _____ el primer presidente de los Estados Unidos?
10. ¿A dónde _____ tú ayer? ¿A la tienda?
11. Carlos y Roberto _____ al laboratorio anoche.
12. ¿Le _____ tú el paraguas a tu prima?
13. María y yo _____ a Santiago el año pasado.
14. Yo les _____ a mis hermanos esos zapatos.

## 3. THE EXPRESSION **acabar de**

**Acabar de** means *to have just.* While English uses the present perfect tense plus the word *just*, Spanish uses this formula:

| *subject* | + | **acabar** (present tense) | + | **de** | + | *infinitive* |
|-----------|---|----------------------------|---|--------|---|--------------|
| **Pedro** | | **acaba** | | **de** | | **llegar** |

| | |
|---|---|
| ¿Tiene Elena un puesto? | *Does Helen have a job?* |
| Sí, **acaba de encontrar** uno. | *Yes, she has just found one.* |
| ¿Quieres un poco de sopa? | *Do you want some soup?* |
| No, gracias. **Acabo de comer.** | *No, thanks. I have just eaten.* |

• Notice that the conjugation of **acabar** is completely regular.

### Exercise

Complete the following sentences with the correct form of **acabar de** + *infinitive:*

1. Juan (*has just arrived*) _____ a esta ciudad.
2. Yo (*have just bought*) _____ esta casa.
3. Ellas (*have just found*) _____ un puesto.
4. Él (*has just eaten*) _____ un poco de carne.
5. Elena (*has just got dressed*) _____ .
6. Uds. (*have just gone*) _____ a la oficina.
7. Elena (*has just written*) _____ la carta.
8. Tú (*have just read*) _____ la revista.
9. Yo (*have just bathed*) _____ .
10. Ellos (*have just lent me*) _____ el periódico.
11. Nosotros (*have just found*) _____ las maletas.
12. Marta y Ana (*have just gotten dressed*) _____ .

## 4. THE ABSOLUTE SUPERLATIVE

Sometimes a high degree of a given quality is expressed without comparing it to the same quality of another person or thing. Spanish has two ways of expressing this:

A. By modifying the adjective with an adverb (**muy, sumamente**):

| | |
|---|---|
| ¿Cómo es tu novia? | *What is your girlfriend like?* |
| Es **muy** inteligente y **sumamente** buena. | *She is very intelligent and extremely kind.* |

B. By adding the suffix **-ísimo** (**-a, -os, -as**) to the adjective. If the word ends in a vowel, the vowel is dropped before adding the suffix. Notice that the **í** of the suffix always has a written accent:

| | | | |
|---|---|---|---|
| alto | alt- | ísimo | altísimo |
| ocupada | ocupad- | ísima | ocupadísima |
| lentos | lent- | ísimos | lentísimos |
| buenas | buen- | ísimas | buenísimas |
| difícil | dificil- | ísimo | dificilísimo |

| | |
|---|---|
| ¿Fuiste a Madrid el verano pasado? | *Did you go to Madrid last summer?* |
| Sí, es una cíudad **bellísima**, pero es **dificilísimo** conducir allí. | *Yes, it is a very beautiful city, but it is extremely difficult to drive there.* |
| ¿Pueden ir a la tienda con nosotros? | *Can you go to the store with us?* |
| No, estamos **ocupadísimas**. | *No, we are extremely busy.* |

**Exercise**

Change the following sentences, using the absolute superlative:

1. Mis padres son muy inteligentes.
2. Mi novio es sumamente alto.
3. Ellos están muy ocupados.
4. Es muy fácil conducir en esta ciudad.
5. Ellas son muy buenas.
6. La enfermera está sumamente ocupada.
7. Ellos son muy lentos.
8. La lección es sumamente difícil.

## 5. WEATHER EXPRESSIONS

In the following expressions, Spanish uses the verb **hacer** (*to make*) followed by a noun, whereas English uses the verb *to be* followed by an adjective:

> **Hace** (mucho) frío. *It is (very) cold.*
> **Hace** (mucho) calor. *It is (very) hot.*
> **Hace** (mucho) viento. *It is (very) windy.*
> **Hace** sol. *It is sunny.*

The following weather expressions do not combine with **hacer**:

> **llover** (**o** > **ue**) (*to rain*): **llueve**
> **nevar** (**e** > **ie**) (*to snow*): **nieva**

As in English, Spanish uses the impersonal verbs in the infinitive, present or past participle, and third person singular forms only.

| | |
|---|---|
| ¿**Hace viento** hoy? | *Is it windy today?* |
| Sí y también **está lloviendo** mucho. | *Yes and it is raining a lot also.* |
| ¿Qué tiempo hace hoy, Marta? | *How's the weather today, Martha?* |
| **Hace** mucho **frío** y **está nevando.** | *It is very cold and it is snowing.* |

## Exercises

A. Study these words and then complete the following sentences:

**el paraguas**      umbrella
**el impermeable**   raincoat
**el suéter**        sweater

1. ¿Necesitas un paraguas? — Sí, porque _____.
2. ¿No necesitas un abrigo? — No, porque _____.
3. ¿Quieres un impermeable? — No, no está _____.
4. ¿Necesitas un suéter? — No, hoy _____.
5. Está nevando. Lleve el _____.

B. Give the Spanish equivalent:

1. It is very windy today.
2. It is very cold and it is also snowing.
3. It is very hot in Cuba.
4. How is the weather today?
5. Is it sunny?

## STUDY OF COGNATES

1. These words are the same in Spanish and English, except for a final vowel:

   **el dentista**      dentist

2. Spanish words ending in **-ia** or **-io** instead of English *y:*

   **el laboratorio**   laboratory

3. Approximate cognates:

   **la bicicleta**     bicycle
   **la economía**      economics
   **el suéter**        sweater

## NEW VOCABULARY

### NOUNS

| | |
|---|---|
| la enfermera<br>el enfermero | nurse |
| el impermeable | raincoat |
| la novia | girl friend |
| el novio | boy friend |
| los padres | parents |
| el paraguas | umbrella |
| el puesto | job, position |
| la tienda | store |

### VERBS

| | |
|---|---|
| encontrar<br>  (o > ue) | to find |
| llover (o > ue) | to rain |
| nevar (e > ie) | to snow |

### ADJECTIVES

| | |
|---|---|
| bello(a) | pretty |
| bueno(a) | kind |
| ocupado(a) | busy |

### OTHER WORDS AND EXPRESSIONS

| | |
|---|---|
| anoche | last night |
| ayer | yesterday |
| ¿Qué tiempo<br>hace hoy? | How's the<br>  weather<br>  today? |
| sumamente | extremely |
| un poco de | some |

# Test Yourself: Lessons 6-10

## LESSON 6

A. Some uses of the definite article

Give the Spanish equivalent:

1. Today is Wednesday.
2. Women want equality with men.
3. Freedom is important.
4. We're going to study next week.
5. I don't have classes on Fridays.

B. Stem-changing verbs (o > ue)

Answer the following questions:

1. ¿A qué hora vuelve Ud. a su casa?
2. Cuando Uds. van a México, ¿vuelan o van en coche?
3. ¿Recuerdan Uds. los verbos irregulares?
4. ¿Cuántas horas duermes tú?
5. ¿Pueden Uds. ir al cine hoy?

C. Affirmative and negative expressions

Change the following sentences to the affirmative:

1. Ellos no recuerdan nada.
2. No hay nadie en el cine.
3. Yo no quiero volar tampoco.
4. No recibimos ningún regalo.
5. Nunca tiene éxito.

D. Ordinal numbers

For each of the following cardinal numbers, give the corresponding ordinal number:

| | | |
|---|---|---|
| cinco | tres | seis |
| ocho | nueve | cuatro |
| diez | dos | siete |
| uno | | |

E. Uses of **tener que** and **hay que**

Give the Spanish equivalent:

1. To succeed, one must work.
2. You have to come back next week, Mr. Vega.

3. She has to work tomorrow.
4. One must start early.
5. Do we have to begin at eight?

# LESSON 7

A. Stem-changing verbs (**e > i**)

Answer the following questions:

1. ¿Qué sirven Uds., sopa o ensalada?
2. ¿Qué pide Ud. para beber cuando va a un restaurante?
3. ¿Dice Ud. su edad?
4. ¿Sigue Ud. en la clase de español?
5. ¿Uds. siempre piden postre?

B. More about irregular verbs

Complete the sentences with the present indicative of the verbs in the following list. Use each verb once:

traer      traducir    conducir
caber      poner       saber
conocer    hacer       ver
salir

1. Yo _____ mi coche.
2. Yo siempre _____ con ella.
3. Yo _____ los documentos en el fichero.
4. Yo _____ del inglés al español.
5. Yo no _____ al maestro de mi hijo.
6. Yo no _____ aquí. Soy muy grande.
7. Yo _____ el postre.
8. Yo no _____ el regalo. ¿Dónde está?
9. Yo no _____ nadar.
10. Yo _____ la carne.

C. **Saber** vs. **Conocer**

Give the Spanish equivalent:

1. I know your son.
2. He doesn't know French.
3. Can you (do you know how to) swim, Miss Vera?
4. Do you know the ambassador?
5. Do the students know Cervantes' novels?

D.  Direct object pronouns

Complete the following sentences with the Spanish equivalent of the direct object pronouns in parentheses. Follow the models:

*Modelos:*  Yo veo   (*him*)
**Yo lo veo.**

Yo quiero ver   (*him*)
**Yo quiero verlo.**

1.  Yo conozco                     (*them, fem.*)
2.  Uds. van a comprar             (*it, masc.*)
3.  **Nosotros** no queremos ver   (*you, familiar*)
4.  Ella sirve                     (*it, fem.*)
5.  ¿Ud. no conoce . . . ?         (*me*)
6.  Él escribe                     (*them, masc.*)
7.  Carlos va a traer              (*us*)
8.  Nosotros no vemos              (*you, formal, sing., masc.*)

E.  Formation of adverbs

Write the adverbs corresponding to the following adjectives:

1.  feliz               4.  fácil
2.  especial            5.  lento y cuidadoso
3.  rápido

# LESSON 8

A.  Demonstrative adjectives / Demonstrative pronouns

Give the Spanish equivalent:

1.  I need these magazines and those ones (over there).
2.  Do you want this notebook or that one?
3.  I prefer these newspapers, not those ones (over there).
4.  Do you want to buy this tie or that one?
5.  I don't want to eat at this restaurant. I prefer that one (over there).
6.  I don't understand that. (*neuter form*)

B.  Present progressive

Complete the following sentences with the present progressive of **leer, decir, estudiar, comprar,** or **comer,** as needed:

1.  Él _____ la lección.
2.  Ella _____ en la cafetería.
3.  Nosotros _____ el periódico.

4. Tú no _____ la verdad.
5. Yo _____ un abrigo.

C. Indirect object pronouns

Answer the following questions, according to the model:

*Modelo:* ¿Qué me vas a traer de México?  (un abrigo)
**Te voy a traer un abrigo.**

1. ¿Qué te va a comprar Carlos?  (los pasajes)
2. ¿Qué le das tú a Luis?  (las revistas)
3. ¿En qué idioma les habla a Uds. el profesor?  (en español)
4. ¿Qué va a decirles Ud. a los niños?  (la verdad)
5. ¿Qué nos pregunta Ud.?  (la dirección de la oficina)
6. ¿A quién están escribiéndole Uds.?  (a nuestro profesor)
7. ¿Cuándo le escribe Ud. a su esposo?  (los lunes)
8. ¿A quién le da Ud. la información?  (al señor Vera)
9. ¿En qué idioma me hablas tú?  (en inglés)
10. ¿Qué te compran tus hijos?  (nada)

D. Direct and indirect object pronouns used together

Give the Spanish equivalent:

1. The money? I'm giving it to you tomorrow, Mr. Peña.
2. I know you need the dictionary, Anita, but I can't lend it to you.
3. I need my coat. Can you bring it to me, Miss López?
4. The pens? She is bringing them to us.
5. When I need new shoes, my mother buys them for me.

E. **Pedir** vs. **Preguntar**

Give the Spanish equivalent:

1. I'm going to ask her where she lives.
2. I always ask my husband for money.
3. She always asks how you are, Mrs. Nieto.
4. They are going to ask me for the chemistry books.
5. We aren't going to ask you any (questions), sir.

## LESSON 9

A. Possessive pronouns

Answer the following questions in the negative, according to the model:

*Modelo:* ¿Estos pantalones son *de Juan?*
**No, no son de él.**

1. ¿Son *tuyas* estas maletas?
2. ¿Estos zapatos son *de Julia*?
3. ¿El vestido que está en la tintorería es *suyo*, señora?
4. ¿Es *de Uds.* esta cama?
5. ¿Este talonario de cheques es *de Eva y Gustavo*?
6. ¿Son *tuyos* estos muebles?
7. ¿Es *de Uds.* este sofá?
8. ¿Es *nuestro* este escritorio?

B. Reflexive constructions

Give the Spanish equivalent:

1. I get up at seven, I bathe, I get dressed, and leave at seven-thirty.
2. What time do the children wake up?
3. She doesn't want to sit down.
4. You always worry about your son, Mrs. Cruz.
5. Do you remember your teachers, Carlitos?
6. They are always complaining.
7. First she puts the children to bed. She goes to bed at ten.
8. Do you want to try on this coat, miss?
9. Where are you putting the money, ladies?
10. The students always fall asleep in this class.

C. The command forms: **Ud.** and **Uds.**

Complete the sentences with the command forms of the verbs in the following list, as needed, and read each sentence aloud. Use each verb once:

| escribir | venir | dar | hablar | doblar |
|----------|-------|--------|--------|--------|
| servir | cerrar | volver | seguir | ser |
| estar | poner | ir | abrir | traer |

1. _____ la puerta, señor Benítez.
2. _____ español, señores.
3. _____ sus documentos, señorita.
4. _____ mañana por la mañana, señoras.
5. No _____ la ventana, señorita. Hace calor.
6. _____ a la izquierda, señores.
7. _____ derecho, señorita.
8. _____ su nombre y dirección, señores.
9. _____ en la oficina mañana por la tarde, señores.
10. ¡No _____ tan impacientes, señoritas!
11. _____ a la casa del director, señor Vega.

12. _____ el martes, señora. El doctor no está.
13. _____ el café en la terraza, señorita.
14. _____ las maletas aquí, señores.
15. _____ las cartas mañana, señoras.

D. Uses of object pronouns and reflexive pronouns with the command forms

Give the Spanish equivalent:

1. Tell them yes, Mr. Mena.
2. The dessert? Don't bring it to me now, Miss Ruiz.
3. Don't tell (it to) Ana, please.
4. Bring the chairs, gentlemen. Bring them to the terrace.
5. Don't get up, Mrs. Miño.
6. The tea? Bring it to her at four o'clock in the afternoon, Mr. Vargas.

# LESSON 10

A. Preterit of regular verbs / Preterit of **ser, ir,** and **dar**

Rewrite the following sentences according to the new beginnings. Follow the model:

*Modelo:* Voy al cine. (Ayer . . . )
          **Ayer fui al cine.**

1. Ella entra en la cafetería y come una ensalada. (Ayer . . . )
2. María le escribe a Pedro. (Ayer . . . )
3. Ella me presta su bicicleta. (Anoche . . . )
4. Ellos son los mejores estudiantes. (El año pasado . . . )
5. Ellos te esperan cerca¹ del cine. (El sábado pasado . . . )
6. Mis hermanos van a Buenos Aires. (El verano pasado . . . )
7. Le doy dinero. (Ayer . . . )
8. Nosotros decidimos comprar la bicicleta. (El lunes pasado . . . )
9. Le pregunto la hora. (Anoche . . . )
10. Tú no entiendes la lección. (Ayer . . . )
11. Somos los primeros. (El jueves pasado . . . )
12. Me dan muchos problemas. (Ayer . . . )
13. Marta no bebe café. (Anoche . . . )
14. Yo no voy a la clase. (El miércoles pasado . . . )
15. Te damos té. (Ayer por la mañana . . . )

¹ **cerca (de)** near

B. The expression **acabar de**

Answer the following questions, according to the model:

*Modelo:* ¿Ya llegó Juan? **Sí, acaba de llegar.**

1. ¿Ya comieron Uds.?
2. ¿Ya se levantó Pedro?
3. ¿Ya hablaste con Susana?
4. ¿Ya compraron ellos la casa?
5. ¿Ya te bañaste?
6. ¿Ya llegaron los estudiantes?

C. The absolute superlative

Answer the following questions, according to the model:

*Modelo:* ¿Es inteligente el hijo de Yolanda?
   **¡Ah, sí! Es inteligentísimo.**

1. ¿Es alto Roberto?
2. ¿Están Uds. ocupadas?
3. ¿Son lentos los niños?
4. ¿Es buena la profesora?
5. ¿Es difícil esta lección?
6. ¿Es bella la ciudad donde viven Uds.?
7. ¿Es fácil el español?
8. ¿Estás ocupado?

D. Weather expressions

Look at the following pictures and say what kind of weather they show:

Lesson 11

# 1. TIME EXPRESSIONS WITH **hacer** AND **llevar**

A. English uses the present perfect tense to express how long something has been going on:

*I **have lived** in this city for fifteen years.*

Spanish follows this formula:

| | | | | |
|---|---|---|---|---|
| **Hace** + | length of time | + | **que** | + *verb* (in the present tense) |
| **Hace** | **quince años** | | **que** | **vivo en esta ciudad.** |

| | |
|---|---|
| ¿Cuánto tiempo **hace que** trabaja Ud. para el gobierno? | *How long have you been working for the government?* |
| **Hace** tres años **que** trabajo para el gobierno. | *I have worked for the government for three years.* |
| ¿Cuánto tiempo **hace que** Uds. viven aquí? | *How long have you lived here?* |
| **Hace** un mes **que** vivimos aquí. | *We have lived here for one month.* |

B. English uses ***has (have) been*** + *gerund* to describe an action that started in the past and is still going on in the present:

*I **have been studying** for three hours.*

Spanish uses the verb **llevar** followed by a period of time and a gerund, as shown below:

| | | | | |
|---|---|---|---|---|
| **Llevar** | + | length of time | + | *gerund* |
| **Llevo** | | **tres horas** | | **estudiando.** |

| | |
|---|---|
| ¿Cuánto tiempo **llevas escribiendo?** | *How long have you been writing?* |
| **Llevo** media hora **escribiendo.** | *I've been writing for half an hour.* |
| ¿Cuánto tiempo **llevan** Uds. **estudiando** español? | *How long have you been studying Spanish?* |
| **Llevamos** dos años **estudiando** español. | *We've been studying Spanish for two years.* |

**Exercise**

Answer the following questions, according to the model:

*Modelo:* ¿Cuánto tiempo llevan Uds. trabajando?  (dos horas)
**Llevamos dos horas trabajando.**

1. ¿Cuánto tiempo hace que Ud. estudia español?  (tres meses)
2. ¿Cuánto tiempo lleva Ud. trabajando en este puesto?  (un año)
3. ¿Cuánto tiempo hace que Ud. no come?  (media hora)
4. ¿Cuánto tiempo llevan Uds. viviendo en esta ciudad?  (un mes)
5. ¿Cuánto tiempo hace que no llueve aquí?  (cuatro meses)
6. ¿Cuánto tiempo llevan ellos trabajando para el gobierno?  (un mes)
7. ¿Cuánto tiempo hace que el presidente vive en Washington?  (un año)
8. ¿Cuánto tiempo hace que Uds. no van a clase?  (cinco días)

## 2. IRREGULAR PRETERITS

The following Spanish verbs are irregular in the preterit:

| | |
|---|---|
| **tener:** | tuve, tuviste, tuvo, tuvimos, tuvieron |
| **estar:** | estuve, estuviste, estuvo, estuvimos, estuvieron |
| **poder:** | pude, pudiste, pudo, pudimos, pudieron |
| **poner:** | puse, pusiste, puso, pusimos, pusieron |
| **hacer:** | hice, hiciste, hizo, hicimos, hicieron |
| **venir:** | vine, viniste, vino, vinimos, vinieron |
| **querer:** | quise, quisiste, quiso, quisimos, quisieron |
| **decir:** | dije, dijiste, dijo, dijimos, dijeron |
| **traer:** | traje, trajiste, trajo, trajimos, trajeron |
| **conducir:** | conduje, condujiste, condujo, condujimos, condujeron |

ATENCIÓN: Notice that the third person singular of the verb **hacer** changes the **c** to **z** in order to maintain the soft sound of the **c** in the infinitive.

● All verbs ending in **-ducir** follow the same pattern as the verb **conducir: traducir,** *to translate;* **producir,** *to produce.*

| | |
|---|---|
| ¿Llamaste por teléfono a Juan? | *Did you phone John?* |
| No, porque él **vino** a mi casa. | *No, because he came to my house.* |
| | |
| ¿Qué **hiciste** ayer? | *What did you do yesterday?* |
| Caminé por la ciudad. | *I walked around the city.* |

¿Dónde **pusieron** Uds. el dinero?

*Where did you put the money?*

Lo **pusimos** en el banco.

*We put it in the bank.*

### Exercise

Complete the following paragraph with the preterit of the verbs in parentheses:

*Isabel le escribe una carta a Teresa:*

Toledo, 15 de julio de 19..

Querida Teresa:

Ayer yo _____ (estar) en Madrid, pero no _____ (poder) ir a verte. Salí de Toledo por la mañana y _____ (conducir) por tres horas hasta llegar a Madrid. Allí _____ (tener) que ir al hospital para ver a Gustavo. Caminé por la ciudad y _____ (querer) llamarte por teléfono, pero no _____ (poder) encontrar uno. Como siempre, ayer _____ (hacer) mucho calor. _____ (Venir) de Madrid muy cansada. Esta mañana hablé por teléfono con Ramón. Él me _____ (decir) muchas cosas interesantes. ¡Ah . . . ! Me _____ (poner) el vestido que compré en Madrid y salí con Jorge. El sábado vuelvo a Madrid para verte.

Tu amiga,

Isabel

## 3. ¿De quién . . . ? FOR "WHOSE?"

¿**De quién** . . . ? is the interrogative form that Spanish uses to express the English *whose*. It can be singular or plural.

¿**De quién** es esta máquina de escribir?

*Whose typewriter is this?*

Es del contador.

*It's the accountant's.*

¿**De quiénes** son estos televisores?

*Whose TV sets are these?*

Éste es de Pedro y ése es mío.

*This one is Peter's and that one is mine.*

### Exercise

Give the Spanish equivalent:

1. Whose typewriter is that?
2. Whose books are these? The accountant's?
3. Whose revolver is this?
4. Whose raincoat is this?
5. Whose umbrellas are these?

## 4. THE IMPERFECT TENSE

A. There are two simple past tenses in Spanish: the preterit, which you studied in lessons 10 and 11, and the imperfect. The imperfect is a descriptive tense: it does not express a completed action. It expresses a continued, habitual or repeated action in the past.

To form the imperfect tense, add the following endings to the stem:

| -ar *Verbs* | -er *and* -ir *Verbs* | |
|---|---|---|
| **hablar** | **comer** | **vivir** |
| habl- **aba** | com- **ía** | viv- **ía** |
| habl- **abas** | com- **ías** | viv- **ías** |
| habl- **aba** | com- **ía** | viv- **ía** |
| habl- **ábamos** | com- **íamos** | viv- **íamos** |
| habl- **aban** | com- **ían** | viv- **ían** |

● Notice that the endings of the **-er** and **-ir** verbs are the same. Notice also that there is a written accent mark on the final í of the **-er** and **-ir** verbs.

● The Spanish imperfect tense is equivalent to three English forms:

Yo **vivía** en Chicago.
$\begin{cases} \textbf{\textit{I used to live}} \textit{ in Chicago.} \\ \textbf{\textit{I was living}} \textit{ in Chicago.} \\ \textbf{\textit{I lived}} \textit{ in Chicago.} \end{cases}$

| | |
|---|---|
| ¿De qué te **hablaba** Pedro? | *What was Peter talking to you about?* |
| Me **hablaba** de la inflación. | *He was talking to me about inflation.* |
| | |
| ¿Qué **comían** ellos? | *What were they eating?* |
| **Comían** arroz con pollo. | *They were eating chicken and rice.* |
| | |
| ¿Dónde **vivía** Ud. en esa época? | *Where did you live in those days?* |
| Yo **vivía** en La Habana. | *I lived in Havana.* |
| | |
| Yo siempre **depositaba** todo mi dinero en el banco. | *I always used to deposit all my money in the bank.* |
| Yo también **ahorraba** mi dinero, pero ahora lo gasto. | *I used to save my money too, but now I spend it.* |

### Exercise

Complete the following sentences with the imperfect tense of the verbs in this list. Use each verb once:

acostarse      creer      dormir
gastar         dar        ahorrar
poder          servir     hablar
comenzar       tener      depositar
preferir

1. Ellos no _____ ir a la universidad porque las clases _____ a las ocho de la mañana.
2. Mamá siempre me _____ dinero para comprar café.
3. En esa época yo _____ en Santa Claus.
4. ¿Tú _____ todo tu dinero en el banco o lo _____?
5. ¿Qué _____ Uds.? ¿Arroz con pollo o sopa?
6. Yo no _____ muy bien por la noche.
7. Papá siempre _____ su dinero.
8. En esa época nosotros _____ muy temprano porque _____ que ir a trabajar.
9. Yo siempre _____ la sopa.
10. Nosotros siempre _____ de la inflación en esa época.

---

B. There are only three verbs that are irregular in the imperfect tense: **ser, ir,** and **ver.**

| ser | ir | ver |
|---|---|---|
| era | iba | veía |
| eras | ibas | veías |
| era | iba | veía |
| éramos | íbamos | veíamos |
| eran | iban | veían |

¿Dónde **vivías** tú cuando **eras** chico?

*Where did you live when you were little?*

Yo **vivía** en Arizona cuando **era** chico.

*I lived in Arizona when I was little.*

Los vi esta mañana en la calle Quinta. ¿Adónde **iban** Uds.?

*I saw you this morning on Fifth Street. Where were you going?*

**Íbamos** a la escuela.

*We were going to school.*

Cecilia siempre **veía** a sus abuelos, ¿no?

*Cecilia always used to see her grandparents, didn't she?*

Veía a su abuela a veces, pero
casi nunca veía a su abuelo.

*She used to see her
grandmother sometimes, but
she hardly ever saw her
grandfather.*

### Exercise

Item Substitution. Change the verbs according to the new subjects.
Make any additional change needed:

1. Cuando yo **era** chica vivía con mis abuelos.  (nosotros / tú / Gustavo / ellos / Uds.)
2. Ellos casi nunca **iban** a la escuela.  (Yo / María / Nosotros / Tú / Uds.)
3. Nosotros **veíamos** que venía la inflación.  (Ud. / Ellos / Yo / Tú / El presidente)

## STUDY OF COGNATES

1. Spanish word ending in **-ción** instead of English -*tion:*

   **la inflación**  inflation

2. Approximate cognates:

   | **el banco** | bank |
   |---|---|
   | **la escuela** | school |
   | **La Habana** | Havana |

## NEW VOCABULARY

| NOUNS | | VERBS | |
|---|---|---|---|
| **la abuela** | grandmother | **ahorrar** | to save |
| **el abuelo** | grandfather | | (money) |
| **los abuelos** | grandparents | **caminar** | to walk |
| **el arroz** | rice | **depositar** | to deposit |
| **el contador** | accountant | **gastar** | to spend |
| **el gobierno** | government | | (money) |
| **la máquina de** | | **llamar** | to call |
| **escribir** | typewriter | | |
| **el pollo** | chicken | ADJECTIVE | |
| **el televisor** | TV set | **chico(a)** | little |

OTHER WORDS AND EXPRESSIONS

| | | | |
|---|---|---|---|
| **arroz con pollo** | chicken and rice | **en esa época** | in those days |
| **a veces** | sometimes | **llamar por teléfono** | to phone |
| **casi nunca** | hardly ever | **media hora** | half an hour |
| **¿de quién?** | whose? | **por** | around |

Lesson 12

# 1. THE PAST PROGRESSIVE

To stress the idea of action in progress in the past, Spanish uses the imperfect tense of the verb **estar** and the gerund of the conjugated verb.

| | |
|---|---|
| ¿En qué **estabas pensando** tú cuando tu coche chocó con el ómnibus? | *What were you thinking about when your car collided with the bus?* |
| **Estaba pensando** en todas las cuentas que tengo que pagar. | *I was thinking about all the bills (that) I have to pay.* |
| ¿Qué **estaba haciendo** la secretaria cuando Ud. la llamó? | *What was the secretary doing when you called her?* |
| **Estaba escribiendo** a máquina. | *She was typing.* |
| ¿Qué **estaban haciendo** Uds. cuando llegó el policía? | *What were you doing when the policeman arrived?* |
| **Estábamos leyendo** el periódico. | *We were reading the paper.* |
| ¿A quién **estaban esperando** los niños? | *Who were the children waiting for?* |
| **Estaban esperando** al señor García. | *They were waiting for Mr. García.* |

### Exercise

Answer the following questions:

1. ¿Qué estaban haciendo Uds. cuando llegó el policía?
2. ¿Qué estabas haciendo tú con esa pluma?
3. ¿En qué estaba Ud. pensando cuando yo le hablé?
4. ¿Estaba Ud. escribiendo a máquina cuando yo vine?
5. ¿Con quién estaba hablando Ud. por teléfono cuando yo lo (la) vi?
6. ¿Qué estaban leyendo Uds.?
7. Esta mañana mi auto chocó con un ómnibus. ¿En qué cree Ud. que yo estaba pensando?
8. ¿Estaban Uds. hablando de la inflación o de las cuentas que tienen que pagar?

# 2. PRETERIT VS. IMPERFECT

Spanish has two simple past tenses: the imperfect and the preterit. The difference between the two can be visualized this way:

The continuous moving line of the imperfect represents an action or state as it was taking place in the past. We don't know when the action started or ended. The vertical line represents the event as a completed unit in the past, and the preterit records such action.

The following table summarizes the uses of the preterit and the imperfect:

| Preterit | Imperfect |
|---|---|
| 1. Records, narrates, and reports an independent act or event as a completed and undivided whole, regardless of its duration.<br>2. Sums up a condition or state viewed as a whole. | 1. Describes an action in progress at a certain time in the past.<br>2. Indicates a continuous and habitual action: *"used to . . ."*<br>3. Describes a physical, mental, or emotional state or condition in the past.<br>4. Expresses time in the past.<br>5. Is used in indirect discourse. |

THE PRETERIT:

¿A qué hora **se acostó** Ud. anoche?

Anoche **me acosté** a las once y media.

*What time did you go to bed last night?*

*Last night I went to bed at eleven-thirty.*

Ayer **estuve** enferma.
Yo también.

*Yesterday I was sick.*
*Me too.*

THE IMPERFECT:

Cuando **íbamos** al cine vimos a María Ortiz.

¿Sí? Ella y yo **estudiábamos** inglés juntas.

*When we were going to the movies we saw Maria Ortiz.*

*Yeah? She and I used to study English together.*

| | |
|---|---|
| Me fui porque no **me sentía** muy bien. | *I left because I wasn't feeling very well.* |
| ¡Pero **eran** las ocho de la noche! | *But it was eight o'clock in the evening!* |
| ¿Qué dijo Eduardo? | *What did Edward say?* |
| Dijo que **quería** salir con María. | *He said he wanted to go out with Maria.* |

### Exercise

Complete the following sentences with the preterit or the imperfect of the verbs in parentheses, as needed:

1. Anoche él y yo _____ (ir) al cine juntos.
2. Cuando nosotros _____ (ser) chicos, _____ (ir) a casa de nuestros abuelos.
3. _____ (ser) las cuatro de la tarde cuando él _____ (llegar).
4. Anoche Roberto me _____ (decir) que _____ (necesitar) el coche.
5. La semana pasada yo _____ (estar) muy enfermo también.
6. Yo _____ (venir) por la calle Octava cuando _____ (ver) a los niños que _____ (ir) al cine.
7. Ellos _____ (irse) porque no _____ (sentirse) bien.
8. Yo siempre los _____ (ver) cuando ellos _____ (ir) al teatro.
9. Ellos no _____ (estar) en casa anoche.
10. ¿Qué hora _____ (ser) cuando Uds. lo _____ (ver)?

## 3. **en** AND **a** FOR "AT"

**A. En** is used in Spanish to indicate a certain place or location:

| | |
|---|---|
| ¿Dónde están los chicos? ¿No están **en** casa? | *Where are the boys? Aren't they (at) home?* |
| No, están **en** la estación de policía. | *No, they are at the police station.* |
| ¿Qué hacen allí? | *What are they doing there?* |
| Tuvieron un accidente **en** la esquina de Domínguez y Figueroa. | *They had an accident at the corner of Dominguez and Figueroa.* |

**B. A** is used in Spanish:

1. To refer to a specific moment in time:

| | |
|---|---|
| ¿Cuándo tuvieron el accidente? | *When did they have the accident?* |
| Esta mañana **a** las once. | *This morning at eleven.* |

2. After the verb **llegar** to indicate direction towards a point:

¿Cuándo llegaron **al** aeropuerto?

*When did they arrive at the airport?*

Llegaron **al** aeropuerto ayer.

*They arrived at the airport yesterday.*

### Exercise

Complete the following sentences using **a** or **en:**

1. Ellos están _____ la universidad.
2. Hoy no voy a estar _____ casa.
3. Mamá llegó _____ aeropuerto _____ las diez y media.
4. Llegó _____ la estación de policía.
5. Estoy _____ la esquina de Montevideo y Séptima.
6. El accidente fue _____ las ocho.
7. ¿Están _____ el aeropuerto?
8. Tuvimos un accidente cuando llegamos _____ la esquina.

## 4. CHANGES IN MEANING WITH IMPERFECT AND PRETERIT OF conocer, saber, querer, AND poder

In Spanish, a few verbs change their meaning when used in the preterit or the imperfect:

| Preterit | | Imperfect | |
|---|---|---|---|
| **conocer** | | **conocer** | |
| conocí | *I met* | conocía | *I knew, I was acquainted with* |
| **saber** | | **saber** | |
| supe | *I found out* | sabía | *I knew (a fact, how to)* |
| **querer** | | **querer** | |
| quise | *I tried* | quería | *I wanted* |
| no quise | *I refused* | no quería | *I didn't want to* |
| **poder** | | **poder** | |
| pude | *I succeeded, I was able* | podía | *I had the ability or chance* |

| | |
|---|---|
| Mario, ¿**conocías** a los suegros de Luisa? | *Mario, did you know Louise's parents-in-law?* |
| No, los **conocí** ayer. | *No, I met them yesterday.* |
| Rita, ¿**sabías** que teníamos examen hoy? | *Rita, did you know that we had an exam today?* |
| No, lo **supe** esta mañana. | *No, I found out this morning.* |
| ¿Por qué no fuiste el domingo a la fiesta? | *Why didn't you go to the party on Sunday?* |
| Yo **quería** ir, pero Carlos **no quiso** llevarme. | *I wanted to go, but Charles refused to take me.* |
| Ramón, ayer me dijiste que **podías** ayudarme con la tarea y no viniste. | *Raymond, yesterday you told me you could help me with the homework and you didn't come.* |
| No **pude** salir porque mamá estaba enferma. | *I wasn't able to go out because mother was sick.* |

### Exercise

Give the Spanish equivalent:

1. We met Julia's father yesterday.
2. She said she couldn't help you with the homework.
3. My father-in-law wasn't able to take his wife to the party.
4. They found out that they had an exam.
5. I didn't know your mother-in-law.
6. He refused to help me.
7. Did you know my address and my telephone number?
8. They wanted to go but weren't able to.

---

## STUDY OF COGNATES

1. This word is the same in Spanish and English, except for a final vowel:

   **el accidente**    accident

2. Approximate cognates:

   | | |
   |---|---|
   | **el aeropuerto** | airport |
   | **la estación** | station |
   | **el examen** | exam |
   | **el policía** | policeman |
   | **la policía** | police (organization) |

## NEW VOCABULARY

### Nouns

| | |
|---|---|
| **la cuenta** | bill |
| **la esquina** | corner |
| **la fiesta** | party |
| **la suegra** | mother-in-law |
| **el suegro** | father-in-law |
| **la tarea** | homework |

### Verbs

| | |
|---|---|
| **ayudar** | to help |
| **chocar** | to collide, to run into |
| **escribir a máquina** | to type |
| **irse** | to leave, to go away |
| **llevar** | to take (someone or something somewhere) |
| **pensar (e > ie)** | to think |
| **sentirse (e > ie)** | to feel |

### Other words and expressions

| | |
|---|---|
| **en casa** | at home |
| **juntos(as)** | together |
| **también** | also, too |

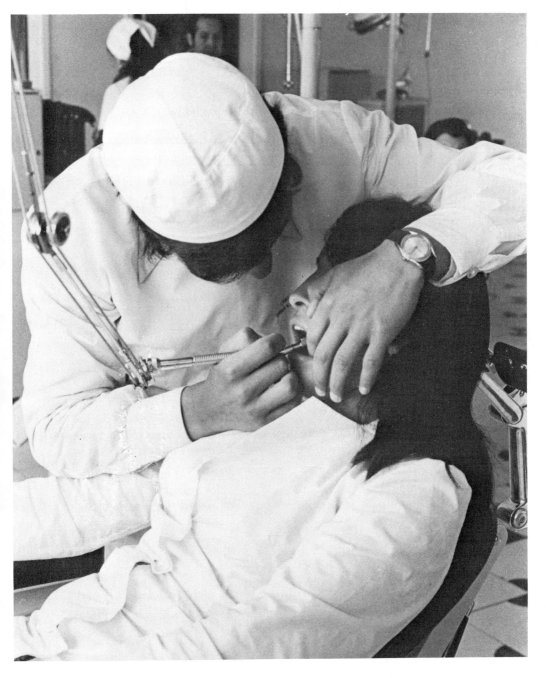

Lesson 13

# 1. MORE ABOUT IRREGULAR PRETERITS

Stem-changing verbs of the -ir conjugation change e to i or o to u in the third person singular and plural of the preterit:

| **sentir** (*to feel*) | | **dormir** (*to sleep*) | |
|---|---|---|---|
| sentí | sentimos | dormí | dormimos |
| sentiste | | dormiste | |
| sintió | sintieron | durmió | durmieron |

Other verbs that follow the same pattern:

pedir            servir           conseguir
reir(se) (*to laugh*)   repetir          morir (*to die*)
mentir (*to lie*)    seguir           despedirse (*to say good-bye*)

Sra. López, ¿**sintió** Ud. dolor
    cuando le sacaron la
    muela?
No, no sentí nada.

*Mrs. López, did you feel (any)*
    *pain when they took out*
    *your tooth?*
*No, I didn't feel anything.*

¿Cuántas horas **durmió** Ud.
    anoche?
Yo dormí seis horas, pero Ana y
    Luis sólo **durmieron** tres.

*How many hours did you sleep*
    *last night?*
*I slept six hours, but Anna and*
    *Louis slept only three.*

¿A quién le **pidieron** Uds. los
    documentos?
Se los **pedimos** al director.

*Whom did you ask for the*
    *documents?*
*We asked the director (for*
    *them).*

## Exercise

Complete the sentences with the preterit of the following verbs, as needed. Use each verb only once: **sentir, dormir, pedir, mentir, servir, repetir, seguir, conseguir, morir, reir:**

1. Ellos no me _____ la información.
2. Ayer yo no _____ dolor cuando me sacaron la muela.
3. Ella no me _____. Me dijo la verdad.
4. ¿_____ ellos los refrescos o los _____ tú?
5. El hijo de Carmen no _____ el puesto.
6. Pedro _____ en el accidente de anoche.
7. ¿Dónde _____ Uds. anoche? Yo _____ en el sofá.
8. ¿A quién le _____ Ud. la maleta?
9. Los niños _____ a la maestra.
10. Las niñas se _____ mucho.

## 2. USES OF **por** AND **para**

A. The preposition **por** is used to indicate:

1. Motion (*through, along, by*):

| | |
|---|---|
| ¿**Por** dónde entró el ladrón? | *How (through where) did the burglar get in?* |
| Entró **por** la ventana. | *He got in through the window.* |
| ¿A qué hora pasaste **por** mi casa ayer? | *At what time did you go by my house yesterday?* |
| Pasé **por** tu casa a las tres. | *I went by your house at three o'clock.* |

2. Cause or motive of an action (*because of, on account of, in behalf of*):

| | |
|---|---|
| ¿Por qué no vinieron anoche? | *Why didn't you come last night?* |
| No pudimos venir **por** la lluvia. | *We weren't able to come on account of the rain.* |

3. Agency, means, manner, unit of measure (*by, for, per*):

| | |
|---|---|
| ¿Vas a San Francisco **por** avión? | *Are you going to San Francisco by plane?* |
| No, llevo el coche. | *No, I'm taking the car.* |
| ¿Cuál es el límite de velocidad en California? | *What's the speed limit in California?* |
| Cincuenta y cinco millas **por** hora. | *Fifty-five miles per hour.* |

4. *In exchange for:*

| | |
|---|---|
| ¿Cuánto pagaste **por** ese abrigo? | *How much did you pay for that coat?* |
| Pagué[1] cien dólares **por** él. | *I paid one hundred dollars for it.* |

B. The preposition **para** is used to indicate:

1. Destination in space:

| | |
|---|---|
| ¿A qué hora hay vuelos **para** México? | *What time are there flights to Mexico?* |
| A las diez y a las doce de la noche. | *At ten and twelve P.M.* |

[1] Verbs ending in **-gar** change **g** to **gu** before **e** in the first person of the preterit. (See Verb paradigms in Appendix, p. 213.

2. Direction in time (*by, for*); a certain date in the future:

| | |
|---|---|
| ¿Cuándo necesita Ud. las cartas? | *When do you need the letters?* |
| Las necesito **para** mañana. | *I need them for tomorrow.* |

3. Direction toward a recipient:

| | |
|---|---|
| ¿**Para** quién es ese vestido? | *Who is that dress for?* |
| Es **para** mi suegra. | *It's for my mother-in-law.* |

4. *In order to:*

| | |
|---|---|
| ¿**Para** qué necesita Ud. el dinero? | *What do you need the money for?* |
| Lo necesito **para** pagar la cuenta del hospital. | *I need it (in order) to pay the hospital bill.* |

### Exercise

Complete the following sentences using **para** or **por**, as needed:

1. Salimos _____ México mañana. Vamos _____ avión.
2. Necesito los exámenes _____ mañana.
3. Anoche Juan pasó _____ mi casa _____ verme.
4. Hoy no hay vuelos _____ Madrid.
5. El ladrón no entró _____ la ventana.
6. ¿Cuánto pagaste _____ esos zapatos?
7. El abrigo no es _____ mi suegra.
8. Conduzco mi coche a 55 millas _____ hora. Ése es el límite de velocidad.
9. No puedo conducir a mucha velocidad _____ la lluvia.
10. Pagué diez dólares _____ este libro.

## 3. SPECIAL CONSTRUCTION WITH **gustar, doler,** AND **hacer falta**

A. The English verb *to like* is translated in Spanish by the verb **gustar,** which means *to be pleasing:*

---

| | | |
|---|---|---|
| *English:* | **I** like **your suit.** | |
| | Subj. | D.O. |
| *Spanish:* | **Me gusta tu traje.** | |
| | I.O. | Subject |
| *Literally:* | *Your suit is pleasing to me.* | |

---

Notice that the subject of the English sentence (*I*) becomes the indirect object (**me**) of the Spanish sentence. The direct object of the English sentence (*your suit*) becomes the subject of the Spanish sentence (**tu traje**).

ATENCIÓN:

1. When the Spanish subject is plural, the verb is also plural:

Me gust**an esos trajes**                I like those suits.
　　　　Subj.

¿**Le gustan** estos edificios?          Do you like these buildings?
No, no **me gustan.**                    No, I don't like them.

2. This construction may also be followed by an infinitive:

¿**Te gusta** caminar?                   Do you like to walk?
Sí, **me gusta** mucho.                  Yes, I like it very much.

3. **Más** is the equivalent of *better*. It is placed directly after **gustar:**

¿**Les gusta** a Uds. este modelo?   Do you like this model?
Sí, pero **nos gusta más** el otro.      Yes, but we like the other (one)
　　　　　　　　　　　　　　　　　　 better.

B. The verbs **doler** (*to hurt, to ache*) and **hacer falta** (*to need*) are
constructed in the same way as **gustar:**

¿Por qué estás tomando                 Why are you taking aspirins?
　 aspirinas?
Porque **me duele** la cabeza.           Because my head hurts.

¿Qué **les hace falta,** señoras?        What do you need, ladies?
**Nos hacen falta** toallas y jabón.     We need towels and soap.

## Exercises

A. Give the Spanish equivalent:

1. They like those buildings.
2. I need a suit.
3. I like this model.
4. We don't like to take aspirins.
5. Does your head hurt, madam?
6. Do you need towels or soap?

B. Answer the following questions:

1. ¿Qué le duele?
2. ¿Qué le hace falta a Ud.?
3. ¿Qué te gusta más, el piano o la radio?
4. ¿Les hacen falta a Uds. más toallas?
5. ¿Le duele a Ud. la cabeza?
6. ¿Te gusta caminar?
7. ¿Cuándo toman Uds. aspirinas?
8. ¿Les gusta a Uds. el español?

## 4. PRONOUNS AS OBJECT OF A PREPOSITION

| mí | me | | nosotros | us | |
|----|----|----|----------|----|----|
| ti | you | (familiar) | | | |
| Ud. | you | (formal) | Uds. | you | (formal, plural) |
| él | him | | ellos | them | (masc.) |
| ella | her | | ellas | them | (fem.) |

- Notice that the first and second persons singular have special forms. The other persons use the subject pronouns.
- When used with the preposition **con**, the first and second person singular forms become **conmigo** and **contigo**:

¿Viene Ud. a la conferencia **conmigo?**

*Are you coming to the lecture with me?*

No. Voy **con ellos.**

*No. I'm going with them.*

¿Quieres darle las toallas **a ella?**

*Do you want to give the towels to her?*

No. Te las doy **a ti.**

*No. I'm giving them to you.*

¿Es **para nosotros** el regalo?

*Is the gift for us?*

Sí, el regalo es **para Uds.**

*Yes, the gift is for you.*

### Exercise

Complete the following sentences with the correct forms of the pronouns:

1. Ella va a la conferencia con _____ (us).
2. Le doy el regalo a _____ (him).
3. Yo les traigo el jabón a _____ (you, pl.)
4. El regalo es para _____ (her).
5. Nosotros venimos con _____ (you, fam. sing.).
6. Juan se los da a _____ (them, masc.).
7. Yo se lo pregunto a _____ (you, form. sing.).
8. A _____ (them, fem.) les duele la cabeza.
9. La botella de plástico es para _____ (you, form. sing.).
10. Ud. viene a clase con _____ (me).

## STUDY OF COGNATES

1. These words are the same in Spanish and English, except for a final vowel or a single consonant:

   | | |
   |---|---|
   | **la aspirina** | aspirin |
   | **el límite** | limit |
   | **el modelo** | model |

2. Approximate cognates:

   | | |
   |---|---|
   | **el dólar** | dollar |
   | **la milla** | mile |

## NEW VOCABULARY

NOUNS

| | |
|---|---|
| **el avión** | plane |
| **la cabeza** | head |
| **la conferencia** | lecture |
| **el dolor** | pain |
| **el edificio** | building |
| **el jabón** | soap |
| **el ladrón** | burglar |
| **la lluvia** | rain |
| **la muela** | tooth (molar) |
| **el regalo** | present, gift |

| | |
|---|---|
| **la toalla** | towel |
| **el traje** | suit |
| **la velocidad** | speed |
| **el vuelo** | flight |

VERBS

| | |
|---|---|
| **doler (o > ue)** | to hurt, to ache |
| **entrar** | to enter |
| **pasar** | to go by |
| **sacar** | to take out |
| **tomar** | to take |

Lesson 14

## 1. ¿qué? AND ¿cuál? FOR "WHAT?"

A. When asking for a definition, opinion, or explanation, use ¿qué? to translate *what:*

| | |
|---|---|
| ¿**Qué** es un termómetro? | *What is a thermometer?* |
| Un termómetro es un instrumento que usamos para medir la temperatura. | *A thermometer is an instrument we use to measure temperature.* |
| ¿**Qué** piensa Ud. de ese perfume? | *What do you think about that perfume?* |
| Me gusta mucho. Es mi perfume favorito. | *I like it very much. It is my favorite perfume.* |
| ¿**Qué** haces aquí? | *What are you doing here?* |
| Estoy esperando a un amigo. | *I'm waiting for a friend.* |

B. When asking for a choice, use ¿**cuál?** to translate *what.* ¿**Cuál?** carries the idea of selection from among many objects or ideas:

| | |
|---|---|
| ¿**Cuál** es su número de seguro social? | *What is your social security number?* |
| Mi número de seguro social es 243-50-8139. | *My social security number is 243-50-8139.* |
| ¿**Cuáles** son sus ideas sobre la economía? | *What are your ideas about the economy?* |
| Está muy mal. | *It is very bad.* |

### Exercise

Use **qué** or **cuál** to complete the following questions:

1. ¿_____ piensan ellos de la economía?
2. ¿_____ es su número de seguro social?
3. ¿_____ es un termómetro? ¿Un instrumento?
4. ¿_____ hacen ellos aquí?
5. ¿_____ son sus ideas sobre la economía?
6. ¿_____ usamos para medir la temperatura?
7. ¿_____ es su estado civil?
8. ¿_____ es tu perfume favorito?
9. ¿_____ hace el profesor en clase?
10. ¿_____ es tu libro?

## 2. **hace** MEANING "AGO"

With sentences in the preterit, **hace** + period of time is equivalent to *ago*. When **hace** is placed at the beginning of the sentence, the construction is **hace** + period of time + **que**.

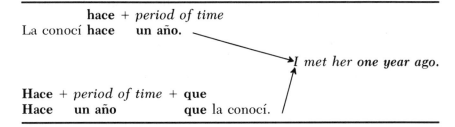

**hace** + *period of time*
La conocí **hace    un año.**

*I met her one year ago.*

**Hace** + *period of time* + **que**
**Hace    un año        que** la conocí.

| | |
|---|---|
| ¿Cuánto tiempo **hace que** conoció al profesor? | *How long ago did you meet the professor?* |
| **Hace un año que** lo conocí. | *I met him a year ago.* |
| ¿Cuánto tiempo **hace que** llegó? | *How long ago did you arrive?* |
| Llegué **hace dos horas.** | *I arrived two hours ago.* |

### Exercise

Answer the following questions in complete sentences:

1. ¿Cuánto tiempo hace que comenzó la clase?
2. ¿Cuánto tiempo hace que Ud. comió?
3. ¿Cuánto tiempo hace que Uds. empezaron a estudiar español?
4. ¿Cuánto tiempo hace que Uds. terminaron la lección trece?
5. ¿Cuánto tiempo hace que Ud. vino a esta ciudad?

## 3. USES OF **hacía . . . que**

**Hacía . . . que** is used:

1. To describe a situation that had been going on for a period of time and was still going on at a given moment in the past:

| | |
|---|---|
| ¿Cuánto tiempo **hacía que** Ud. vivía allí? | *How long had you been living there?* |
| **Hacía diez años que** vivía allí. | *I had been living there for ten years.* |

2. To tell of something that was going on in the past when something else happened:

| | |
|---|---|
| ¿Cuánto tiempo **hacía que** esperabas cuando él llegó? | *How long had you been waiting when he arrived?* |
| **Hacía dos horas y media que** esperaba cuando él llegó. | *I had been waiting for two and a half hours when he arrived.* |

ATENCIÓN: Notice that in the **hacía . . . que** construction, the verb that follows it is always in the imperfect tense:

| | |
|---|---|
| ¿Cuánto tiempo **hacía que** **estudiabas?** | *How long had you been studying?* |
| **Hacía** tres años **que estudiaba.** | *I had been studying for three years.* |

### Exercise

Give the Spanish equivalent:

1. She had been living there for two months when she met him.
2. How long had you been living there?
3. They had been studying for four years.
4. I had been working for two weeks when she arrived.
5. How long had you known him?

## 4. MORE USES OF THE DEFINITE ARTICLE

Spanish uses the definite article in the following cases:

1. With parts of the body or with articles of clothing in place of the possessive adjectives:

| | |
|---|---|
| ¿Dónde le duele? | *Where does it hurt?* |
| Me duele **el** estómago. | *My stomach hurts.* |
| Lávese **las** manos, por favor. | *Wash your hands, please.* |
| ¿Por qué te quitas **el** abrigo? | *Why are you taking your coat off?* |
| Porque tengo calor. | *Because I'm hot.* |

2. With the nouns **cárcel, iglesia,** and **escuela** when they are preceded by a preposition:

| | |
|---|---|
| ¿Por qué está Jorge en **la** cárcel? | *Why is George in jail?* |
| Porque mató a un hombre. | *Because he killed a man.* |
| ¿A dónde va esa mujer todos los domingos? | *Where does that woman go every Sunday?* |
| Va a **la** iglesia. | *She goes to church.* |
| ¿Dónde está Felipe? | *Where is Philip?* |
| Está en **la** escuela. | *He is at school.* |

3. Before titles such as **señor, señora, doctor, profesora,** etc., when talking about the person and not directly to him or her:

Buenos días, señor García.          *Good morning, Mr. Garcia.*
¿Cómo está **el** doctor Orta?      *How is Doctor Orta?*
Está bien, gracias.                 *He is well, thank you.*

## Exercise

Give the Spanish equivalent:

1. I want to see Mrs. Mata.
2. Does your stomach hurt?
3. I washed my hands and put on my dress.
4. Good afternoon, doctor Morales.
5. The man is in jail because he killed a woman.
6. They are not in school. They went to church.

## 5. PAST PARTICIPLES

A. Regular past participles are formed by adding the following endings to the stem of the verb:

| Part Participle Endings | | |
|---|---|---|
| **-ar** *Verbs* | **-er** *Verbs* | **-ir** *Verbs* |
| habl- **ado** | ten- **ido** | ven- **ido** |

B. The following verbs have irregular past participles in Spanish:

| abrir | **abierto** | morir | **muerto** |
|---|---|---|---|
| cubrir | **cubierto** | poner | **puesto** |
| decir | **dicho** | ver | **visto** |
| escribir | **escrito** | volver | **vuelto** |
| hacer | **hecho** | romper | **roto** |

● The past participle is used with the auxiliary verb **haber** (*to have*)[1] to form the compound tenses. These will be discussed in Lesson 15.

## Exercise

Give the past participles of the following verbs:

1. dormir      6. cubrir      11. caminar      16. abrir
2. romper      7. recibir     12. pedir        17. ver
3. estar       8. hacer       13. decir        18. volver
4. comer       9. cerrar      14. comprar      19. aprender
5. poner       10. ser        15. morir        20. escribir

[1] Note that *to have* has two equivalents in Spanish: **haber** (used only as an auxiliary verb) and **tener.**

## STUDY OF COGNATES

1. Exact cognates:

   **la idea**        idea
   **el perfume**     perfume

2. This word is the same in Spanish and English, except for a final vowel:

   **el instrumento**   instrument

3. Approximate cognates:

   **favorito**        favorite
   **la temperatura**  temperature
   **el termómetro**   thermometer

## NEW VOCABULARY

NOUNS

**la cárcel**      jail
**el estómago**    stomach
**la iglesia**     church

VERBS

**cubrir**         to cover
**lavar(se)**      to wash
                   (oneself)

**matar**          to kill
**medir (e > i)**  to measure
**quitar(se)**     to take off
**romper**         to break
**usar**           to use

OTHER WORDS AND EXPRESSIONS

**sobre**          about
**todos**          every, all

Lesson 15

## 1. THE PRESENT PERFECT TENSE

A. The present indicative of the auxiliary verb **haber** is as follows:

| | | | |
|---|---|---|---|
| yo | he | nosotros | hemos |
| tú | has | | |
| Ud. ⎤ | | Uds. ⎤ | |
| él ⎬ | ha | ellos ⎬ | han |
| ella ⎦ | | ellas ⎦ | |

B. The present perfect tense is formed by using the present tense of
the auxiliary verb **haber** and the past participle of the verb to be
conjugated:

| Present Perfect Tense | | | | | |
|---|---|---|---|---|---|
| **hablar** | | **tener** | | **venir** | |
| **he** | hablado | **he** | tenido | **he** | venido |
| **has** | hablado | **has** | tenido | **has** | venido |
| **ha** | hablado | **ha** | tenido | **ha** | venido |
| **hemos** | hablado | **hemos** | tenido | **hemos** | venido |
| **han** | hablado | **han** | tenido | **han** | venido |

¿**Ha terminado** Ud. su lección
de matemáticas?
No, no la **he terminado** todavía.

*Have you finished your math
lesson?*
*No, I haven't finished it yet.*

¿Cuántas veces **ha venido** ella
a este lugar?
Ella **ha venido** muchas veces.

*How many times has she come
to this place?*
*She has come many times.*

¿De qué **han hablado** Uds.?
**Hemos hablado** de negocios.

*What have you talked about?*
*We have talked about business.*

¿Qué les **ha dicho** el
gerente?
El gerente nos **ha dicho** que
tenemos que terminar el
trabajo para mañana.

*What has the manager said to
you?*
*The manager has told us that
we have to finish the work
for tomorrow.*

ATENCIÓN: Note that when the past participle is part of a perfect
tense, it is invariable and cannot be separated from the auxiliary
verb **haber**:

¿Qué **ha hecho** Ud. hoy?
Hoy, no **he hecho** nada.

*What **have you done** today?*
*Today, I haven't done
anything.*

### Exercise

Item Substitution:

1. El gerente **ha hablado** de negocios. (Yo, Ud., Nosotras, Ella, Tú)
2. Ellos ya **han terminado** el trabajo. (Ud., Nosotros, Tú, Él, Yo)
3. Yo **he escrito** la carta. (Nosotros, Uds., Ella, Yo, Tú)
4. Ud. **ha abierto** la puerta. (Yo, Él, Uds., Nosotras, Ellas)
5. Uds. **han venido** a este lugar. (Tú, Ellos, Yo, Él, Nosotros)

## 2. THE PAST PERFECT TENSE (PLUPERFECT)

The pluperfect tense is formed by using the imperfect tense of the auxiliary verb **haber** and the past participle of the verb to be conjugated:

| Past Perfect Tense | | | | | |
|---|---|---|---|---|---|
| **hablar** | | **tener** | | **venir** | |
| **había** | hablado | **había** | tenido | **había** | venido |
| **habías** | hablado | **habías** | tenido | **habías** | venido |
| **había** | hablado | **había** | tenido | **había** | venido |
| **habíamos** | hablado | **habíamos** | tenido | **habíamos** | venido |
| **habían** | hablado | **habían** | tenido | **habían** | venido |

| | |
|---|---|
| ¿No trajiste las sábanas? | *Didn't you bring the sheets?* |
| Ya las **había traído** Ernesto. | *Ernest had already brought them.* |
| ¿De qué **había hablado** el doctor Peña? | *What had Dr. Peña talked about?* |
| El Dr. Peña **había hablado** de sus experimentos con plantas tropicales. | *Dr. Peña had talked about his experiments with tropical plants.* |
| ¿Para qué **habían venido** ellos? | *What had they come for?* |
| **Habían venido** para ver al administrador. | *They had come to see the administrator.* |

### Exercise

Change the following sentences to the past perfect:

1. Ella está enferma.
2. Vinieron a ver al administrador.
3. Ud. cubrió los instrumentos.
4. Yo hablo de mis experimentos con plantas tropicales.
5. Nosotros vimos las sábanas.

6. Uds. rompieron la puerta.
7. Yo salí a las cinco.
8. Ellas ya estudiaron la lección de matemáticas.
9. Tú puedes hacerlo.
10. Ud. durmió hasta muy tarde.

## 3. PAST PARTICIPLES USED AS ADJECTIVES

In Spanish most past participles may be used as adjectives. As such, they agree in number and gender with the nouns they modify:

| | |
|---|---|
| ¿Ha tenido Ud. un accidente? | *Have you had an accident?* |
| Sí, y tengo **la pierna rota**. | *Yes, and I have a broken leg.* |
| ¿Y el brazo? | *And your arm?* |
| No, **el brazo** no está **roto**. | *No, my arm is not broken.* |
| Entonces, ¿no ha terminado los artículos? | *Then, haven't you finished the articles?* |
| Sí, **los artículos** ya están **escritos**. | *Yes, the articles are already written.* |

### Exercise

Complete the following sentences with the past participle of the verbs in parentheses. Read the completed sentences aloud:

1. Los niños están _____ (morir).
2. Pedro y yo estamos _____ (cansar).
3. Juan tiene las piernas _____ (romper).
4. El libro _____ (abrir) es del administrador.
5. Entonces la lección está _____ (terminar).
6. Los instrumentos están _____ (cubrir).
7. Las puertas no están _____ (abrir).
8. El brazo del niño no está _____ (romper).
9. Las ventanas estaban _____ (cerrar).
10. Todos los artículos están _____ (escribir).

## 4. DIMINUTIVE SUFFIXES

To express the idea of size, and also to denote affection, Spanish uses different suffixes. The most common suffixes are **-ito(a)** and **-cito(a)**. There are no set rules for forming the diminutive, but usually if the word ends in **-a** or **-o,** these vowels are dropped and **-ito(a)** is added:

| | | |
|---|---|---|
| niño | niñ + **ito** = | **niñito** (*little boy*) |
| niña | niñ + **ita** = | **niñita** (*little girl*) |
| abuelo | abuel + **ito** = | **abuelito** (*grandpa*) |
| Ana | An + **ita** = | **Anita** |

If the word ends in a consonant other than **-n** or **-r**, the suffix **ito(a)** is added:

| | | |
|---|---|---|
| árbol | + **ito** = | **arbolito** (*little tree*) |
| Luis | + **ito** = | **Luisito** |

If the word ends in **-e, -n** or **-r**, the suffix **-cito(a)** is added:

| | | |
|---|---|---|
| coche | + **cito** = | **cochecito** (*little car*) |
| mujer | + **cita** = | **mujercita** (*little woman*) |
| Carmen | + **cita** = | **Carmencita** |

| | |
|---|---|
| Hola, **abuelito.** ¿Me trajiste el **arbolito** de Navidad? | *Hello, grandpa. Did you bring me the little Christmas tree?* |
| Sí, **Tomasito.** | *Yes, Tommy.* |
| Me gusta tu **cochecito.** | *I like your little car.* |
| Gracias, **Carmencita.** | *Thanks, Carmen.* |

## Exercise

Give the diminutive corresponding to each of the following:

| | |
|---|---|
| 1. primo | 6. hermana |
| 2. escuela | 7. favor |
| 3. árbol | 8. Juan |
| 4. Raúl | 9. Adela |
| 5. coche | 10. mamá |

## STUDY OF COGNATES

1. Exact cognate:

   **tropical**      tropical

2. These words are the same in Spanish and English, except for a final vowel:

   | | |
   |---|---|
   | **la planta** | plant |
   | **el experimento** | experiment |

3. Approximate cognates:

   | | |
   |---|---|
   | **el administrador** | administrator |
   | **el artículo** | article |
   | **las matemáticas** | mathematics |

## NEW VOCABULARY

<table>
<tr><td colspan="2">Nouns</td><td colspan="2">Verb</td></tr>
<tr><td>el árbol</td><td>tree</td><td>terminar</td><td>to finish</td></tr>
<tr><td>el brazo</td><td>arm</td><td></td><td></td></tr>
<tr><td>el gerente</td><td>manager</td><td colspan="2">Other words and expressions</td></tr>
<tr><td>el lugar</td><td>place</td><td>¿cuántas veces?</td><td>how many</td></tr>
<tr><td>los negocios</td><td>business</td><td></td><td>times?</td></tr>
<tr><td>la Navidad</td><td>Christmas</td><td>entonces</td><td>then</td></tr>
<tr><td>la niña</td><td>girl, child</td><td>muchas veces</td><td>many times,</td></tr>
<tr><td>el niño</td><td>boy, child</td><td></td><td>often</td></tr>
<tr><td>la pierna</td><td>leg</td><td></td><td></td></tr>
<tr><td>la sábana</td><td>sheet</td><td></td><td></td></tr>
<tr><td>el trabajo</td><td>work</td><td></td><td></td></tr>
</table>

# Test Yourself: Lessons 11-15

## LESSON 11

A. Time expressions with **hacer** and **llevar**

Give two Spanish equivalents for each of the sentences. Follow the models:

*Modelos:* How long have you lived in California?
   a) **¿Cuánto tiempo hace que vive en California?**
   b) **¿Cuánto tiempo lleva viviendo en California?**

   I have been living in California for two months.
   a) **Hace dos meses que vivo en California.**
   b) **Llevo dos meses viviendo en California.**

1. How long have you worked in Lima?
2. We have worked in Lima for five years.
3. How long have they waited?
4. They have waited for three hours.
5. How long has she studied Spanish?
6. She has studied Spanish for two years.

B. Irregular preterits

Rewrite the sentences, according to the new beginnings. Follow the model:

*Modelo:* Tenemos que salir. (Ayer)
   **Ayer tuvimos que salir.**

1. María está muy ocupada. (Ayer)
2. No pueden venir. (Anoche)
3. Pongo el dinero en el banco. (La semana pasada)
4. No haces nada. (El domingo pasado)
5. Ella viene con Juan. (Ayer)
6. No queremos venir a clase. (La semana pasada)
7. Yo no digo nada. (Anoche)
8. Traemos la máquina de escribir. (Ayer)
9. Yo conduzco mi coche. (Anoche)
10. Ellos traducen las lecciones. (Ayer)

C. **¿De quién . . . ?** for "Whose?"

Ask who these items belong to. Follow the model:

*Modelo:* esta máquina de escribir
   **¿De quién es esta máquina de escribir?**

1. ese paraguas
2. esos revólveres
3. estos zapatos
4. este dinero
5. aquella silla

D. The imperfect tense

Answer the following questions, according to the model:

*Modelo:* ¿Qué querían ellos?   (arroz con pollo)
**Querían arroz con pollo.**

1. ¿Dónde vivían Uds. cuando eran chicos?   (en Alaska)
2. ¿Qué idioma hablabas tú cuando eras chico(a)?   (inglés)
3. ¿A quién veías siempre cuando eras chico(a)?   (a mi abuela)
4. ¿En qué banco depositaban Uds. el dinero?   (en el Banco de América)
5. ¿A qué hora se acostaban los niños?   (a las nueve)
6. ¿A dónde iba Rosa?   (al cine)
7. ¿Qué compraba Ud.?   (café)
8. ¿En qué gastaban Uds. su dinero?   (en libros)

# LESSON 12

A. The past progressive

Complete the sentences with the past progressive of the following verbs, as needed. Use each verb once: **hacer, hablar, estudiar, comer, pensar, leer, trabajar, escribir**

1. Nosotros _____ arroz con pollo cuando llegó Elsa.
2. ¿Qué _____ Uds. cuando yo llamé?
3. Elena _____ a máquina cuando llegó el doctor Vargas.
4. Yo _____ por teléfono con mi hijo.
5. ¿En qué _____ tú cuando yo te hablé?
6. Ud. _____ el periódico cuando yo vine.
7. Los niños _____ la lección.
8. Roberto _____ en el garaje cuando yo lo vi.

B. Preterit vs. imperfect

Give the Spanish equivalent:

1. We went to bed at eleven last night.
2. She was very busy when I saw her.
3. We used to go to Buenos Aires.
4. It was ten-thirty when I called him.
5. She said she wanted to read.

C. **En** and **a** for "at"

Write sentences, using these items. Follow the model:

*Modelo:* Yo / estar / universidad / anoche
**Yo estuve en la universidad anoche.**

1. Nosotros / llegar / aeropuerto / seis y media
2. Mi hermana / estar / casa
3. Ellos / estar / esquina de Unión y Figueroa
4. El accidente / ser / las doce
5. Yo / estar / la estación de policía / ayer

D. Changes in meaning with imperfect and preterit of **conocer, saber, querer,** and **poder**

Complete the sentences with the preterit or the imperfect of the verbs **conocer, saber, querer,** and **poder,** as needed:

1. Yo no _____ a los abuelos de María. Los _____ ayer.
2. Nosotros no _____ que ella era casada. Lo _____ anoche.
3. Pedro dijo que no _____ venir, pero vino a eso de las dos.
4. Ellos no _____ llamarte por teléfono porque estaban trabajando. Por eso no te llamaron.
5. Mamá no vino a la reunión porque no _____ venir.
6. Yo no _____ ir a la fiesta, pero cuando _____ que Carlos iba a ir, decidí ir también.

# LESSON 13

A. More about irregular preterits

Rewrite the sentences, according to the new beginnings. Follow the model:

*Modelo:* Él no pide dinero.  (Ayer)
**Ayer él no pidió dinero.**

1. Él siente mucho dolor.  (Ayer)
2. Marta no duerme bien.  (Anoche)
3. No le pido nada.  (Ayer)
4. Ella te miente.  (La semana pasada)
5. Ellos sirven los refrescos.  (El sábado pasado)
6. No lo repito.  (Ayer)
7. Ella sigue estudiando.  (Anoche)
8. Tú no consigues nada.  (El lunes pasado)

B. Uses of **por** and **para**

Give the Spanish equivalent:

1. The thief went in through the window.
2. She went by my house.
3. She wasn't able to come on account of the rain.
4. There are flights to Mexico on Saturdays.
5. We are going by plane.
6. He needs the shirt for tomorrow.
7. He was going at ninety miles per hour.
8. Who is the newspaper for?
9. I need the money to pay the bill.
10. She paid two hundred dollars for that dress.

C. Special construction with **gustar, doler,** and **hacer falta**

Complete the sentences with the appropriate forms of **gustar, doler,** and **hacer falta,** as needed:

1. No _____ esos edificios. Prefiero aquéllos.
2. ¿Qué _____ señora? ¿Jabón?
3. A Marta _____ la cabeza. ¿Tienes aspirinas?
4. A nosotros no _____ dinero. No necesitamos comprar nada.
5. ¿_____ a Ud. este modelo, o prefiere el otro?
6. _____ toallas. ¿Puede traérmelas, por favor?
7. _____ la muela. Tengo que ir al dentista.
8. ¿No _____ caminar? ¡Podemos ir en coche!

D. Pronouns as object of a preposition

Give the Spanish equivalent:

1. Can you come with me?
2. Are you going to work with them?
3. To whom did she give the towels? To you?
4. The gift is not for me. It is for her.
5. No, Charlie. I can't go with you.

# LESSON 14

A. **¿Qué?** and **¿cuál?** for "what?"

Give the Spanish equivalent:

1. What is freedom?
2. What are you doing here?

3. What does the teacher think about him?
4. What is your telephone number?
5. What are his ideas about this?

B. **Hace** meaning "ago"

Write two sentences for each set of items. Follow the model:

*Modelo:*  Un año / yo / conocer / él
   **Hace un año que yo lo conocí.**
   **Yo lo conocí hace un año.**

1. tres meses / nosotros / llegar / a California
2. doce horas / Ud. / comer
3. dos días / ellos / terminar / el trabajo
4. veinte años / ella / ver / él
5. quince días / tú / venir / a esta ciudad

C. Uses of **hacía . . . que**

Answer the following questions, according to the model:

*Modelo:*  ¿Cuánto tiempo hacía que Ud. vivía allí?  (tres años)
   **Hacía tres años que yo vivía allí.**

1. ¿Cuánto tiempo hacía que Ud. no comía?  (diez horas)
2. ¿Cuánto tiempo hacía que Uds. lo esperaban cuando él llegó?  (media hora)
3. ¿Cuánto tiempo hacía que estudiabas español cuando fuiste a Madrid?  (dos meses)
4. ¿Cuánto tiempo hacía que ella no bebía?  (cuatro años)
5. ¿Cuánto tiempo hacía que Uds. trabajaban para el gobierno?  (quince años)

D. More uses of the definite article

Write sentences using these items. Follow the model:

*Modelo:*  A mí / doler / estómago
   **Me duele el estómago.**

1. Ana / estar / escuela
2. Ella / lavarse / manos
3. Tú / quitarse / abrigo
4. Mamá / ir / iglesia / domingos
5. Felipe / estar / cárcel
6. Nosotros / visitar / señorita García

E. Past participles

Complete the following chart:

| Infinitive | Past Participle |
|---|---|
| 1. trabajar | 1. trabajado |
| 2. recibir | 2. _____ |
| 3. _____ | 3. vuelto |
| 4. hablar | 4. _____ |
| 5. escribir | 5. _____ |
| 6. _____ | 6. ido |
| 7. aprender | 7. _____ |
| 8. _____ | 8. abierto |
| 9. cubrir | 9. _____ |
| 10. comer | 10. _____ |
| 11. _____ | 11. visto |
| 12. hacer | 12. _____ |
| 13. ser | 13. _____ |
| 14. _____ | 14. dicho |
| 15. cerrar | 15. _____ |
| 16. _____ | 16. muerto |
| 17. _____ | 17. roto |
| 18. dormir | 18. _____ |
| 19. estar | 19. _____ |
| 20. _____ | 20. puesto |

# LESSON 15

A. The present perfect tense

Complete the sentences with the present perfect of the following verbs. Use each verb once: **hablar, hacer, abrir, venir, decir, terminar, escribir, tener, poner.**

1. Yo _____ muchas veces a este lugar.
2. ¿_____ Uds. la lección de matemáticas?
3. Nosotros todavía no _____ de negocios con el gerente del hotel.
4. Ellos me _____ que tengo que venir el sábado y el domingo.
5. ¿No _____ (tú) las cartas todavía?
6. Hoy nosotros no _____ nada, porque no _____ tiempo.
7. ¿Quién _____ las puertas?
8. ¿Dónde _____ Ud. las sillas?

B. The past perfect tense

Give the Spanish equivalent:

1. I had already brought the sheets.
2. We had written to him about our experiments with tropical plants.
3. They had broken the pencils.
4. He had already seen the administrator.
5. Had you covered the tables, Miss Peña?

C. Past participles used as adjectives

Give the Spanish equivalent:

1. The article is written.
2. These are the broken chairs.
3. The door is open.
4. Are the books closed?
5. The work is finished.

D. Diminutive suffixes

Complete the following sentences with the Spanish equivalent of the words in parentheses:

1. Yo ya compré el _____ (*little tree*) de Navidad.
2. Mi _____ (*little sister*) se llama _____ (*little Theresa*).
3. Puedes hacerme un _____ (*little dress*) para mi _____ (*little daughter*)
4. Fuimos a Disneylandia con _____ (*little John*).
5. Tenemos un _____ (*little car*) muy bueno.

Lesson 16

# 1. THE FUTURE TENSE

A. Most Spanish verbs are regular in the future. The infinitive serves as the stem of almost all verbs. The endings are the same for all three conjugations. The English equivalent is *will* plus *verb*.

| The Future Tense | | | |
|---|---|---|---|
| *Infinitive* | | *Stems* | *Endings* |
| trabajar | yo | trabajar- | é |
| aprender | tú | aprender- | ás |
| escribir | Ud. | escribir- | á |
| hablar | él | hablar- | á |
| decidir | ella | decidir- | á |
| entender | nosotros | entender- | **emos** |
| caminar | Uds. | caminar- | án |
| perder | ellos | perder- | án |
| recibir | ellas | recibir- | án |

ATENCIÓN: Notice that all the endings, except the one for the **nosotros** form, have written accent marks.

¿**Irán** ustedes a la conferencia sobre la civilización y la cultura de México?

Sí, **iremos** todos, sin falta.

¿Ud. cree que el paciente **mejorará** pronto?

Yo creo que sí.

¿Cuándo **estarán** listos los análisis?

**Estarán** listos mañana por la tarde.

*Will you go to the lecture on the civilization and the culture of Mexico?*

*Yes, we'll all go without fail.*

*Do you think the patient will improve soon?*

*I think so.*

*When will the tests be ready?*

*They will be ready tomorrow afternoon.*

## Exercise

Change the following sentences to the future tense:

1. Nosotros somos los primeros.
2. ¿El paciente mejora?
3. Los alumnos entienden la lección.
4. Los análisis están listos.
5. Él no entiende los problemas de la economía.
6. ¿Tú aprendes español?
7. Yo compro las sábanas.
8. Uds. lo deciden el próximo mes.

9. Ellos escriben sobre la cultura y la civilización de México.
10. Ella va a clase sin falta.
11. Roberto habla con el profesor.
12. Los estudiantes comen en la cafetería.
13. Nosotros caminamos por la ciudad.
14. Tú no trabajas aquí.
15. ¿Van Uds. a la conferencia?

B. A small number of verbs are irregular in the future. These verbs use a modified form of the infinitive as a stem. The endings are the same.

| Infinitive | Modified Form (Stem) | Future Tense | | |
|---|---|---|---|---|
| decir | dir- | yo | **dir-** | é |
| hacer | har- | tú | **har-** | ás |
| saber | sabr- | Ud. | **sabr-** | á |
| haber | habr- | él | **habr-** | á |
| poder | podr- | ella | **podr-** | á |
| poner | pondr- | nosotros | **pondr-** | emos |
| venir | vendr- | Uds. | **vendr-** | án |
| tener | tendr- | ellos | **tendr-** | án |
| salir | saldr- | ellas | **saldr-** | án |

¿Les has dicho la fecha de la reunión?
No, se la **diré** después.

*Have you told them the date of the meeting?*
*No, I'll tell (it to) them later.*

¿Cuándo **sabrán** Uds. el resultado de los análisis?
Lo **sabremos** la semana próxima.

*When will you know the result of the tests?*
*We will know it next week.*

¿**Vendrá** hoy el mecánico a arreglar el coche?
Sí, **vendrá** por la tarde.

*Will the mechanic come today to fix the car?*
*Yes, he will come in the afternoon.*

## Exercise

Complete the following sentences with the future tense of the verbs in parentheses:

1. ¿Qué les _____ Ud. a sus pacientes?  (decir)
2. Los padres de ella _____ después.  (salir)
3. Nosotros _____ con el director del banco.  (venir)
4. Yo _____ los resultados mañana.  (tener)
5. El mecánico no _____ arreglar el coche.  (poder)

6. ¿Cuándo _____ Ud. la fecha del examen?  (saber)
7. ¿Qué _____ tú en el verano?  (hacer)
8. Mañana _____ una reunión.  (haber)
9. ¿_____ Uds. el dinero en el banco?  (poner)
10. ¿Crees tú que él _____ con nosotros? ¡Yo creo que sí!  (venir)

## 2. THE CONDITIONAL TENSE

A. The Spanish conditional tense is equivalent in meaning to the English conditional (*should* or *would*). Like the future, the conditional has only one ending for all three conjugations. It also uses the infinitive as the stem.

| The Conditional Tense | | | |
|---|---|---|---|
| *Infinitive* | | *Stem* | *Endings* |
| trabajar | yo | trabajar- | ía |
| aprender | tú | aprender- | ías |
| escribir | Ud. | escribir- | ía |
| ir | él | ir- | ía |
| ser | ella | ser- | ía |
| dar | nosotros | dar- | íamos |
| servir | Uds. | servir- | ían |
| estar | ellos | estar- | ían |
| preferir | ellas | preferir- | ían |

¿**Vendería** Ud. su casa por cincuenta mil dólares?

*Would you sell your house for fifty thousand dollars?*

No, yo no la **vendería** a ese precio.

*No, I wouldn't sell it at that price.*

¿**Preferirían** Uds. ir conmigo a Europa?

*Would you prefer to go to Europe with me?*

Sí, **preferiríamos** ir contigo.

*Yes, we would prefer going with you.*

The conditional is also used to describe a future action in relation to the past:

Mi sobrino **dijo** que **trabajaría** en una estación de servicio el verano próximo.

*My nephew said he would work at a service station next summer.*

¡Buena idea!

*Good idea!*

**Exercise**

Item substitution:

1. Yo no vendería mi casa a ese precio. (Uds., Tú, Ella, Nosotros)
2. Nosotros no le escribiríamos. (Yo, Tú, Ellos, Él, Uds.)
3. Ellas serían felices. (Nosotros, Yo, Ud., Tú, Ella)
4. Mi sobrino trabajaría en la estación de servicio. (Yo, Nosotros, Uds., Tú, Ud., Ellos)
5. Ud. dijo que serviría el café. (Yo, Nosotros, Tú, Ella, Ellos)

---

B. The same verbs that have irregular stems in the future tense are also irregular in the conditional. The endings are the same as the ones for regular verbs.

| Infinitive | Modified Form (Stem) | Conditional Tense | | |
|---|---|---|---|---|
| decir | dir- | yo | **dir-** | ía |
| hacer | har- | tú | **har-** | ías |
| saber | sabr- | Ud. | **sabr-** | ía |
| haber | habr- | él | **habr-** | ía |
| poder | podr- | ella | **podr-** | ía |
| poner | pondr- | nosotros | **pondr-** | íamos |
| venir | vendr- | Uds. | **vendr-** | ían |
| tener | tendr- | ellos | **tendr-** | ían |
| salir | saldr- | ellas | **saldr-** | ían |

¿Lo **harían** Uds.?                     *Would you do it?*
No, no lo **haríamos.**                  *No, we wouldn't do it.*

¿**Saldrías** conmigo?                   *Would you go out with me?*
No, no **saldría** contigo.              *No, I wouldn't go out with you.*

¿**Podría** él llegar a tiempo?          *Would he be able to arrive on time?*

No, no **podría** llegar a tiempo.       *No, he wouldn't be able to arrive on time.*

**Exercises**

A. Change the following sentences according to the model:

*Modelo:* Dice que lo **hará.** (Dijo)
         **Dijo que lo haría.**

1. Digo que vendré. (Dije)
2. Decimos que saldremos. (Dijimos)
3. Dices que lo pondrás en el banco. (Dijiste)
4. Ud. dice que lo sabrá mañana. (Ud. dijo)
5. Dicen que se lo dirán hoy. (Dijeron)

6. Dice que habrá una reunión.  (Dijo)
7. Digo que no podré ir.  (Dije)
8. Dices que lo tendrás listo hoy.  (Dijiste)

B.  Give the Spanish equivalent:

1. Would the men arrive on time?
2. My mother wouldn't do it.
3. They wouldn't know what to say.
4. Would you like to go to Europe?
5. Would the mechanic be at the service station?
6. We wouldn't tell (it to) him.
7. Did she say there would be a meeting?
8. She said she wouldn't be able to work.

# 3. THE PRESENT SUBJUNCTIVE

## Use of the Present Subjunctive

A.  The present subjunctive is used almost exclusively in subordinate clauses when the speaker has doubts, uncertainty, or strong feelings about an action or assertion. For example, it is used when a contrary-to-fact supposition is made. The subjunctive expresses the subjectivity or mental uncertainty of the speaker.

B.  The subjunctive is also used in English, although not as often as in Spanish. For example:

   *I suggest that he **arrive** tomorrow.*

As in Spanish, the expression that requires the use of the subjunctive is in the main clause (*I suggest*). The subjunctive itself appears in the subordinate clause (*that he **arrive** tomorrow*).

C.  There are three main concepts that call for the use of the subjunctive in Spanish:

1. Command: indirect or implied:

   Ella quiere que yo le **escriba.**

2. Emotion: pity, joy, fear, surprise, hope, desire, etc.:

   Espero que Uds. **puedan** venir.

3. Unreality: indefiniteness, doubt, uncertainty, nonexistence:

   No hay nadie que **sepa** hacerlo.

## Formation of the Present Subjunctive

The present subjunctive is formed by adding the following endings to the stem of the first person singular of the present indicative, after dropping the **-o:**

| The Present Subjunctive of Regular Verbs | | |
|---|---|---|
| **-ar** *Verbs* | **-er** *Verbs* | **-ir** *Verbs* |
| **trabajar** | **comer** | **vivir** |
| trabaj- **e** | com- **a** | viv- **a** |
| trabaj- **es** | com- **as** | viv- **as** |
| trabaj- **e** | com- **a** | viv- **a** |
| trabaj- **emos** | com- **amos** | viv- **amos** |
| trabaj- **en** | com- **an** | viv- **an** |

ATENCIÓN: Notice that the endings for the **-er** and **-ir** verbs are the same.

The following table shows you how to form the first person singular of the present subjunctive from the infinitive of the verb:

| Verb | *First Person Singular (Indicative)* | *Stem* | *First Person Singular (Present Subjunctive)* |
|---|---|---|---|
| hab**lar** | hablo | habl- | hable |
| apren**der** | aprendo | aprend- | aprenda |
| escrib**ir** | escribo | escrib- | escriba |
| de**cir** | digo | dig- | diga |
| ha**cer** | hago | hag- | haga |
| tra**er** | traigo | traig- | traiga |
| ven**ir** | vengo | veng- | venga |
| cono**cer** | conozco | conozc- | conozca |

## Exercise

Give the present subjunctive of the following verbs:

1. **yo:**       comer, venir, hablar, hacer, salir, ponerse
2. **tú:**        decir, ver, traer, trabajar, escribir, acostarse
3. **él:**        vivir, aprender, salir, estudiar, levantarse
4. **nosotros:**  escribir, caminar, poner, desear, tener, afeitarse
5. **ellos:**     salir, hacer, llevar, conocer, ver, bañarse

## Subjunctive Forms of Stem-changing Verbs

1. **-ar** and **-er** verbs maintain the basic pattern of the present indicative. That is, their stems undergo the same changes in the present subjunctive:

| **recomendar** (to recommend) | | **recordar** (to remember) | |
|---|---|---|---|
| recomiende | recomendemos | recuerde | recordemos |
| recomiendes | | recuerdes | |
| recomiende | recomienden | recuerde | recuerden |

| **entender** (to understand) | | **mover** (to move) | |
|---|---|---|---|
| entienda | entendamos | mueva | movamos |
| entiendas | | muevas | |
| entienda | entiendan | mueva | muevan |

2. **-ir** verbs change the unstressed **e** to **i** and the unstressed **o** to **u** in the first person plural:

| **mentir** (to lie) | | **dormir** (to sleep) | |
|---|---|---|---|
| mienta | mintamos | duerma | durmamos |
| mientas | | duermas | |
| mienta | mientan | duerma | duerman |

## Verbs That Are Irregular in the Subjunctive

| dar | estar | haber | saber | ser | ir |
|---|---|---|---|---|---|
| dé | esté | haya | sepa | sea | vaya |
| des | estés | hayas | sepas | seas | vayas |
| dé | esté | haya | sepa | sea | vaya |
| demos | estemos | hayamos | sepamos | seamos | vayamos |
| den | estén | hayan | sepan | sean | vayan |

### Exercise

Give the present subjunctive of the following verbs:

1. **yo:** dormir, mover, cerrar, sentir, ser
2. **tú:** mentir, volver, ir, dar, recordar
3. **ella:** estar, saber, perder, dormir, ser
4. **nosotros:** pensar, recordar, dar, morir, cerrar
5. **ellos:** ver, preferir, dar, ir, saber

## STUDY OF COGNATES

1. Spanish word ending in **-ción** instead of English *-tion:*

   **la civilización**   civilization

2. Approximate cognates:

   | | |
   |---|---|
   | **la cultura** | culture |
   | **Europa** | Europe |
   | **el mecánico** | mechanic |
   | **el paciente** | patient |
   | **el resultado** | result |

## NEW VOCABULARY

### NOUNS

| | |
|---|---|
| **el análisis** | test |
| **la estación de servicio** | service station |
| **la fecha** | date |
| **el precio** | price |
| **la sobrina** | niece |
| **el sobrino** | nephew |

### VERBS

| | |
|---|---|
| **arreglar** | to fix, to arrange |
| **mejorar** | to improve |
| **vender** | to sell |

### OTHER WORDS AND EXPRESSIONS

| | |
|---|---|
| **a tiempo** | on time |
| **después** | later, afterwards |
| **estar listo(a)** | to be ready |
| **sin falta** | without fail |
| **yo creo que sí** | I think so |
| **pronto** | soon |

Lesson 17

## 1. THE SUBJUNCTIVE IN INDIRECT OR IMPLIED COMMANDS

A. All indirect and implied commands use the present subjunctive. In this type of sentence, there must be a different subject in the subordinate clause in order to maintain the indirect command in the main clause. Some common verbs used in the indirect command are: **querer, aconsejar** (*to advise*), **sugerir** (*to suggest*), etc. Notice the structure in the use of the subjunctive:

| I   want | you to study. |
|---|---|
| **Yo quiero que** | **Ud. estudie.** |
| main clause | subordinate clause |

| | |
|---|---|
| Mañana tengo examen de geografía física. | *I have an exam in physical geography tomorrow.* |
| Pues te aconsejo que **estudies**. | *Well, I advise you to study.* |
| ¿Qué quiere que yo **haga**? | *What do you want me to do?* |
| Quiero que Ud. me **traiga** esos paquetes. | *I want you to bring me those packages.* |

ATENCIÓN: If there is no change of subject, the infinitive is used:

| | |
|---|---|
| ¿Qué quiere **hacer** Ud.? | *What do you want to do?* |
| Yo quiero **traer** esos paquetes. | *I want to bring those packages.* |

### Exercise

Complete the following sentences with the present subjunctive of the verbs in parentheses:

1. Yo te sugiero que _____ (hacer) el trabajo hoy.
2. Nosotros queremos que Ud. _____ (sentarse).
3. Ud. me aconseja que yo _____ (venir) temprano.
4. Ellos necesitan que él _____ (traer) los paquetes.
5. Él me pide que yo lo _____ (ayudar).
6. Uds. les dicen a ellas que _____ (abrir) la puerta.
7. Ellos prefieren que nosotros _____ (ir) a la oficina.
8. La doctora Rivas quiere que Ud. _____ (venir) por la tarde.
9. El profesor nos dice que _____ (estudiar) geografía física.
10. Yo no quiero que Uds. me _____ (dar) nada.

B. Sometimes the main clause in which the command is expressed is omitted in Spanish, but the expression of the speaker's will is easily understood:

| | |
|---|---|
| ¿Qué quiere Ud. que **hagan** los muchachos? | *What do you want the boys to do?* |

| | |
|---|---|
| (Quiero) Que **estudien.** | *I want them to study.* |
| ¿Va Ud. a hacer el trabajo? | *Are you going to do the work?* |
| No. Que lo **haga** Jorge. | *No. Let George do it.* |

### Exercise

Respond, following the models:

*Modelo:* ¿Quién va a hacerlo? ¿Ud.?
   **¡Yo no! ¡Que lo haga ella!**

1. ¿Quién va a salir? ¿Ud.?
2. ¿Quién va a comer? ¿Ud.?
3. ¿Quién va a ir? ¿Ud.?
4. ¿Quién va a hablar? ¿Ud.?
5. ¿Quién va a traerlo? ¿Ud.?

*Modelo:* ¿No va a entrar Ud.?
   **No, ¡que entren ellos!**

1. ¿No va a dormir Ud.?
2. ¿No va a volver Ud.?
3. ¿No va a trabajar Ud.?
4. ¿No va a venir Ud.?
5. ¿No va a beber Ud.?

## 2. THE SUBJUNCTIVE TO EXPRESS EMOTION

In Spanish the subjunctive is always used in the subordinate clause when the verb in the main clause expresses any kind of emotion, such as fear, joy, pity, hope, pleasure, surprise, anger, regret, and sorrow. Some of the verbs that call for the subjunctive are **temer** (*to fear*), **alegrarse (de)**, (*to be glad*), **sentir** (*to regret*), **esperar** (*to hope*).

| | |
|---|---|
| ¿Vas a ir a cortarte el pelo hoy? | *Are you going to get a haircut today?* |
| No. **Temo** que el barbero **tenga** muchos clientes. | *No. I'm afraid the barber will have many customers.* |
| ¿Cuándo vienen tus padres? | *When are your parents coming?* |
| **Espero** que ellos **lleguen** mañana. | *I hope they will arrive tomorrow.* |

ATENCIÓN: The subject of the subordinate clause must be different from that of the main clause. If there is no change of subject, the infinitive is used instead:

¿Vas a terminar el trabajo para las cinco?      *Are you going to finish the work by five?*

Temo no **poder** terminarlo tan pronto.      *I'm afraid I can't finish it so soon.*

(**Yo temo** in main clause. **Yo no puedo** in subordinate clause.)

¿Cuándo se van Uds.?      *When are you leaving?*

Esperamos **irnos** esta noche.      *We hope to leave tonight.*

(**Nosotros esperamos** in main clause. **Nosotros nos vamos** in subordinate clause.)

### Exercise

Complete the following sentences with the subjunctive or infinitive of the verbs in parentheses, as needed:

1. Espero que los niños _____ (cortarse) el pelo hoy.
2. Me alegro de _____ (estar) aquí.
3. Temen no _____ (poder) terminar para la una.
4. Ella espera _____ (salir) mañana.
5. Uds. esperan que el barbero no _____ (tener) muchos clientes.
6. Siento que ellos no _____ (volver) tan pronto.
7. Espero que no _____ (llover) hoy pues tengo que salir.
8. Espero que ellos lo _____ (traer).
9. Siento _____ (estar) tan enferma.
10. Temo que Ud. no _____ (tener) trabajo pronto.
11. Temo no _____ (recordar) su dirección.
12. Me alegro de que nosotros _____ (poder) salir mañana.

## 3. THE SUBJUNCTIVE WITH IMPERSONAL EXPRESSIONS

Certain impersonal expressions indicate emotion, doubt, uncertainty, unreality, or an indirect or implied command. These expressions require the subjunctive in the main clause if a subject is expressed in the subordinate clause. The most common of these expressions are:

| | |
|---|---|
| **conviene** | it is advisable |
| **es difícil** | it is unlikely |
| **es importante** | it is important |
| **es (im)posible** | it is (im)possible |
| **es lástima** | it is a pity |

| | |
|---|---|
| **es mejor** | it is better |
| **es necesario** | it is necessary |
| **¡ojalá!** | if only . . .! *or* I hope |
| **puede ser** | it may be |

| | |
|---|---|
| ¿Viene hoy el plomero? | *Is the plumber coming today?* |
| **Es difícil** que **venga** hoy. | *It is unlikely that he'll come today.* |
| | |
| ¿Cuándo quiere Ud. que escriba las cartas? | *When do you want me to write the letters?* |
| **Es importante** que las **escriba** hoy. | *It is important that you write them today.* |
| | |
| ¿Cuándo quiere que los estudiantes tomen el examen? | *When do you want the students to take the exam?* |
| **Es mejor** que lo **tomen** en seguida. | *It is better that they take it right away.* |
| | |
| **Es lástima** que Ud. no **pueda** hacerlo. | *It is a pity you can't do it.* |
| Lo sé, pero no tengo tiempo. | *I know, but I don't have time.* |
| | |
| ¿Lloverá mañana? | *Will it rain tomorrow?* |
| Espero que no llueva porque **es posible** que Enrique me **lleve** a la playa. | *I hope it won't rain, because it's possible that Henry will take me to the beach.* |

ATENCIÓN:

1. When the impersonal expression implies certainty, the indicative is used:

| | |
|---|---|
| ¿Vienen ellos hoy? | *Are they coming today?* |
| Sí, **es seguro** que **vienen** hoy. | *Yes, it is certain that they'll come today.* |

2. Impersonal expressions that are *not* followed by a subordinate clause containing a specific subject are followed by an infinitive construction:

| | |
|---|---|
| ¿Cuándo vamos a firmar el contrato? | *When are we going to sign the contract?* |
| Conviene **firmarlo** esta semana. | *It is advisable to sign it this week.* |

### Exercise

Give the Spanish equivalent:

1. It is unlikely that the plumber will come today.
2. It is important that the students take the test right away.
3. It's a pity that your mother is sick.
4. It is necessary to finish the job this week.
5. I hope he doesn't say anything.
6. It is certain that it is going to rain tonight.
7. It is better to see the client now.
8. It is advisable to sign the contract this week.
9. Well, is it possible to do it today?
10. It is better to go to the beach now than later.

## STUDY OF COGNATES

1. These words are the same in Spanish and English, except for a final vowel or a single consonant:

   | | |
   |---|---|
   | **el barbero** | barber |
   | **importante** | important |
   | **posible** | possible |

2. Approximate cognates:

   | | |
   |---|---|
   | **el contrato** | contract |
   | **la geografía** | geography |
   | **físico(a)** | physical |

## NEW VOCABULARY

NOUNS

| | |
|---|---|
| **el cliente** | customer |
| **el paquete** | package |
| **la playa** | beach |
| **el plomero** | plumber |

VERBS

| | |
|---|---|
| **aconsejar** | to advise |
| **alegrarse (de)** | to be glad |
| **esperar** | to hope |
| **firmar** | to sign |
| **sentir (e > ie)** | to regret |

| | |
|---|---|
| **sugerir (e > ie)** | to suggest |
| **temer** | to fear |

OTHER WORDS AND EXPRESSIONS

| | |
|---|---|
| **conviene** | it is advisable |
| **cortarse el pelo** | to get a haircut |
| **es difícil** | it's unlikely |
| **es lástima** | it is a pity |
| **en seguida** | right away |
| **es seguro** | it is certain |
| **¡ojalá!** | if only . . . ! |
| **pues** | well |

Lesson 18

# 1. THE SUBJUNCTIVE TO EXPRESS DOUBT AND UNREALITY

A. The subjunctive is always used in the subordinate clause when the verb in the main clause expresses doubt, uncertainty, denial, negation, disbelief, indefiniteness, or nonexistence:

1. Uncertainty or doubt:

¿Viene tu hermana a la oficina hoy?
**Dudo** que ella **venga** hoy.

*Is your sister coming to the office today?*
*I doubt whether she's coming today.*

¿Está Ud. seguro de que el jefe sale mañana?
No, **no estoy seguro** de que **salga** mañana.

*Are you sure (that) the boss is leaving tomorrow?*
*No, I'm not sure (that) he's leaving tomorrow.*

ATENCIÓN: The verb **dudar** (in the affirmative) takes the subjunctive in the subordinate clause even when there is no change of subject:

¿Puedes ir conmigo al médico?

**(Yo) dudo** que **(yo) pueda** ir contigo hoy.

*Can you go to the doctor's with me?*
*I doubt whether I can go with you today.*

• When no doubt is expressed, and the speaker is certain of the reality, the indicative is used:

¿Viene tu hermana hoy?
**No dudo** (de) que ella **viene.**

*Is your sister coming today?*
*I don't doubt that she's coming.*

¿Está Ud. seguro de que él sale mañana?
Sí, estoy seguro de que él **sale** mañana.

*Are you sure (that) he's leaving tomorrow?*
*Yes, I'm sure (that) he's leaving tomorrow.*

2. The verb **creer** (*to believe, to think*) is followed by the indicative when used in affirmative sentences, and by the subjunctive when used in negative sentences:

¿Cuántos cuartos tiene la casa?

**Creo** que **tiene** veinte y cinco cuartos.
¡Vamos! **No creo** que **tenga** veinte y cinco cuartos.

*How many rooms does the house have?*
*I think it has twenty-five rooms.*
*Come on! I don't believe it has twenty-five rooms.*

3. When the main clause negates the statement made in the subordinate clause, the subjunctive is used:

¿Es verdad que tu padre está preso?

No, **no es verdad** que mi padre **esté** preso.

*Is it true that your father is in jail?*

*No, it isn't true that my father is in jail.*

ATENCIÓN: When the main clause does not negate the statement made in the subordinate clause, the indicative is used:

¿Es verdad que tu padre está preso?

Sí, **es verdad** que mi padre **está** preso.

*Is it true that your father is in jail?*

*Yes, it is true that my father is in jail.*

B. The subjunctive is always used when the subordinate clause refers to someone or something that is indefinite, unspecified, or nonexistent:

¿Qué clase de casa necesitan ellos?

Ellos necesitan una casa que **sea** grande y que **quede** cerca del centro.

*What kind of house do they need?*

*They need a house that is big and (that is) located near the downtown area.*

Buscamos un profesor que **hable** tres idiomas.

Pues yo busco un profesor que **sepa** inglés.

*We're looking for a professor who speaks three languages.*

*Well, I'm looking for a professor who knows English.*

¿Hay alguien aquí que **sepa** hacer traducciones?

No, no hay nadie que **sepa** hacer traducciones.

*Is there anybody here who knows how to do translations?*

*No, there is no one who knows how to do translations.*

ATENCIÓN: If the subordinate clause refers to existent, definite, or specific persons or things, the indicative is used:

¿Dónde viven ellos?

Ellos viven en una casa que **es** grande y que **queda** cerca del centro.

*Where do they live?*

*They live in a house that is big and that is located near the downtown area.*

¿Tienen Uds. secretaria?      *Do you have a secretary?*
Sí, tenemos una secretaria que      *Yes, we have a secretary who*
  **habla** tres idiomas y que      *speaks three languages and*
  **sabe** escribir muy bien a      *who can (knows how to)*
  máquina.      *type very well.*

Aquí hay alguien que **sabe**      *There is someone here who*
  hacer traducciones.      *knows how to do*
       *translations.*

¡Fantástico!      *Fantastic!*

### Exercise

Complete the sentences using either the present indicative or the present subjunctive of the verbs in the following list, as needed. Read each sentence aloud:

| | | |
|---|---|---|
| tener | saber | querer |
| poder | ser | escribir |
| entender | servir | venir |
| salir | hablar | estar |
| abrirse | quedar | ir |

1. Dudo que la maestra _____ a la escuela hoy, niños, porque está muy enferma.
2. No estoy seguro de que (nosotros) _____ terminar el trabajo para esta tarde.
3. Dudo que (yo) _____ a la reunión esta noche.
4. Estamos seguros de que Uds. _____ la situación.
5. No creo que el avión _____ el sábado por la noche.
6. Creo que el banco _____ a las nueve de la mañana.
7. ¡Vamos! No es verdad que el jefe _____ preso.
8. Es verdad que la casa de Tomás _____ sólo tres cuartos.
9. Tengo una secretaria que _____ cuatro idiomas.
10. ¿Hay alguien aquí que _____ escribir a máquina?
11. María busca una casa que _____ cerca del centro.
12. Busca una esposa que _____ inteligente.
13. En esta ciudad no hay ningún restaurante que _____ comida italiana.
14. Aquí hay tres personas que _____ hacer traducciones del inglés al español. ¡Fantástico!
15. Necesito una pluma que _____ bien.

## 2. THE FAMILIAR COMMAND (**tú** FORM)

### The Affirmative Command

The affirmative command for **tú** has exactly the same form as the third person singular of the present indicative.

| Verb | Present Indicative Third Person Singular | Familiar Command ( tú Form) |
|---|---|---|
| hablar | él habla | habla |
| comer | él come | come |
| abrir | él abre | abre |
| cerrar | él cierra | cierra |
| volver | él vuelve | vuelve |
| pedir | él pide | pide |
| traer | él trae | trae |

| | |
|---|---|
| ¿Qué pido? | *What shall I order?* |
| **Pide** un coctel para mí y una limonada para ti. | *Order a cocktail for me and a lemonade for you.* |
| **Cierra** las ventanas y **apaga** las luces antes de salir. | *Close the windows and turn off the lights before going out.* |
| Muy bien. **Espérame** en el coche. | *Very well. Wait for me in the car.* |
| ¿Puedo jugar afuera? | *May I play outside?* |
| No, **quédate** adentro. Hace mucho frío. | *No, stay inside. It's very cold.* |

ATENCIÓN: Notice that direct, indirect, and reflexive pronouns are always placed *after* an affirmative command.

● Eight Spanish verbs have irregular forms for the affirmative command of **tú:**

| | | | | |
|---|---|---|---|---|
| decir: | **di** (*say, tell*) | salir: | **sal** (*go out, leave*) |
| hacer: | **haz** (*do, make*) | ser: | **sé** (*be*) |
| ir: | **ve** (*go*) | tener: | **ten** (*have*) |
| poner: | **pon** (*put*) | venir: | **ven** (*come*) |

| | |
|---|---|
| Carlitos, **ven** aquí. **Haz**me un favor. **Ve** y **di**le a tu mamá que quiero hablar con ella. | *Charlie, come here. Do me a favor. Go and tell your mom I want to speak with her.* |
| ¿Dónde pongo las plantas? **Pon**las en la mesa. | *Where shall I put the plants? Put them on the table.* |
| Marcos, **sé** bueno y **sal** con los niños esta tarde. Necesito trabajar. | *Mark, be nice (kind) and go out with the kids this afternoon. I need to work.* |
| Bueno. Pero ¿cuándo vas a terminar ese trabajo? | *Okay. But, when are you going to finish that job?* |
| **Ten** paciencia. Estará listo mañana por la tarde. | *Have patience. It will be ready tomorrow afternoon.* |

## The Negative Command

The negative command for **tú** uses the corresponding form of the present subjunctive:

| | |
|---|---|
| Tengo mil dólares para gastar durante mis vacaciones. | *I have a thousand dollars to spend during my vacation.* |
| **No lleves** dinero. Lleva cheques de viajeros. | *Don't take money. Take travelers' checks.* |
| Tengo que ir a la oficina de correos. **No me esperes** para cenar. | *I have to go to the post office. Don't wait for me to (have) dinner.* |
| **No vayas** hoy. Ve mañana. | *Don't go today. Go tomorrow.* |
| **No te bañes** todavía. No hay agua caliente. | *Don't bathe yet. There is no hot water.* |
| **No me digas** que otra vez no tenemos agua caliente. | *Don't tell me that we don't have hot water again.* |

ATENCIÓN: All object pronouns are placed *before* a negative command.

## Exercises

A. Answer the following questions, according to the model:

> *Modelo:* ¿Traigo las plantas?
> **Sí, tráelas, por favor.**

1. ¿Pido el coctel?
2. ¿Hago la limonada?
3. ¿Apago la luz?
4. ¿Te espero en el coche?
5. ¿Me quedo aquí?
6. ¿Juego afuera?
7. ¿Vengo con Eva?
8. ¿Lo pongo adentro?
9. ¿Se lo digo?
10. ¿Voy con Alberto?
11. ¿Salgo temprano?
12. ¿Llevo las plantas?
13. ¿Abro las ventanas?
14. ¿Cierro las puertas?
15. ¿Traigo los cheques de viajeros?

B. Make the following commands negative:

1. Gasta todo el dinero.
2. Vete.
3. Dile que venga con nosotros.
4. Sal con Roberto.
5. Ven esta tarde.
6. Pídele que salga con los chicos.
7. Dile que necesitas trabajar.
8. Báñate con agua caliente.
9. Hazlo otra vez.
10. Pon las plantas en la mesa.
11. Sé bueno.
12. Ten paciencia.
13. Quédate con ella.
14. Dale el dinero al médico.
15. Llévala al cine.

C. Give the Spanish equivalent (Use the **tú** form.):

1. Tell him what kind of house you want.
2. Go to the post office.
3. Don't have supper now.
4. Do me a favor.
5. Wash your hands before going out.

## STUDY OF COGNATES

1. Exact cognate:

   **el favor**        favor

2. The following words are the same in Spanish and English except for a final vowel or an accent:

   **fantástico**(a)    fantastic

3. Spanish word ending in **-ción,** instead of English *-tion:*

   **las vacaciones**[1]    vacation

4. Approximate cognates:

   **el coctel**      cocktail
   **el cheque**      check
   **la limonada**    lemonade
   **la paciencia**   patience

## NEW VOCABULARY

NOUNS

**el agua** (f.)[2]    water
**el centro**        downtown
**la clase**         kind, type
**el cuarto**        room
**el jefe**          boss, chief
**la luz**           light
**el médico**        medical doctor
**la oficina**
 **de correos**      post office
**la traducción**    translation
**el viajero**       traveler

VERBS

**apagar**      to turn off
**buscar**      to look for
**cenar**       to have supper,
                 to dine

**dudar**       to doubt
**jugar**[3]     to play (a game)
**quedar**      to be located
**quedarse**    to stay,
                 to remain

ADJECTIVES

**caliente**     hot
**seguro**(a)    sure

OTHER WORDS AND EXPRESSIONS

**adentro**           inside
**afuera**            outside
**antes de**          before
**cerca (de)**        near, next to
**estar preso**(a)    to be in jail
**otra vez**          again
**¡vamos!**           come on!

---

[1] **Vacaciones** is always used in the plural form in Spanish.
[2] When a singular, feminine noun begins with a stressed **a** or **ha,** the masculine article is used.
[3] Present indicative: juego, juegas, juega, jugamos, juegan

Lesson 19

# 1. THE SUBJUNCTIVE AFTER CONJUNCTIONS IMPLYING UNCERTAINTY OR UNFULFILLMENT

A. Certain conjunctions of time, such as **tan pronto como, en cuanto** (both meaning *as soon as*), **hasta que** (*until*), and **cuando** (*when*), may take the indicative or the subjunctive. They take the subjunctive when the action in the subordinate clause has not yet been completed. This is because there is always some uncertainty as to whether a future action will be completed:

Eva, ¿cuándo va a llamarte el doctor?
*Eva, when is the doctor going to call you?*

Me llamará **tan pronto como sepa** el resultado de los análisis.
*He is going to call me as soon as he finds out the result of the tests.*

Carlos, ¿a qué hora vamos a empezar la asamblea?
*Charles, at what time are we going to begin the assembly?*

La vamos a empezar **en cuanto lleguen** todos los empleados.
*We are going to start it as soon as all the employees arrive.*

Tomás, ¿cuándo vamos a salir para el aeropuerto?
*Thomas, when are we going to leave for the airport?*

No podemos salir **hasta que** el carro **esté** arreglado.
*We can't leave until the car is fixed.*

**Cuando llegue** Carlos dígale que saque copia de estas cartas y las eche al correo.
*When Charles arrives tell him to photocopy these letters and mail them.*

Muy bien, se lo diré **cuando venga.**
*OK, I'll tell him when he arrives.*

If there is no indication of a future action, the indicative is used after the conjunction of time:

Eva, ¿cuándo te llamó el doctor?
*Eva, when did the doctor call you?*

Me llamó **tan pronto como supo** el resultado de los análisis.
*He called me as soon as he found out the result of the tests.*

Carlos, ¿a qué hora vamos a empezar la asamblea?
*Charles, at what time are we going to begin the assembly?*

Siempre empezamos **en cuanto llegan** todos los empleados.
*We always begin as soon as all the employees arrive.*

| | |
|---|---|
| Pedro, ¿cuándo salieron Uds. para el aeropuerto? | *Peter, when did you leave for the airport?* |
| No pudimos salir **hasta que** el coche **estuvo** arreglado. | *We were not able to leave until the car was fixed.* |

B. There are some conjunctions that by their very meaning imply uncertainty or condition, such as **sin que** (*without*) and **a menos que** (*unless*). These conjunctions are always followed by the subjunctive:

| | |
|---|---|
| ¿Va Ud. a firmar el testamento hoy? | *Are you going to sign the will today?* |
| No puedo firmarlo **sin que** mi abogado lo **lea.** | *I can't sign it without my lawyer reading it.* |
| ¿Piensa Ud. vender su casa? | *Are you thinking of selling your house?* |
| Voy a venderla **a menos que pueda** alquilarla. | *I'm going to sell it unless I can rent it.* |

### Exercise

Complete the sentences with the subjunctive or the indicative of the following verbs, as needed: **venir, dar, llegar, pedir, firmar, llover, salir, preguntar, ver, estar.** Use each verb only once.

1. Vamos a echar las cartas al correo tan pronto como el jefe las _____ .
2. Siempre cierro las ventanas cuando _____ .
3. Me llamó tan pronto como _____ de la asamblea.
4. No puede salir sin que ellos lo _____ .
5. No me lo dirán a menos que se lo _____ .
6. No podré alquilarlo hasta que Ud. me _____ el dinero.
7. Le dimos el carro tan pronto como nos lo _____ .
8. Dígale al empleado que saque copia del testamento en cuanto _____ terminado.
9. Siempre espero hasta que él _____ del trabajo.
10. Te llamaré por teléfono cuando _____ a casa.

## 2. THE PRESENT PERFECT SUBJUNCTIVE

The present perfect subjunctive is formed with the present subjunctive of the auxiliary verb **haber** plus the past participle of the main verb.

| Present Perfect Subjunctive | | |
|---|---|---|
| *Present Subjunctive of* **haber** | + | *Past Participle of the Main Verb* |
| yo | haya | amado |
| tú | hayas | comido |
| él | haya | vivido |
| ella | haya | conseguido |
| nosotros | hayamos | hecho |
| ellos | hayan | puesto |
| ellas | hayan | traducido |

### Exercise

Conjugate the following verbs in the present perfect subjunctive for each subject given:

1. **yo:**       hacer, venir, comer, levantarse
2. **tú:**       trabajar, poner, decir, acostarse
3. **ella:**     escribir, cerrar, abrir, sentarse
4. **nosotros:** morir, hablar, llegar, vestirse
5. **ellos:**    romper, vender, alquilar, bañarse

## 3. USES OF THE PRESENT PERFECT SUBJUNCTIVE

The present perfect subjunctive is used in the same way as the present perfect in English, but only in sentences that call for the subjunctive in the subordinate clause:

| | |
|---|---|
| ¿Ya han pagado Uds. la cuenta del teléfono? | *Have you already paid the phone bill?* |
| No recuerdo . . . no, **no creo** que la **hayamos pagado** todavía. | *I don't remember . . . No, I don't think we've paid it yet.* |
| Estoy tan ocupado que no he tenido tiempo de revisar los informes. | *I'm so busy (that) I haven't had time to check the reports.* |
| **Espero** que por lo menos su ayudante los **haya visto.** | *I hope at least your assistant has seen them.* |
| Hubo un accidente en la autopista. Chocaron dos autobuses, y **temo** que **hayan muerto** todos los pasajeros. | *There was an accident on the freeway. Two buses collided and I'm afraid all the passengers have died.* |
| ¡Qué horrible!¹ **Ojalá** que algunos **hayan sobrevivido.** | *How horrible! I hope some (of them) have survived.* |

¹ The Spanish equivalent of *"how"* + *adjective* is **qué** + *adjective.*

### Exercise

Complete the sentences with the present perfect subjunctive of the verbs in the following list, as needed: **estar, ir, sobrevivir, conseguir, pagar, chocar, poder, revisar, morir, llegar.** Use each verb only once.

1. No creo que ellos _____ la cuenta.
2. Siento que tú _____ tan ocupado.
3. Espero que Uds. _____ los informes.
4. Ojalá que mi ayudante _____ a la oficina.
5. No es verdad que _____ dos autobuses.
6. Temo que ninguno de los pasajeros del avión _____. ¡Qué horrible!
7. Dudo que él _____ vender la casa a ese precio.
8. Ojalá que no _____ todos los pasajeros en el accidente de la autopista.
9. No creo que todos los empleados _____ a la reunión.
10. Siento que tú no _____ el puesto.

---

## STUDY OF COGNATES

1. Exact cognates:

   **horrible**    horrible

2. These words are the same in Spanish and English, except for a written accent or a final vowel:

   **el autobús**    bus, autobus
   **el testamento**    will, testament

3. Approximate cognates:

   **la asamblea**    assembly
   **el pasajero**    passenger

---

## NEW VOCABULARY

| NOUNS | | VERBS | |
|---|---|---|---|
| **la autopista** | freeway | **alquilar** | to rent |
| **el, la ayudante** | assistant | **revisar** | to check |
| **el carro** | car | **sobrevivir** | to survive |
| **el empleado** | employee | | |
| **el informe** | report | OTHER WORDS AND EXPRESSIONS | |
| | | **echar al correo** | to mail |
| | | **sacar copia** | to photocopy |
| | | **por lo menos** | at least |

Lesson 20

# 1. THE IMPERFECT SUBJUNCTIVE

The imperfect subjunctive is the simple past tense of the subjunctive. It is formed in the same way for all verbs, regular and irregular: the **-ron** ending of the third person plural of the preterit is dropped and the following endings are added to the stem: **-ra, -ras, -ra, -ramos, -ran.**

| | Formation of the Imperfect Subjunctive | | |
|---|---|---|---|
| *Verb* | *Preterit, Third Person Plural* | *Stem* | *Imperfect Subjunctive* |
| hablar | hablaron | habla- | que yo habla- **ra** |
| comer | comieron | comie- | que tú comie- **ras** |
| vivir | vivieron | vivie- | que Ud. vivie- **ra** |
| traer | trajeron | traje- | que él traje- **ra** |
| ir | fueron | fue- | que ella fue- **ra** |
| saber | supieron | supie- | que nosotros supié- **ramos** |
| decir | dijeron | dije- | que Uds. dije- **ran** |
| poner | pusieron | pusie- | que ellos pusie- **ran** |
| estar | estuvieron | estuvie- | que ellas estuvie- **ran** |

●Notice the written accent mark in the first person plural form.

## Exercise

Conjugate the following verbs in the imperfect subjunctive for each subject given:

1. **yo:**        caminar, aprender, abrir, cerrar, acostarse
2. **tú:**        salir, sentir, temer, recordar, ponerse
3. **Ud.:**       llevar, romper, morir, terminar, volar, alegrarse
4. **nosotros:**  esperar, traer, pedir, volver, servir, vestirse
5. **ellos:**     tener, ser, dar, estar, poder, irse

# 2. USES OF THE IMPERFECT SUBJUNCTIVE

A. The imperfect subjunctive is always used in a subordinate clause when the verb of the main clause is in the past:

Señorita Peña, ayer le **dije** que **archivara** las solicitudes de empleo.

*Miss Peña, yesterday I told you to file the job applications.*

Pero el jefe de personal me **pidió** que las **dejara** en su escritorio.

*But the personnel director asked me to leave them on his desk.*

Carlitos, te **dije** que **te lavaras**
  la cara y las manos antes de
  hacer la tarea.
Ya me las lavé.

*Charlie, I told you to wash*
  *your face and hands before*
  *doing your (the) homework.*
*I already washed them.*

B. The imperfect subjunctive is also used when the verb of the main
   clause is in the present, but the subordinate clause refers to the
   past:

**Es** una lástima que no
  **asistieras ayer** a la
  conferencia de la Dra. Ruiz.
No pude, porque tuve que ir al
  consulado a recoger mi
  pasaporte.

*It's a pity that you didn't*
  *attend Dr. Ruiz's lecture*
  *yesterday.*
*I wasn't able to (make it)*
  *because I had to go to the*
  *consulate to pick up my*
  *passport.*

## Exercises

A. Complete the sentences with the imperfect subjunctive of the
   following verbs, as needed: **escribir, asistir, sacar, archivar,
   lavarse, venir, recoger, firmar.** Use each verb once.

1. El jefe de personal nos dijo que _____ los documentos.
2. Sentí mucho que Ud. no _____ a la conferencia el sábado
   pasado.
3. Le pedí a papá que _____ mi pasaporte en el consulado.
4. Ella no les dijo que _____ las cartas.
5. Es una lástima que el plomero no _____ ayer.
6. El director me pidió que _____ copias de las solicitudes de
   empleo.
7. El profesor quería que nosotros _____ a máquina las lecciones.
8. Tú no me dijiste que _____ la cara y las manos antes de hacer la
   tarea.

B. Give the Spanish equivalent:

1. They wanted me to leave my car.
2. I told you not to play with him, Robert.
3. I'm sorry you were sick yesterday, Mr. Vera.
4. We asked them to attend the lecture.
5. He told us to get dressed.
6. I'm glad you were able to come last Friday.

## 3. "IF" CLAUSES

In Spanish, as in English, the imperfect subjunctive is used when a contrary-to-fact statement is made:

*If I were you . . .*
**Si yo fuera Ud. . . .**

| | |
|---|---|
| Si yo **tuviera** dinero iría de vacaciones con Uds. | *If I had money I would go on vacation with you.* |
| ¿No te lo puede prestar tu padre? | *Can't your father lend it to you?* |
| No, porque si mi padre me lo **prestara,** tendría que devolvérselo antes de septiembre, y yo necesito el dinero para pagar la matrícula. | *No, because if my father were to lend it to me, I would have to give it back to him before September and I need the money to pay for registration.* |
| Si los muchachos **vinieran** hoy, podríamos ir a la playa o al parque. | *If the boys (young men) came today, we could go to the beach or to the park.* |
| Sí, pero ellos no llegan hasta mañana por la tarde. | *Yes, but they are not arriving until tomorrow afternoon.* |

ATENCIÓN: When an "if" clause is *not* contrary to fact, the indicative is used.

Si los muchachos **vienen** hoy, podemos ir a la playa.

• The present subjunctive is *never* used with an "if" clause.

### Exercises

A. Complete the following sentences with the present indicative or the imperfect subjunctive of the verbs in parentheses, as needed:

1. Si yo _____ (tener) tiempo, te llevaré al cine.
2. Si tú _____ (poder), ¿lo harías?
3. Si Federico me _____ (devolver) el dinero, podré pagar la matrícula.
4. Si ella _____ (venir) iríamos a la playa.
5. Si el jefe me _____ (dar) una semana de vacaciones, iría a Francia.
6. Nosotros visitaríamos a nuestros abuelos si (nosotros) no _____ (estar) enfermos.
7. Compraré la casa si _____ (conseguir) el dinero.
8. Si yo _____ (ser) tú, no conduciría a esa velocidad.
9. Mamá dice que me va a comprar el vestido si _____ (salir) temprano de la oficina.
10. Si ellos lo _____ (saber), te lo dirían.

B. Give the Spanish equivalent:

1. I would help you if I could, Charlie.
2. If she has time, she'll take you to the movies.
3. If you study, you will learn.
4. We would go on vacation if we had the money.
5. I would attend the lecture if I weren't sleepy.
6. We are going to go to the park if she comes back early.

---

## STUDY OF COGNATES

Approximate cognates:

| | |
|---|---|
| **el consulado** | consulate |
| **Francia** | France |
| **el parque** | park |
| **el pasaporte** | passport |
| **el personal** | personnel |

---

## NEW VOCABULARY

NOUNS

| | |
|---|---|
| **la cara** | face |
| **el empleo** | job |
| **la matrícula** | registration |
| **la solicitud** | application |

VERBS

| | |
|---|---|
| **archivar** | to file |
| **asistir** | to attend |
| **dejar** | to leave (behind) |

| | |
|---|---|
| **devolver** (o > ue) | to return, to give back |
| **lavarse** | to wash oneself |
| **recoger** | to pick up |

OTHER WORDS AND EXPRESSIONS

| | |
|---|---|
| **ir(se) de vacaciones** | to go on vacation |

# Test Yourself: Lessons 16-20

## LESSON 16

A. The future tense

Answer the following questions, according to the model:

*Modelo:* ¿Cuándo comprarán Uds. un coche?  (el año próximo)
**Compraremos un coche el año próximo.**

1. ¿Cuál será el tema de la conferencia?  (la civilización y la cultura de México)
2. ¿Cuándo estarán listos los análisis?  (la semana que viene)
3. ¿Qué idioma aprenderán Uds.?  (el español)
4. ¿A dónde irán Uds. el verano próximo?  (a Santiago)
5. ¿Qué le dirán Uds. a Raquel?  (que sí)
6. ¿Qué harás tú el domingo?  (nada)
7. ¿Cuándo sabremos el resultado?  (el próximo mes)
8. ¿Quién abrirá las puertas?  (el señor Reyes)
9. ¿Quiénes podrán venir?  (María y Carlos)
10. ¿Dónde pondrás el dinero?  (en el banco)
11. ¿Cuándo volverán Uds. de México?  (el sábado próximo)
12. ¿Con quién vendrá Ud. a la reunión?  (con la señorita Vargas)
13. ¿Qué tendrán que hacer Uds.?  (estudiar para el examen)
14. ¿Cuándo me dará Ud. las cartas?  (mañana)
15. ¿Con quiénes saldrán Uds. el sábado?  (con Raúl y Mario)

B. The conditional tense

Complete the sentences with the conditional tense of the following verbs: **servir, poner, quejarse, haber, trabajar, seguir, vender, levantarse, preferir, ir.** Use each verb once:

1. Él dijo que nosotros _____ a Europa el verano próximo.
2. Ellos no _____ su casa a ese precio.
3. ¿Dijo Ud. que _____ una reunión esta tarde?
4. Yo no _____ el café en la terraza.
5. Tú no _____ en una estación de servicio.
6. ¿_____ Ud. su dinero en ese banco?
7. ¿Qué _____ Uds.: ir a México o ir a Guatemala?
8. ¿_____ Uds. estudiando español?
9. ¿_____ tú a las tres de la mañana?
10. Nosotros no _____ del profesor.

C. The subjunctive

Complete the sentences with the Spanish equivalent of the verbs in parentheses. Use the present subjunctive. Follow the model:

*Modelo:* . . . que yo _____ (speak)
    **. . . que yo hable**

1. . . . que nosotros _____ (*work*)
2. . . . que yo _____ (*eat*)
3. . . . que Uds. _____ (*write*)
4. . . . que tú _____ (*live*)
5. . . . que él _____ (*say*)
6. . . . que Ud. _____ (*close*)
7. . . . que ellos _____ (*come*)
8. . . . que ella _____ (*get up*)
9. . . . que yo _____ (*ask for, request*)
10. . . . que Uds. _____ (*do*)
11. . . . que Ana _____ (*bring*)
12. . . . que Ud. _____ (*recommend*)
13. . . . que nosotros _____ (*move*)
14. . . . que yo _____ (*go*)
15. . . . que Luis _____ (*shave*)
16. . . . que nosotros _____ (*sleep*)
17. . . . que ella _____ (*give*)
18. . . . que ellos _____ (*know*)
19. . . . que yo _____ (*go out*)
20. . . . que tú _____ (*have*)

## LESSON 17

A. The subjunctive in indirect or implied commands

Give the Spanish equivalent:

1. She wants me to bring the packages.
2. I prefer that we go to your office, Miss Diaz.
3. At what time do you want me to be here tomorrow, Mr. Acevedo?
4. Ask him to help you, Mrs. Portillo.
5. Tell them not to be afraid.
6. (Let) Robert do it.
7. (Let) them come in.
8. She wants me to be her friend.
9. Do you need them to give you the money today, Mr. Ortiz?
10. I don't want you to do anything, Johnny.

B. The subjunctive to express emotion

Give the Spanish equivalent:

1. I hope you can get a haircut this afternoon, Robbie.
2. I'm glad your mother is feeling better, Mr. Gómez.
3. I'm afraid we can't meet next week, Miss Herrero.

4. We're glad to be here today.
5. She hopes to leave tomorrow morning.
6. I hope you can come to the meeting, Mr. Peña.
7. We're afraid we can't finish the job tonight.
8. I'm sorry you are sick, Mrs. Treviño.

C. The subjunctive with impersonal expressions

Complete the following sentences with the subjunctive, the indic-active, or the infinitive of the verb in parentheses, as needed:

1. Es difícil que ellos _____ (poder) venir hoy.
2. Es necesario _____ (estudiar) mucho.
3. Es mejor _____ (escribir) ahora mismo.
4. Es verdad que nosotros _____ (terminar) mañana.
5. Es lástima que el plomero no _____ (estar) aquí ahora.
6. Es importante _____ (hacer) bien el trabajo.
7. Es seguro que ellos _____ (llegar) el lunes.
8. Es posible _____ (firmar) los contratos hoy.

# LESSON 18

A. The subjunctive to express doubt and unreality

Change the following sentences, according to the model:

*Modelo:* Estoy seguro de que el jefe *viene* hoy.  (Dudo)
   **Dudo que el jefe venga hoy.**

1. Dudo que ellos *puedan* venir.  (Estoy seguro de que)
2. Creo que Pedro *va* con nosotros.  (No creo que)
3. Es verdad que María *está* muy enferma.  (No es verdad que)
4. Tengo una casa que *queda* cerca del centro.  (Busco)
5. ¿Hay alguien aquí que *sepa* escribir a máquina?  (Aquí hay una chica que)
6. Hay muchas personas que *quieren* hacer traducciones.  (No hay muchas personas que)
7. No creo que él se *levante* a las cuatro de la mañana.  (Creo que)
8. Necesito una casa que *tenga* seis cuartos.  (Vivo en una casa que)

B. The affirmative familiar command (**tú** form)

Change the commands from the **Ud.** (formal) form to the **tú** (infor-mal) form. Follow the model:

*Modelo:* Salga con los niños.
   **Sal con los niños.**

1. Venga acá, por favor.
2. Hable con la maestra.
3. Dígame su dirección.
4. Escriba la carta.

5. Póngase el abrigo.
6. Tráiganos agua caliente.
7. Termine el trabajo.
8. Hágame el favor.
9. Apague la luz.
10. Vaya al centro.

11. Salga temprano.
12. Quédese afuera.
13. Tenga paciencia.
14. Sea buena.
15. Cene con nosotros.

C. The negative familiar command (**tú** form)

Give the Spanish equivalent:

1. Don't tell (it to) him.
2. Don't go out now.
3. Don't get up.
4. Don't do the translations.
5. Don't drink the lemonade.
6. Don't break it (*masc.*).
7. Don't talk to them.
8. Don't go downtown.
9. That dress? Don't put it on!
10. Don't do that.

# LESSON 19

A. The subjunctive after conjunctions implying uncertainty or un-fulfillment

Give the Spanish equivalent:

1. I'll speak to him as soon as I see him.
2. Stay here in case he calls, Miss Gonzalez.
3. He wrote to me as soon as he arrived.
4. We are going to wait until he comes.
5. I can't go without my parents knowing (it).
6. We'll buy the car when we have the money.

B. The present perfect subjunctive

Complete the following sentences with the Spanish equivalent of the verbs in parentheses. Use the present perfect subjunctive. Follow the model:

*Modelo:* . . . que él _____ (*speak*)
       **que él haya hablado**

1. . . . que yo _____ (*see*)
2. . . . que Uds. _____ (*do*)
3. . . . que tú _____ (*learn*)
4. . . . que ellos _____ (*sign*)
5. . . . que Ud. _____ (*fix*)
6. . . . que nosotros _____ (*file*)

7. . . . que Ana _____ (return)
8. . . . que Luis _____ (go to bed)

C. Uses of the present perfect subjunctive

Write sentences using the following items. Follow the model:

Modelo:  Yo / alegrarse / tú / venir
**Yo me alegro de que tú hayas venido.**

1. Ellos / sentir / Uds. / estar enfermos
2. Rosa / no creer / yo / hacerlo
3. Nosotros / temer / él / morir
4. No es verdad / nosotros / escribir / esa carta
5. Ojalá / papá / poder / venir

## LESSON 20

A. The imperfect subjunctive (forms)

Complete the sentences with the Spanish equivalent of the verbs in parentheses. Use imperfect subjunctive. Follow the model:

Modelo:  . . . que yo _____ (live)
**que yo viviera**

1. . . . que nosotros _____ (attend)
2. . . . que tú _____ (leave behind)
3. . . . que ellos _____ (wash themselves)
4. . . . que yo _____ (pick up)
5. . . . que Ud. _____ (can)
6. . . . que Carlos _____ (bring)
7. . . . que Uds. _____ (give back)
8. . . . que ella _____ (have)

B. Uses of the imperfect subjunctive

Change the following sentences according to the models:

Modelo 1:  Me dice que hable con él.
**Me dijo que hablara con él.**

Modelo 2:  Siento que tú estés enferma.  (ayer)
**Siento que tú estuvieras enferma ayer.**

1. Le pido que venga en seguida.
2. Me alegro de que puedas terminarlo.  (anoche)
3. No creo que ella lo haga.
4. No es verdad que mi hermano esté preso.  (el año pasado)
5. Tememos que ella no sepa escribir a máquina.
6. Dudo que la conferencia sea hoy.  (el sábado pasado)

C. "If" clauses

Complete the following sentences:

1. Yo compraría una casa si . . .
2. Iremos a verte si . . .
3. Yo iría al médico si . . .
4. Mañana saldremos si . . .
5. Ellos nos ayudarían si . . .
6. Nosotros se lo diremos si . . .
7. Yo dormiría si . . .
8. Vamos a comer algo si . . .

# APPENDICES

# Appendix A: Pronunciation

## 1. SPANISH SOUNDS

### A. The Vowels

Spanish has five distinctive vowels: **a, e, i, o, u.** Each vowel has only one basic sound that is produced with considerable muscular tension. The pronunciation of each vowel is constant, clear, and brief. The sound is never prolonged; in fact, the length of the sound is almost the same whether it is produced in a stressed or an unstressed syllable.[1]

To produce the English stressed vowels that most closely resemble Spanish, the speaker changes the position of the tongue, lips, and lower jaw during the production of the sound, so that the vowel actually starts as one sound, and then *glides* into another. In Spanish, however, the tongue, lips, and jaw keep a constant position during the production of the sound.

|  |  |
|---|---|
| *English* | *Spanish* |
| banana | banana |

The stress falls on the same vowel and syllable in both Spanish and English, but the stressed English *a* is longer in comparison to Spanish stressed **a.**

|  |  |
|---|---|
| *English* | *Spanish* |
| banana | banana |

Also notice that the stressed English *a* has a sound different from the other *a*'s in the word, while the Spanish **a** sound remains constant and is similar to the other **a** sounds in the Spanish word.

**a**   in Spanish has a sound somewhat similar to the English *a* in the word *father:*

| | | | |
|---|---|---|---|
| alta | palma | cama | alma |
| casa | Ana | Panamá | apagar |

**e**   is pronounced like the English *e* in the word *met:*

| | | | |
|---|---|---|---|
| mes | este | ese | teme |
| entre | deje | encender | prender |

**i**   has a sound similar to the English *ee* in the word *see:*

| | | |
|---|---|---|
| fin | sí | dividir | difícil |
| ir | sin | Trini |

[1] In a stressed syllable the prominence of the vowel is indicated by its loudness.

199

**o**   is similar to the English *o* in the word *know*, but without the glide:

| | | | |
|---|---|---|---|
| toco | poco | corto | solo |
| como | roto | corro | loco |

**u**   is pronounced like the English *oo* sound in the word *shoot*, or the *ue* sound in the word *Sue:*

| | | | |
|---|---|---|---|
| su | Úrsula | un | sucursal |
| Lulú | cultura | luna | Uruguay |

*Diphthongs and Triphthongs:*

When unstressed **i** or **u** falls next to another vowel in a syllable, it unites with it to form a *diphthong*. Both vowels are pronounced as one syllable. Their sounds do not change; they are only pronounced more rapidly and with a glide. For example:

| | | | | | |
|---|---|---|---|---|---|
| traiga | Lidia | treinta | siete | oigo | adiós |
| Aurora | agua | bueno | antiguo | ciudad | Luis |

A *triphthong* is the union of three vowels, a stressed vowel between unstressed **i** or **u,** in the same syllable. For example:

Paraguay        estudiáis

NOTE: Stressed **i** and **u** do not form diphthongs with other vowels, except in the combinations **iu** and **ui.** For example:

rí-o        sa-bí-ais

In syllabication, diphthongs and triphthongs are considered as a single vowel. Their components cannot be separated.

## B. The Consonants

Consonant sounds are produced by regulating the flow of air through the mouth with the aid of two speech organs. As the diagrams illustrate, different speech organs can be used to control the air flow. The point of articulation will differ accordingly.

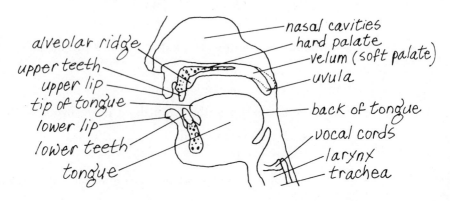

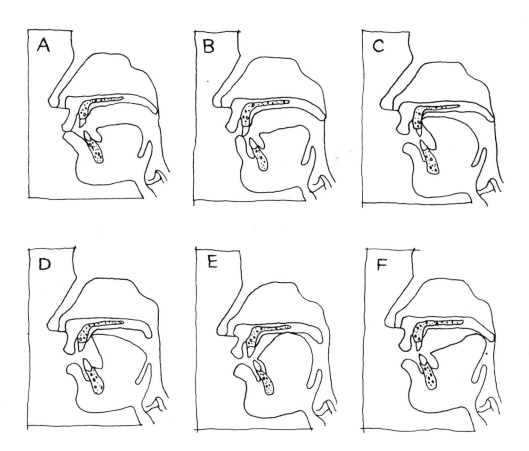

In Spanish the air flow can be controlled in different ways. One such way is called a *stop* because in the articulation of the sound the air is stopped at some point while passing through the oral cavity.

When we bring the speech organs close together, but without closing the air flow completely, we produce a friction sound called a *fricative*, such as the *ff* and the *th* in the English words *offer* and *other*.

p   Spanish **p** is produced by bringing the lips together as a stream of air passes through the oral cavity (see diagram A). It is pronounced in a manner similar to the English *p* sound, but without the puff of air that comes out after the English sound is produced:

pesca   pude   puedo   parte   papá
postre   piña   puente   Paco

k   Spanish **k** sound, represented by the letters **k, c** (before **a, o, u,** or *a consonant*), and **qu,** is produced by touching the velum with the back of the tongue, as in diagram B. The sound is somewhat similar to the English *k* sound but without the puff of air:

| casa   | comer | cuna   | clima  | acción    | que |
|--------|-------|--------|--------|-----------|-----|
| quinto | queso | aunque | kiosko | kilómetro |     |

**t**  The Spanish **t** sound is produced by touching the back of the upper front teeth with the tip of the tongue, as in diagram C. It has no puff of air as in the English *t:*

| todo  | antes | corto | Guatemala | diente |
|-------|-------|-------|-----------|--------|
| resto | tonto | roto  | tanque    |        |

**d**  The Spanish consonant **d** has two different sounds depending on its position. At the beginning of an utterance and after **n** or **l**, the tip of the tongue presses the back of the upper front teeth to produce what is called a *voiced dental stop* (see diagram C):

| día  | doma | dice  | dolor    | dar         |
|------|------|-------|----------|-------------|
| anda | Aldo | caldo | el deseo | un domicilio |

In all other positions the sound of **d** is similar to the *th* sound in the English word *they*, but softer. This sound is called a *voiced dental fricative* (see diagram C). To produce it, place the tip of the tongue behind the front teeth:

| medida | todo | nada  | nadie | medio |
|--------|------|-------|-------|-------|
| puedo  | moda | queda | nudo  |       |

**g**  The Spanish consonant **g** also represents two sounds. At the beginning of an utterance or after **n**, it is a *voiced velar stop* (see diagram B), identical to the English *g* sound in the word *guy:*

| goma    | glotón | gallo  | gloria   |
|---------|--------|--------|----------|
| gorrión | garra  | guerra | angustia |

In all other positions, except before **e** or **i**, it is a *voiced velar fricative* (see diagram B), similar to the English *g* sound in the word *sugar*. To produce it, move the back of the tongue close to the velum, as in diagram F:

| lago | alga      | traga      | amigo   |
|------|-----------|------------|---------|
| algo | Dagoberto | el gorrión | la goma |

**j**  The sound of Spanish **j** (or **g** before **e** and **i**) is called a *voiceless velar fricative*. To produce it, position the back of the tongue close to the velum (see diagram F). (In some Latin American countries the sound is similar to a strongly exaggerated English *h* sound.):

| gemir | juez | jarro | gitano | agente |
|-------|------|-------|--------|--------|
| juego | giro | bajo  | gente  |        |

**b, v**   There is no difference in sound between Spanish **b** and **v**. Both letters are pronounced alike. At the beginning of an utterance or after **m** or **n, b** and **v** have a sound called a *voiced bilabial stop* (see diagram A), which is identical to the English *b* sound in the word *boy:*

| | | | | |
|---|---|---|---|---|
| vivir | beber | vamos | barco | enviar |
| hambre | batea | bueno | vestido | |

In all other positions the Spanish **b** and **v** sound is a *voiced bilabial fricative* (see diagram A). To produce this sound, bring the lips together but do not close them, letting some air pass through.

**y, ll**   At the beginning of an utterance or after **n** or **l**, Spanish **y** and **ll** have a sound similar to the English *dg* in the word *edge*, but somewhat softer (see diagram E):

| | | |
|---|---|---|
| el llavero | el yeso | llama |
| un yelmo | su yunta | yema |

In all other positions the sound is a *voiced palatal fricative* (see diagram E), similar to the English *y* sound in the word *yes:*

| | | |
|---|---|---|
| oye | trayectoria | milla |
| trayecto | mayo | bella |

NOTE: Spanish **y** when it stands alone or is at the end of a word is pronounced like the vowel **i:**

| | | |
|---|---|---|
| rey | doy | voy |
| hoy | buey | estoy |
| y | muy | soy |

**r, rr**   Spanish **r** is produced by tapping the alveolar ridge with the tongue only once and very briefly (see diagram D). The sound is similar to the English *tt* sound in the word *gutter* or the *dd* sound in the word *ladder:*

| | | | | |
|---|---|---|---|---|
| crema | aroma | cara | arena | aro |
| harina | toro | oro | eres | portero |

Spanish **r** in an initial position and after **n, l,** or **s,** and also **rr** in the middle of a word are pronounced with a very strong trill. This trill is produced by bringing the tip of the tongue near the alveolar ridge and letting it vibrate freely while the air passes through the mouth:

| | | | | |
|---|---|---|---|---|
| rama | carro | Israel | cierra | roto |
| perro | alrededor | rizo | corre | Enrique |

**s**  Spanish **s** is represented in most of the Spanish world by the letters **s, z,** and **c** before **e** or **i.** The sound is very similar to the English sibilant *s* in the word *sink:*

| | | | |
|---|---|---|---|
| sale | sitio | presidente | signo |
| salsa | seda | suma | vaso |
| sobrino | ciudad | cima | canción |
| zapato | zarza | cerveza | centro |

When it is in final position, Spanish **s** is less sibilant than in other positions. In many regions of the Spanish world there is a tendency to aspirate word-final **s** and even to drop it altogether:

| | | | | |
|---|---|---|---|---|
| eres | somos | estas | mesas | libros |
| vamos | sillas | cosas | rezas mucho | |

**h**  The letter **h** is silent in Spanish, unless it is combined with the **c** to form **ch:**

| | | | |
|---|---|---|---|
| hoy | hora | hidra | hemos |
| humor | huevo | horror | hortelano |

**ch**  Spanish **ch** is pronounced like the English *ch* in the word *chief:*

| | | | |
|---|---|---|---|
| hecho | chico | coche | Chile |
| mucho | muchacho | salchicha | |

**f**  Spanish **f** is identical in sound to the English *f:*

| | | | |
|---|---|---|---|
| difícil | feo | fuego | forma |
| fácil | fecha | foto | fueron |

**l**  To produce the Spanish **l** sound, touch the alveolar ridge with the tip of the tongue as for the English *l.* Try to keep the rest of the tongue fairly low in the mouth:

| | | | | |
|---|---|---|---|---|
| dolor | lata | ángel | lago | sueldo |
| los | pelo | lana | general | fácil |

**m**  Spanish **m** is pronounced like the English *m* in the word *mother:*

| | | | |
|---|---|---|---|
| mano | moda | mucho | muy |
| mismo | tampoco | multa | cómoda |

**n**  In most cases, Spanish **n** has a sound similar to the English *n* (see diagram D):

| | | | |
|---|---|---|---|
| nada | nunca | ninguno | norte |
| entra | tiene | sienta | |

The sound of Spanish **n** is often affected by the sounds that occur around it. When it appears before **b, v,** or **p,** it is pronounced like an **m:**

tan bueno    toman vino    sin poder
un pobre     comen peras   siguen bebiendo

Before **k, g,** and **j,** Spanish **n** has a voiced velar nasal sound, similar to the English *ng* in the word *sing:*

un kilómetro    incompleto    conjunto    mango
tengo           enjuto        un comedor

**ñ**  Spanish **ñ** is a voiced palatal sound (see diagram E), similar to the English *ny* sound in the word *canyon:*

señor    otoño    ñoño    uña
leña     dueño    niños   años

**x**  Spanish **x** has two pronunciations depending on its position. Between vowels the sound is similar to an English *gs:*

examen    exacto    boxeo       éxito
oxidar    oxígeno   existencia

When Spanish **x** occurs before a consonant it sounds like *s:*

expresión    explicar    extraer    excusa
expreso      exquisito   extremo

NOTE: When the **x** appears in the word **México** or in other words of Mexican origin that are associated with historical or legendary figures or name places, it is pronounced like the letter **j.**

# 2. RHYTHM

Rhythm is the melodic variation of sound intensity that we usually associate with music. Spanish and English each regulate these variations in speech differently, because they have different patterns of syllable length. In Spanish the length of the stressed and unstressed syllables remains almost the same, while in English stressed syllables are considerably longer than unstressed ones:

student       **estudiante**
composition   **composición**
police        **policía**

Since the length of the Spanish syllables remains constant, the greater the number of syllables in a given word or phrase, the longer the phrase will be.

Pronounce the following words trying to keep stressed and unstressed syllables the same length, and enunciating each syllable clearly. (Remember that stressed and unstressed vowels are pronounced alike.)

Úr-su-la                 los-za-pa-tos
la-su-cur-sal            bue-no
Pa-ra-guay               di-fí-cil
la-cul-tu-ra             ba-jan-to-dos
el-ci-ne                 ki-ló-me-tro

## 3. LINKING

In spoken Spanish the different words in a phrase or a sentence are not pronounced as isolated elements but combined together. This is called *linking:*

Pe-pe-co-me-pan          Pepe come pan
To-más-to-ma-le-che      Tomás toma leche
Luis-tie-ne-la-lla-ve    Luis tiene la llave
la-ma-no-de-Ro-ber-to    La mano de Roberto

1. The last consonant of a word is pronounced together with the initial vowel of the following word:

   Car-lo-san-da                         Carlos anda
   u-nán-gel                             un ángel
   e-lo-to-ño                            el otoño
   u-no-ses-tu-dio-sin-te-re-san-tes     unos estudios interesantes

2. A diphthong is formed between the last vowel of a word and the initial vowel of the following word. A triphthong is formed when there is a three vowel combination:

   suher-ma-na              su hermana
   tues-co-pe-ta            tu escopeta
   Ro-ber-toy-Luis          Roberto y Luis
   ne-go-cioim-por-tan-te   negocio importante
   llu-viay-nie-ve          lluvia y nieve
   ar-duaem-pre-sa          ardua empresa

3. When the last vowel of a word and the initial vowel of the following word are the same, they are pronounced slightly longer than one vowel:

   A-nal-can-za   Ana alcanza   tie-ne-so    tiene eso
   lol-vi-do      lo olvido     Ada-tien-de  Ada atiende

   The same rule applies when two equal vowels appear within a word:

   cres           crees
   Te-rán         Teherán
   cor-di-na-ción coordinación

4. When the last consonant of a word and the initial consonant of the following word are the same, they are pronounced like one consonant with slightly longer than normal duration:

| | | | |
|---|---|---|---|
| e-*l*a-do | el lado | tie-ne-*s*ed | tienes sed |
| Car-lo-*s*al-ta | Carlos salta | | |

## 4. INTONATION

Intonation is the rise and fall of pitch in the delivery of a phrase or a sentence. In most languages intonation is one of the most important devices used to express differences of meaning between otherwise identical phrases or sentences. In general, Spanish pitch tends to change less than English pitch, giving the impression that the language is less emphatic.

As a rule, the intonation for normal statements in Spanish starts in a low tone, raises to a higher one on the first syllable, maintains that tone until the last stressed syllable, and then goes back to the initial low tone, with still another drop at the very end:

Tu amigo viene mañana.   José come pan.

Ada está en casa.   Carlos toma café.

## 5. THE ALPHABET

| Letter | Name | Letter | Name | Letter | Name | Letter | Name |
|--------|------|--------|------|--------|------|--------|------|
| a | a | g | ge | m | eme | rr | erre |
| b | be | h | hache | n | ene | s | ese |
| c | ce | i | i | ñ | eñe | t | te |
| ch | che | j | jota | o | o | u | u |
| d | de | k | ka | p | pe | v | ve |
| e | e | l | ele | q | cu | w | doble ve |
| f | efe | ll | elle | r | ere | x | equis |
| | | | | | | y | i griega |
| | | | | | | z | zeta |

## 6. SYLLABLE FORMATION IN SPANISH

General rules for dividing words into syllables:

## A. Vowels

1. A vowel or a vowel combination can constitute a syllable:

   a-lum-no      a-bue-la      Eu-ro-pa

2. Diphthongs and triphthongs are considered single vowels and cannot be divided:

   bai-le      puen-te      Dia-na      es-tu-diáis      an-ti-guo

3. Two stressed vowels do not form a diphthong and are separated into two syllables:

   em-ple-ar      vol-te-ar      lo-a

4. A written accent on unstressed **i** or **u** breaks the diphthong, thus the vowels are separated into two syllables:

   trí-o      dí-a      Ma-rí-a

## B. Consonants

1. A single consonant forms a syllable with the vowel which follows it:

   po-der      ma-no      mi-nu-to

   NOTE: **ch, ll,** and **rr** are considered single consonants, for example:

   a-ma-ri-llo      co-che      pe-rro

2. Consonant clusters composed of **b, c, d, f, g, p,** or **t** with **l** or **r** are considered single consonants and cannot be separated:

   ha-blar      cla-vo      a-tlán-ti-co      Glo-ria

3. When two consonants appear between two vowels, they are separated into two syllables:

   al-fa-be-to      cam-pe-ón      me-ter-se      mo-les-tia

   EXCEPTION: When a consonant cluster appears between two vowels, we apply rule 2, and the cluster joins the following vowel, for example:

   so-bre      o-tros      ca-ble      te-lé-gra-fo

4. When three consonants appear between two vowels, only the last one goes with the following vowel:

ins-pec-tor     trans-por-te     trans-for-mar

EXCEPTION: When a consonant cluster appears, the first consonant joins the preceding vowel and the cluster joins the following vowel, for example:

es-cri-bir    ex-tran-je-ro    im-plo-rar    es-tre-cho

## 7. ACCENTUATION

In Spanish all words are stressed according to specific rules. Words that do not follow the rules must have a written accent to indicate the change of stress. The basic rules for accentuation are as follows:

1. Words ending in a vowel, **n**, or **s** are stressed on the next to the last syllable:

**hi**-jo       **ca**-lle       **me**-sa       fa-**mo**-sos
flo-**re**-cen   **pla**-ya       **ve**-ces

2. Words ending in a consonant, except **n** or **s**, are stressed on the last syllable:

ma-**yor**      na-**riz**
a-**mor**       re-**loj**
tro-pi-**cal**  co-rre-**dor**

3. All words that do not follow these rules, and also those that are stressed on the second syllable from the last, must have the written accent:

ca-**fé**       sa-**lió**      rin-**cón**     fran-**cés**    sa-**lón**      ma-**má**
**án**-gel      **lá**-piz      **dé**-bil      a-**zú**-car    **Víc**-tor
sim-**pá**-tico **lí**-qui-do   **mú**-si-ca    e-**xá**-me-nes de-**mó**-cra-ta

4. Pronouns and adverbs of interrogation and exclamation have a written accent to distinguish them from the relatives:

¿**Qué** comes? *What are you eating?*
La pera que no comió. *The pear that he did not eat.*

¿**Quién** está ahí? *Who is there?*
El hombre a quien vi. *The man whom I saw.*

¿**Dónde** está? *Where is he?*
El lugar donde él trabaja. *The place where he works.*

5. Words that are spelled the same but have a different meaning take a written accent to differentiate one from the other:

| el | the | él | he, him |
|----|-----|-----|---------|
| mi | my | mí | me |
| tu | your | tú | you |
| te | you (pronoun) | té | tea |
| si | if | sí | yes |
| mas | but | más | more |

6. The demonstrative adjectives have a written accent when they are used as pronouns:

| éste | ésta | éstos | éstas | ése | ésa |
|------|------|-------|-------|-----|-----|
| ésos | ésas | aquél | aquélla | aquéllos | aquéllas |

Prefiero **aquél**.  *I prefer that one.*

## 8. COGNATES

When learning a foreign language, being able to recognize cognates is of great value. Let's study some of them:

1. Some exact cognates (only the pronunciation is different):

| general | mineral | central | natural |
|---------|---------|---------|---------|
| idea | musical | cultural | banana |
| terrible | horrible | humor | terror |

2. Some cognates are almost the same, except for a written accent mark, a final vowel, or a single consonant in the Spanish word:

| región | península | México | conversión |
|--------|-----------|--------|------------|
| persona | arte | importante | potente |
| comercial | oficial | posible | imposible |

3. Most nouns ending in -tion in English end in **-ción** in Spanish:

conversación    solución    operación    cooperación

4. English words ending in -ce and -ty end in **-cia, -cio,** and **-dad** in Spanish:

| importancia | competencia | precipicio |
|-------------|-------------|------------|
| universidad | frivolidad | popularidad |

5. The English ending -ous is often equivalent to the Spanish ending **-oso:**

famoso    amoroso    numeroso    malicioso

6. S consonant is often equivalent to **es** consonant in Spanish:

    escuela    estado    estudio    especial

7. Finally, there are less approximate cognates that are still easily recognizable:

| | | | |
|---|---|---|---|
| millón | norte | millonario | monte |
| ingeniero | estudiar | artículo | ordenar |
| deliberadamente | enemigo | mayoría | centro |

# Appendix B: Verbs

## Regular verbs

## Model **-ar, -er, -ir** verbs

| INFINITIVE | | |
|---|---|---|
| **amar** (*to love*) | **comer** (*to eat*) | **vivir** (*to live*) |

| PRESENT PARTICIPLE | | |
|---|---|---|
| **amando** (*loving*) | **comiendo** (*eating*) | **viviendo** (*living*) |

| PAST PARTICIPLE | | |
|---|---|---|
| **amado** (*loved*) | **comido** (*eaten*) | **vivido** (*lived*) |

### SIMPLE TENSES

#### Indicative Mood

| PRESENT | | |
|---|---|---|
| (*I love*) | (*I eat*) | (*I live*) |
| am**o** | com**o** | viv**o** |
| am**as** | com**es** | viv**es** |
| am**a** | com**e** | viv**e** |
| am**amos** | com**emos** | viv**imos** |
| am**áis** | com**éis** | viv**ís** |
| am**an** | com**en** | viv**en** |

| IMPERFECT | | |
|---|---|---|
| (*I used to love*) | (*I used to eat*) | (*I used to live*) |
| am**aba** | com**ía** | viv**ía** |
| am**abas** | com**ías** | viv**ías** |
| am**aba** | com**ía** | viv**ía** |
| am**ábamos** | com**íamos** | viv**íamos** |
| am**abais** | com**íais** | viv**íais** |
| am**aban** | com**ían** | viv**ían** |

### PRETERIT

| (*I loved*) | (*I ate*) | (*I lived*) |
|---|---|---|
| amé | comí | viví |
| amaste | comiste | viviste |
| amó | comió | vivió |
| amamos | comimos | vivimos |
| amasteis | comisteis | vivisteis |
| amaron | comieron | vivieron |

### FUTURE

| (*I will love*) | (*I will eat*) | (*I will live*) |
|---|---|---|
| amaré | comeré | viviré |
| amarás | comerás | vivirás |
| amará | comerá | vivirá |
| amaremos | comeremos | viviremos |
| amaréis | comeréis | viviréis |
| amarán | comerán | vivirán |

### CONDITIONAL

| (*I would love*) | (*I would eat*) | (*I would live*) |
|---|---|---|
| amaría | comería | viviría |
| amarías | comerías | vivirías |
| amaría | comería | viviría |
| amaríamos | comeríamos | viviríamos |
| amaríais | comeríais | viviríais |
| amarían | comerían | vivirían |

## Subjunctive Mood

### PRESENT

| ([*that*] I [*may*] love) | ([*that*] I [*may*] eat) | ([*that*] I [*may*] live) |
|---|---|---|
| ame | coma | viva |
| ames | comas | vivas |
| ame | coma | viva |
| amemos | comamos | vivamos |
| améis | comáis | viváis |
| amen | coman | vivan |

### IMPERFECT

(two forms: **ara, ase**)

| ([*that*] I [*might*] love) | ([*that*] I [*might*] eat) | ([*that*] I [*might*] live) |
|---|---|---|
| amara -ase | comiera -iese | viviera -iese |
| amaras -ases | comieras -ieses | vivieras -ieses |
| amara -ase | comiera -iese | viviera -iese |
| amáramos -ásemos | comiéramos -iésemos | viviéramos -iésemos |
| amarais -aseis | comierais -ieseis | vivierais -ieseis |
| amaran -asen | comieran -iesen | vivieran -iesen |

IMPERATIVE MOOD

| (*love*) | (*eat*) | (*live*) |
|---|---|---|
| am**a** (tú) | com**e** (tú) | viv**e** (tú) |
| am**e** (Ud.) | com**a** (Ud.) | viv**a** (Ud.) |
| am**emos** (nosotros) | com**amos** (nosotros) | viv**amos** (nosotros) |
| am**ad** (vosotros) | com**ed** (vosotros) | viv**id** (vosotros) |
| am**en** (Uds.) | com**an** (Uds.) | viv**an** (Uds.) |

## COMPOUND TENSES

PERFECT INFINITIVE

| **haber amado** | **haber comido** | **haber vivido** |
|---|---|---|

PERFECT PARTICIPLE

| **habiendo amado** | **habiendo comido** | **habiendo vivido** |
|---|---|---|

### Indicative Mood

PRESENT PERFECT

| (*I have loved*) | (*I have eaten*) | (*I have lived*) |
|---|---|---|
| he amado | he comido | he vivido |
| has amado | has comido | has vivido |
| ha amado | ha comido | ha vivido |
| hemos amado | hemos comido | hemos vivido |
| habéis amado | habéis comido | habéis vivido |
| han amado | han comido | han vivido |

PLUPERFECT

| (*I had loved*) | (*I had eaten*) | (*I had lived*) |
|---|---|---|
| había amado | había comido | había vivido |
| habías amado | habías comido | habías vivido |
| había amado | había comido | había vivido |
| habíamos amado | habíamos comido | habíamos vivido |
| habíais amado | habíais comido | habíais vivido |
| habían amado | habían comido | habían vivido |

FUTURE PERFECT

| (*I will have loved*) | (*I will have eaten*) | (*I will have lived*) |
|---|---|---|
| habré amado | habré comido | habré vivido |
| habrás amado | habrás comido | habrás vivido |
| habrá amado | habrá comido | habrá vivido |
| habremos amado | habremos comido | habremos vivido |
| habréis amado | habréis comido | habréis vivido |
| habrán amado | habrán comido | habrán vivido |

CONDITIONAL PERFECT

| (*I would have loved*) | (*I would have eaten*) | (*I would have lived*) |
|---|---|---|
| habría amado | habría comido | habría vivido |
| habrías amado | habrías comido | habrías vivido |
| habría amado | habría comido | habría vivido |
| habríamos amado | habríamos comido | habríamos vivido |
| habríais amado | habríais comido | habríais vivido |
| habrían amado | habrían comido | habrían vivido |

## Subjunctive Mood

PRESENT PERFECT

| ([*that*] *I* [*may*] have loved) | ([*that*] *I* [*may*] have eaten) | ([*that*] *I* [*may*] have lived) |
|---|---|---|
| haya amado | haya comido | haya vivido |
| hayas amado | hayas comido | hayas vivido |
| haya amado | haya comido | haya vivido |
| hayamos amado | hayamos comido | hayamos vivido |
| hayáis amado | hayáis comido | hayáis vivido |
| hayan amado | hayan comido | hayan vivido |

PLUPERFECT

(two forms: -ra, -se)

| ([*that*] *I* [*might*] have loved) | ([*that*] *I* [*might*] have eaten) | ([*that*] *I* [*might*] have lived) |
|---|---|---|
| hubiera(-iese) amado | hubiera(-iese) comido | hubiera(-iese) vivido |
| hubieras(-ieses) amado | hubieras(-ieses) comido | hubieras(-ieses) vivido |
| hubiera(-iese) amado | hubiera(-iese) comido | hubiera(-iese) vivido |
| hubiéramos(-iésemos) amado | hubiéramos(-iésemos) comido | hubiéramos(-iésemos) vivido |
| hubierais(-ieseis) amado | hubierais(-ieseis) comido | hubierais(-ieseis) vivido |
| hubieran(-iesen) amado | hubieran(-iesen) comido | hubieran(-iesen) vivido |

# Stem-changing verbs

## The -ar and -er stem-changing verbs

Stem-changing verbs are those that have a change in the root of the verb. Verbs that end in **-ar** and **-er** change the stressed vowel **e** to **ie**, and the stressed **o** to **ue**. These changes occur in all persons, except the first and second persons plural, of the present indicative, present subjunctive, and imperative.

| INFINITIVE | PRESENT INDICATIVE | IMPERATIVE | PRESENT SUBJUNCTIVE |
|---|---|---|---|
| **perder** (*to lose*) | pierdo | —— | pierda |
| | pierdes | pierde | pierdas |
| | pierde | pierda | pierda |
| | perdemos | perdamos | perdamos |
| | perdéis | perded | perdáis |
| | pierden | pierdan | pierdan |
| **cerrar** (*to close*) | cierro | —— | cierre |
| | cierras | cierra | cierres |
| | cierra | cierre | cierre |
| | cerramos | cerremos | cerremos |
| | cerráis | cerrad | cerréis |
| | cierran | cierren | cierren |
| **contar** (*to count, to tell*) | cuento | —— | cuente |
| | cuentas | cuenta | cuentes |
| | cuenta | cuente | cuente |
| | contamos | contemos | contemos |
| | contáis | contad | contéis |
| | cuentan | cuenten | cuenten |
| **volver** (*to return*) | vuelvo | —— | vuelva |
| | vuelves | vuelve | vuelvas |
| | vuelve | vuelva | vuelva |
| | volvemos | volvamos | volvamos |
| | volvéis | volved | volváis |
| | vuelven | vuelvan | vuelvan |

Verbs that follow the same pattern are:

acordarse   to remember
acostar(se)   to go to bed
almorzar   to have lunch
atravesar   to go through
cocer   to cook
colgar   to hang
comenzar   to begin
confesar   to confess
costar   to cost
demostrar   to demonstrate, to show
despertar(se)   to wake up
empezar   to begin
encender   to light, turn on
encontrar   to find
entender   to understand

llover   to rain
mover   to move
mostrar   to show
negar   to deny
nevar   to snow
pensar   to think, to plan
probar   to prove, to taste
recordar   to remember
rogar   to beg
sentar(se)   to sit down
soler   to be in the habit of
soñar   to dream
tender   to stretch, to unfold
torcer   to twist

## The -ir stem-changing verbs

There are two types of stem-changing verbs that end in -ir: one type changes stressed e to ie in some tenses and to i in others, and stressed o to ue or u; the second type changes stressed e to i only in all the irregular tenses.

Type I    -ir: e > ie / o > ue or u

These changes occur as follows:

Present Indicative: all persons except the first and second plural change e to ie and o to ue. Preterit: third person, singular and plural, changes e to i and o to u. Present Subjunctive: all persons change e to ie and o to ue, except the first and second persons plural which change e to i and o to u. Imperfect Subjunctive: all persons change e to i and o to u. Imperative: all persons except the second person plural change e to ie and o to ue, and first person plural changes e to i and o to u. Present Participle: changes e to i and o to u.

| INFINITIVE | Indicative PRESENT | Indicative PRETERIT | Imperative | Subjunctive PRESENT | Subjunctive IMPERFECT |
|---|---|---|---|---|---|
| **sentir** | siento | sentí | —— | sienta | sintiera (-iese) |
| (*to feel*) | sientes | sentiste | siente | sientas | sintieras |
| | siente | sintió | sienta | sienta | sintiera |
| PRESENT | sentimos | sentimos | sintamos | sintamos | sintiéramos |
| PARTICIPLE | sentís | sentisteis | sentid | sintáis | sintierais |
| sintiendo | sienten | sintieron | sientan | sientan | sintieran |
| **dormir** | duermo | dormí | —— | duerma | durmiera (-iese) |
| (*to sleep*) | duermes | dormiste | duerme | duermas | durmieras |
| | duerme | durmió | duerma | duerma | durmiera |
| PRESENT | dormimos | dormimos | durmamos | durmamos | durmiéramos |
| PARTICIPLE | dormís | dormisteis | dormid | durmáis | durmierais |
| durmiendo | duermen | durmieron | duerman | duerman | durmieran |

Other verbs that follow the same pattern are:

**advertir**  to warn  
**arrepentir(se)**  to repent  
**consentir**  to consent, to pamper  
**convertir(se)**  to turn into  
**divertir(se)**  to amuse oneself  
**herir**  to wound, to hurt  

**mentir**  to lie  
**morir**  to die  
**preferir**  to prefer  
**referir**  to refer  
**sugerir**  to suggest

Type II     **-ir: e > i**

The verbs in this second category are irregular in the same tenses as those of the first type. The only difference is that they only have one change: **e > i** in all irregular persons.

| | Indicative | | Imperative | Subjunctive | |
|---|---|---|---|---|---|
| INFINITIVE | PRESENT | PRETERIT | | PRESENT | IMPERFECT |
| **pedir** | pido | pedí | —— | pida | pidiera (-iese) |
| (*to ask for,* | pides | pediste | pide | pidas | pidieras |
| *request*) | pide | pidió | pida | pida | pidiera |
| PRESENT | pedimos | pedimos | pidamos | pidamos | pidiéramos |
| PARTICIPLE | pedís | pedisteis | pedid | pidáis | pidierais |
| pidiendo | piden | pidieron | pidan | pidan | pidieran |

Verbs that follow this pattern are:

**concebir**  to conceive
**competir**  to compete
**despedir(se)**  to say goodbye
**elegir**  to choose
**impedir**  to prevent
**perseguir**  to pursue

**reir(se)**  to laugh
**repetir**  to repeat
**reñir**  to fight
**seguir**  to follow
**servir**  to serve
**vestir(se)**  to dress

## Orthographic-changing verbs

Some verbs undergo a change in the spelling of the stem in some tenses, in order to keep the sound of the final consonant. The most common ones are those with the consonants **g** and **c**. Remember that **g** and **c** in front of **e** or **i** have a soft sound, and in front of **a, o,** or **u** have a hard sound. In order to keep the soft sound in front of **a, o,** and **u**, we change **g** and **c** to **j** and **z**, respectively. And in order to keep the hard sound of **g** and **c** in front of **e** and **i**, we add a **u** to the **g** (**gu**) and change the **c** to **qu**. Following are the most important verbs of this type:

1. Verbs ending in **-gar** change **g** to **gu** before **e** in the first person of the preterit and in all persons of the present subjunctive.

   **pagar** (*to pay*)
   *Preterit:*      pagué, pagaste, pagó, etc.
   *Pres. Subj.:*   pague, pagues, pague, paguemos, paguéis, paguen

   Verbs with the same change: **colgar, llegar, navegar, negar, regar, rogar, jugar**.

2. Verbs ending in **-ger** and **-gir** change **g** to **j** before **o** and **a** in the first person of the present indicative and in all the persons of the present subjunctive.

**proteger** (*to protect*)
*Pres. Ind.:*    protejo, proteges, protege, etc.
*Pres. Subj.:*   proteja, protejas, proteja, protejamos, protejáis, protejan

Verbs that follow the same pattern: **coger, dirigir, escoger, exigir, recoger, corregir.**

3. Verbs ending in **-guar** change **gu** to **gü** before **e** in the first persons of the preterit and in all persons of the present subjunctive.

**averiguar** (*to find out*)
*Preterit:*      averigüé, averiguaste, averiguó, etc.
*Pres. Subj.:*   averigüe, averigües, averigüe, averigüemos, averigüéis, averigüen

The verb **apaciguar** has the same changes.

4. Verbs ending in **-guir** change **gu** to **g** before **o** and **a** in the first person of the present indicative and in all persons of the present subjunctive.

**conseguir** (*to get*)
*Pres. Ind.:*    consigo, consigues, consigue, etc.
*Pres. Subj.:*   consiga, consigas, consiga, consigamos, consigáis, consigan

Verbs with the same change: **distinguir, perseguir, proseguir, seguir.**

5. Verbs ending in **-car** change **c** to **qu** before **e** in the first person of the preterit and in all persons of the present subjunctive.

**tocar** (*to touch, to play* [*a musical instrument*])
*Preterit:*      toqué, tocaste, tocó, etc.
*Pres. Subj.:*   toque, toques, toque, toquemos, toquéis, toquen

Verbs with the same pattern: **atacar, buscar, communicar, explicar, indicar, sacar, pescar.**

6. Verbs ending in **-cer** and **-cir** preceded by a consonant change **c** to **z** before **o** and **a** in the first person of the present indicative and in all persons of the present subjunctive.

**torcer** (*to twist*)
*Pres. Ind.:*    tuerzo, tuerces, tuerce, etc.
*Pres. Subj.:*   tuerza, tuerzas, tuerza, torzamos, torzáis, tuerzan

Verbs with the same change: **convencer, esparcir, vencer.**

7. Verbs ending in **-cer** and **-cir** preceded by a vowel change **c** to **zc** before **o** and **a** in the first person of the present indicative and in all persons of the present subjunctive.

**conocer** (*to know, to be acquainted with*)
*Pres. Ind.:* conozco, conoces, conoce, etc.
*Pres. Subj.:* conozca, conozcas, conozca, conozcamos, conozcáis, conozcan

Verbs with the same change: **agradecer, aparecer, carecer, establecer, entristecer** (*to sadden*), **lucir, nacer, obedecer, ofrecer, padecer, parecer, pertenecer, relucir, reconocer.**

8. Verbs ending in **-zar** change **z** to **c** before **e** in the first person of the preterit and in all persons of the present subjunctive.

**rezar** (*to pray*)
*Preterit:* recé, rezaste, rezó, etc.
*Pres. Subj.:* rece, reces, rece, recemos, recéis, recen

Verbs with the same pattern: **alcanzar, almorzar, comenzar, cruzar, empezar, forzar, gozar, abrazar.**

9. Verbs ending in **-eer** change the unstressed **i** to **y** between vowels in the third person singular and plural of the preterit, in all persons of the imperfect subjunctive, and in the present participle.

**creer** (*to believe*)
*Preterit:* creí, creíste, creyó, creímos, creísteis, creyeron
*Imp. Subj.:* creyera, creyeras, creyera, creyéramos, creyerais, creyeran
*Pres. Part.:* creyendo
*Past Part.:* creído

**Leer** and **poseer** follow the same change pattern.

10. Verbs ending in **-uir** change the unstressed **i** to **y** between vowels (except **-quir** which has the silent **u**) in the following tenses and persons:

**huir** (*to escape, to flee*)
*Pres. Part.:* huyendo
*Pres. Ind.:* huyo, huyes, huye, huimos, huís, huyen
*Preterit:* huí, huiste, huyó, huimos, huisteis, huyeron
*Imperative:* huye, huya, huyamos, huid, huyan
*Pres. Subj.:* huya, huyas, huya, huyamos, huyáis, huyan
*Imp. Subj.:* huyera(ese), huyeras, huyera, huyéramos, huyerais, huyeran

Verbs with the same change: **atribuir, concluir, constituir, construir, contribuir, destituir, destruir, disminuir, distribuir, excluir, incluir, influir, instruir, restituir, sustituir.**

11. Verbs ending in **-eír** lose one **e** in the third person singular and plural of the preterit, in all persons of the imperfect subjunctive, and in the present participle.

**reír** (*to laugh*)
*Preterit:*      reí, reíste, rio, reímos, reísteis, rieron
*Imp. Subj.:*  riera(ese), rieras, riera, rieramos, rierais, rieran
*Pres. Part.:*  riendo

**Sonreír** and **freír** have the same pattern.

12. Verbs ending in **-iar** add a written accent to the **i**, except in the first and second persons plural of the present indicative and subjunctive.

**fiar(se)** (*to trust*)
*Pres. Ind.:*   fío (me), fías (te), fía (se), fiamos (nos), fiais (os), fían (se)
*Pres. Subj.:*  fíe (me), fíes (te), fíe (se), fiemos (nos), fiéis (os), fíen (se)

Other verbs with the same change: **enviar, ampliar, criar, desviar, enfriar, guiar, telegrafiar, vaciar, variar.**

13. Verbs ending in **-uar** (except **-guar**) add a written accent to the **u**, except in the first and second persons plural of the present indicative and subjunctive.

**actuar** (*to act*)
*Pres. Ind.:*   actúo, actúas, actúa, actuamos, actuáis, actúan
*Pres. Subj.:*  actúe, actúes, actúe, actuemos, actuéis, actúen

Verbs with the same pattern: **continuar, acentuar, efectuar, exceptuar, graduar, habituar, insinuar, situar.**

14. Verbs ending in **-ñir** remove the **i** of the diphthongs **ie** and **ió** in the third person singular and plural of the preterit and in all persons of the imperfect subjunctive. They also change the **e** of stem to **i** in the same persons.

**teñir** (*to dye*)
*Preterit:*      teñí, teñiste, tiñó, teñimos, teñisteis, tiñeron
*Imp. Subj.:*  tiñera (ese), tiñeras, tiñera, tiñéramos, tiñerais, tiñeran

Verbs with the same change: **ceñir, constreñir, desteñir, estreñir, reñir.**

# Some common irregular verbs

Only those tenses with irregular forms will be given.

**acertar** (*to guess right*)
*Pres. Ind.:* acierto, aciertas, acierta, acertamos, acertáis, aciertan
*Pres. Subj.:* acierte, aciertes, acierte, acertemos, acertéis, acierten
*Imperative:* acierta, acierte, acertemos, acertad, acierten

**adquirir** (*to acquire*)
*Pres. Ind.:* adquiero, adquieres, adquiere, adquirimos, adquirís, adquieren
*Pres. Subj.:* adquiera, adquieras, adquiera, adquiramos, adquiráis, adquieran
*Imperative:* adquiere, adquiera, adquiramos, adquirid, adquieran

**andar** (*to walk*)
*Preterit:* anduve, anduviste, anduvo, anduvimos, anduvisteis, anduvieron
*Imp. Subj.:* anduviera (anduviese), anduvieras, anduviera, anduviéramos, anduvierais, anduvieran

**avergonzarse** (*to be ashamed, to be embarrassed*)
*Pres. Ind.:* me avergüenzo, te avergüenzas, se avergüenza, nos avergonzamos, os avergonzáis, se avergüenzan
*Pres. Subj.:* me avergüence, te avergüences, se avergüence, nos avergoncemos, os avergoncéis, se avergüencen
*Imperative:* avergüénzate, avergüéncese, avergoncémonos, avergonzaos, avergüenzense

**caber** (*to fit, to have enough room*)
*Pres. Ind.:* quepo, cabes, cabe, cabemos, cabéis, caben
*Preterit:* cupe, cupiste, cupo, cupimos, cupisteis, cupieron
*Future:* cabré, cabrás, cabrá, cabremos, cabréis, cabrán
*Conditional:* cabría, cabrías, cabría, cabríamos, cabríais, cabrían
*Imperative:* cabe, quepa, quepamos, cabed, quepan
*Pres. Subj.:* quepa, quepas, quepa, quepamos, quepáis, quepan
*Imp. Subj.:* cupiera (cupiese), cupieras, cupiera, cupiéramos, cupierais, cupieran

**caer** (*to fall*)
*Pres. Ind.:* caigo, caes, cae, caemos, caéis, caen
*Preterit:* caí, caíste, cayó, caímos, caísteis, cayeron
*Imperative:* cae, caiga, caigamos, caed, caigan
*Pres. Subj.:* caiga, caigas, caiga, caigamos, ciagáis, caigan
*Imp. Subj.:* cayera (cayese), cayeras, cayera, cayéramos, cayerais, cayeran
*Past Part.:* caído

**cegar** (*to blind*)
*Pres. Ind.:*    ciego, ciegas, ciega, cegamos, cegáis, ciegan
*Imperative:*    ciega, ciegue, ceguemos, cegad, cieguen
*Pres. Subj.:*   ciegue, ciegues, ciegue, ceguemos, ceguéis, cieguen

**conducir** (*to guide, to drive*)
*Pres. Ind.:*    conduzco, conduces, conduce, conducimos, conducís, conducen
*Preterit:*      conduje, condujiste, condujo, condujimos, condujisteis, condujeron
*Imperative:*    conduce, conduzca, conduzcamos, conducid, conduzcan
*Pres. Subj.:*   conduzca, conduzcas, conduzca, conduzcamos, conduzcáis, conduzcan
*Imp. Subj.:*    condujera (condujese), condujeras, condujera, condujéramos, condujerais, condujeran

(All verbs ending in **-ducir** follow this pattern)

**convenir** (*to agree*) See **venir.**

**dar** (*to give*)
*Pres. Ind.:*    doy, das, da, damos, dais, dan
*Preterit:*      di, diste, dio, dimos, disteis, dieron
*Imperative:*    da, dé, demos, dad, den
*Pres. Subj.:*   dé, des, dé, demos, deis, den
*Imp. Subj.:*    diera (diese), dieras, diera, diéramos, dierais, dieran

**decir** (*to say, to tell*)
*Pres. Ind.:*    digo, dices, dice, decimos, decís, dicen
*Preterit:*      dije, dijiste, dijo, dijimos, dijisteis, dijeron
*Future:*        diré, dirás, dirá, diremos, diréis, dirán
*Conditional:*   diría, dirías, diría, diríamos, diríais, dirían
*Imperative:*    di, diga, digamos, decid, digan
*Pres. Subj.:*   diga, digas, diga, digamos, digáis, digan
*Imp. Subj.:*    dijera (dijese), dijeras, dijera, dijéramos, dijerais, dijeran
*Pres. Part.:*   diciendo
*Past. Part.:*   dicho

**detener** (*to stop, to hold, to arrest*) See **tener.**

**elegir** (*to choose*)
*Pres. Ind.:*    elijo, eliges, elige, elegimos, elegís, eligen
*Preterit:*      elegí, elegiste, eligió, elegimos, elegisteis, eligieron
*Imperative:*    elige, elija, elijamos, elegid, elijan
*Pres. Subj.:*   elija, elijas, elija, elijamos, elijáis, elijan
*Imp. Subj.:*    eligiera (eligiese), eligieras, eligiera, eligiéramos, eligierais, eligieran

**entender** (*to understand*)
Pres. Ind.:   entiendo, entiendes, entiende, entendemos, entendéis,
             entienden
Imperative:  entiende, entienda, entendamos, entended, entiendan
Pres. Subj.:  entienda, entiendas, entienda, entendamos, entendáis,
             entiendan

**entretener** (*to entertain, to amuse*) See **tener**.

**extender** (*to extend, to stretch out*) See **tender**.

**errar** (*to err, to miss*)
Pres. Ind.:   yerro, yerras, yerra, erramos, erráis, yerran
Imperative:  yerra, yerre, erremos, errad, yerren
Pres. Subj.:  yerre, yerres, yerre, erremos, erréis, yerren

**estar** (*to be*)
Pres. Ind.:   estoy, estás, está, estamos, estáis, están
Preterit:    estuve, estuviste, estuvo, estuvimos, estuvisteis, estu-
             vieron
Imperative:  está, esté, estemos, estad, estén
Pres. Subj.:  esté, estés, esté, estemos, estéis, estén
Imp. Subj.:   estuviera (estuviese), estuvieras, estuviera, estuvié-
             ramos, estuvierais, estuvieran

**haber** (*to have*)
Pres. Ind.:   he, has, ha, hemos, habéis, han
Preterit:    hube, hubiste, hubo, hubimos, hubisteis, hubieron
Future:      habré, habrás, habrá, habremos, habréis, habrán
Conditional: habría, habrías, habría, habríamos, habríais, habrían
Imperative:  he, haya, hayamos, habed, hayan
Pres. Subj.:  haya, hayas, haya, hayamos, hayáis, hayan
Imp. Subj.:   hubiera (hubiese), hubieras, hubiera, hubiéramos,
             hubierais, hubieran

**hacer** (*to do, to make*)
Pres. Ind.:   hago, haces, hace, hacemos, hacéis, hacen
Preterit:    hice, hiciste, hizo, hicimos, hicisteis, hicieron
Future:      haré, harás, hará, haremos, haréis, harán
Conditional: haría, harías, haría, haríamos, haríais, harían
Imperative:  haz, haga, hagamos, haced, hagan
Pres. Subj.:  haga, hagas, haga, hagamos, hagáis, hagan
Imp. Subj.:   hiciera (hiciese), hicieras, hiciera, hiciéramos, hicierais,
             hicieran
Past Part.:  hecho

**imponer** (*to impose, to deposit*) See **poner**.

**introducir** (*to introduce, to insert, to gain access*) See **conducir**.

**ir** (*to go*)
| | |
|---|---|
| *Pres. Ind.:* | voy, vas, va, vamos, vais, van |
| *Imp. Ind.:* | iba, ibas, iba, íbamos, ibais, iban |
| *Preterit:* | fui, fuiste, fue, fuimos, fuisteis, fueron |
| *Imperative:* | ve, vaya, vayamos, id, vayan |
| *Pres. Subj.:* | vaya, vayas, vaya, vayamos, vayáis, vayan |
| *Imp. Subj.:* | fuera (fuese), fueras, fuera, fuéramos, fuerais, fueran |

**jugar** (*to play*)
| | |
|---|---|
| *Pres. Ind.:* | juego, juegas, juega, jugamos, jugáis, juegan |
| *Imperative:* | juega, juegue, juguemos, jugad, jueguen |
| *Pres. Subj.:* | juegue, juegues, juegue, juguemos, juguéis, jueguen |

**obtener** (*to obtain*) See **tener.**

**oír** (*to hear*)
| | |
|---|---|
| *Pres. Ind.:* | oigo, oyes, oye, oímos, oís, oyen |
| *Preterit:* | oí, oíste, oyó, oímos, oísteis, oyeron |
| *Imperative:* | oye, oiga, oigamos, oid, oigan |
| *Pres. Subj.:* | oiga, oigas, oiga, oigamos, oigáis, oigan |
| *Imp. Subj.:* | oyera (oyese), oyeras, oyera, oyéramos, oyerais, oyeran |
| *Pres. Part.:* | oyendo |
| *Past Part.:* | oído |

**oler** (*to smell*)
| | |
|---|---|
| *Pres. Ind.:* | huelo, hueles, huele, olemos, oléis, huelen |
| *Imperative:* | huele, huela, olamos, oled, huelan |
| *Pres. Subj.:* | huela, huelas, huela, olamos, oláis, huelan |

**poder** (*to be able*)
| | |
|---|---|
| *Pres. Ind.:* | puedo, puedes, puede, podemos, podéis, pueden |
| *Preterit:* | pude, pudiste, pudo, pudimos, pudisteis, pudieron |
| *Future:* | podré, podrás, podrá, podremos, podréis, podrán |
| *Conditional:* | podría, podrías, podría, podríamos, podríais, podrían |
| *Imperative:* | puede, pueda, podamos, poded, puedan |
| *Pres. Subj.:* | pueda, puedas, pueda, podamos, podáis, puedan |
| *Imp. Subj.:* | pudiera (pudiese), pudieras, pudiera, pudiéramos, pudierais, pudieran |
| *Pres. Part.:* | pudiendo |

**poner** (*to place, to put*)
| | |
|---|---|
| *Pres. Ind.:* | pongo, pones, pone, ponemos, ponéis, ponen |
| *Preterit:* | puse, pusiste, puso, pusimos, pusisteis, pusieron |
| *Future:* | pondré, pondrás, pondrá, pondremos, pondréis, pondrán |
| *Conditional:* | pondría, pondrías, pondría, pondríamos, pondríais, pondrían |
| *Imperative:* | pon, ponga, pongamos, poned, pongan |
| *Pres. Subj.:* | ponga, pongas, ponga, pongamos, pongáis, pongan |

*Imp. Subj.:*    pusiera (pusiese), pusieras, pusiera, pusiéramos, pusierais, pusieran
*Past Part.:*    puesto

**querer** *(to want, to wish, to like)*
*Pres. Ind.:*    quiero, quieres, quiere, queremos, queréis, quieren
*Preterit:*    quise, quisiste, quiso, quisimos, quisisteis, quisieron
*Future:*    querré, querrás, querrá, querremos, querréis, querrán
*Conditional:*    querría, querrías, querría, querríamos, querríais, querrían
*Imperative:*    quiere, quiera, queramos, quered, quieran
*Pres. Subj.:*    quiera, quieras, quiera, queramos, queráis, quieran
*Imp. Subj.:*    quisiera (quisiese), quisieras, quisiera, quisiéramos, quisierais, quisieran

**resolver** *(to decide on)*
*Pres. Ind.:*    resuelvo, resuelves, resuelve, resolvemos, resolvéis, resuelven
*Imperative:*    resuelve, resuelva, resolvamos, resolved, resuelvan
*Pres. Subj.:*    resuelva, resuelvas, resuelva, resolvamos, resolváis, resuelvan
*Past Part.:*    resuelto

**saber** *(to know)*
*Pres. Ind.:*    sé, sabes, sabe, sabemos, sabéis, saben
*Preterit:*    supe, supiste, supo, supimos, supisteis, supieron
*Future:*    sabré, sabrás, sabrá, sabremos, sabréis, sabrán
*Conditional:*    sabría, sabrías, sabría, sabríamos, sabríais, sabrían
*Imperative:*    sabe, sepa, sepamos, sabed, sepan
*Pres. Subj.:*    sepa, sepas, sepa, sepamos, sepáis, sepan
*Imp. Subj.:*    supiera (supiese), supieras, supiera, supiéramos, supierais, supieran

**salir** *(to leave, to go out)*
*Pres. Ind.:*    salgo, sales, sale, salimos, salís, salen
*Future:*    saldré, saldrás, saldrá, saldremos, saldréis, saldrán
*Conditional:*    saldría, saldrías, saldría, saldríamos, saldríais, saldrían
*Imperative:*    sal, salga, salgamos, salid, salgan
*Pres. Subj.:*    salga, salgas, salga, salgamos, salgáis, salgan

**ser** *(to be)*
*Pres. Ind.:*    soy, eres, es, somos, sois, son
*Imp. Ind.:*    era, eras, era, éramos, erais, eran
*Preterit:*    fui, fuiste, fue, fuimos, fuisteis, fueron
*Imperative:*    sé, sea, seamos, sed, sean
*Pres. Subj.:*    sea, seas, sea, seamos, seáis, sean
*Imp. Subj.:*    fuera (fuese), fueras, fuera, fuéramos, fuerais, fueran

**suponer** *(to assume)* See **poner**.

**tener** (*to have*)
*Pres. Ind.:*    tengo, tienes, tiene, tenemos, tenéis, tienen
*Preterit:*    tuve, tuviste, tuvo, tuvimos, tuvisteis, tuvieron
*Future:*    tendré, tendrás, tendrá, tendremos, tendréis, tendrán
*Conditional:* tendría, tendrías, tendría, tendríamos, tendríais, tendrían
*Imperative:*    ten, tenga, tengamos, tened, tengan
*Pres. Subj.:*    tenga, tengas, tenga, tengamos, tengáis, tengan
*Imp. Subj.:*    tuviera (tuviese), tuvieras, tuviera, tuviéramos, tuvierais, tuvieran

**tender** (*to spread out, to hang out*)
*Pres. Ind.:*    tiendo, tiendes, tiende, tendemos, tendéis, tienden
*Imperative:*    tiende, tienda, tendamos, tended, tiendan
*Pres. Subj.:*    tienda, tiendas, tienda, tendamos, tendáis, tiendan

**traducir** (*to translate*)
*Pres Ind.:*    traduzco, traduces, traduce, traducimos, traducís, traducen
*Preterit:*    traduje, tradujiste, tradujo, tradujimos, tradujisteis, tradujeron
*Imperative:*    traduce, traduzca, traduzcamos, traducid, traduzcan
*Pres. Subj.:*    traduzca, traduzcas, traduzca, traduzcamos, traduzcáis, traduzcan
*Imp. Subj.:*    tradujera (tradujese), tradujeras, tradujera, tradujéramos, tradujerais, tradujeran

**traer** (*to bring*)
*Pres. Ind.:*    traigo, traes, trae, traemos, traéis, traen
*Preterit:*    traje, trajiste, trajo, trajimos, trajisteis, trajeron
*Imperative:*    trae, traiga, traigamos, traed, traigan
*Pres. Subj.:*    traiga, traigas, traiga, traigamos, traigáis, traigan
*Imp. Subj.:*    trajera (trajese), trajeras, trajera, trajéramos, trajerais, trajeran
*Pres. Part:*    trayendo
*Past Part.:*    traído

**valer** (*to be worth*)
*Pres. Ind.:*    valgo, vales, vale, valemos, valéis, valen
*Future:*    valdré, valdrás, valdrá, valdremos, valdréis, valdrán
*Conditional:* valdría, valdrías, valdría, valdríamos, valdríais, valdrían
*Imperative:*    vale, valga, valgamos, valed, valgan
*Pres. Subj.:*    valga, valgas, valga, valgamos, valgáis, valgan

**venir** (*to come*)
*Pres. Ind.:*    vengo, vienes, viene, venimos, venís, vienen
*Preterit:*    vine, viniste, vino, vinimos, vinisteis, vinieron
*Future:*    vendré, vendrás, vendrá, vendremos, vendréis, vendrán

| | |
|---|---|
| *Conditional:* | vendría, vendrías, vendría, vendríamos, vendríais, vendrían |
| *Imperative:* | ven, venga, vengamos, venid, vengan |
| *Pres. Subj.:* | venga, vengas, venga, vengamos, vengáis, vengan |
| *Imp. Subj.:* | viniera (viniese), vinieras, viniera, viniéramos, vinierais, vinieran |
| *Pres. Part.:* | viniendo |

**ver** (*to see*)

| | |
|---|---|
| *Pres. Ind.:* | veo, ves, ve, vemos, veis, ven |
| *Imp. Ind.:* | veía, veías, veía, veíamos, veíais, veían |
| *Preterit:* | vi, viste, vio, vimos, visteis, vieron |
| *Imperative:* | ve, vea, veamos, ved, vean |
| *Pres. Subj.:* | vea, veas, vea, veamos, veáis, vean |
| *Imp. Subj.:* | viera (viese), vieras, viera, viéramos, vierais, vieran |
| *Past Part.:* | visto |

# Appendix C: Glossary of Grammatical Terms

**adjective:** A word that is used to describe a noun: *tall* girl, *difficult* lesson.

**adverb:** A word that modifies a verb, an adjective, or another adverb. It answers the questions "How?", "When?", "Where?": She walked *slowly*. She'll be here *tomorrow*. She is *here*.

**agreement:** A term usually applied to adjectives. An adjective is said to show agreement with the noun it modifies when its ending changes in accordance with the gender and number of the noun. In Spanish, a feminine plural noun requires a feminine plural ending in the adjective that describes it (**casas amarillas**) and a masculine singular noun requires a masculine singular ending in the adjective (**libro negro**).

**article:** See *definite article* and *indefinite article*.

**auxiliary verb:** A verb that helps in the conjugation of another verb: I *have* finished. He *was* called. She *will* go. He *would* eat.

**command form:** The form of the verb used to give an order or a direction: *Go! Come back! Turn* to the right!

**conjugation:** The process by which the forms of the verb are presented in their different moods and tenses: I *am*, you

*are*, he *is*, she *was*, we *were*, etc.

**contraction:** The combination of two or more words into one: *isn't, don't, can't*.

**definite article:** A word used before a noun indicating a definite person or thing: *the* woman, *the* money.

**demonstrative:** A word that refers to a definite person or object: *this, that, these, those*.

**diphthong:** A combination of two vowels forming one syllable. In Spanish, a diphthong is composed of one *strong* vowel (**a, e, o**) and one *weak* vowel (**u, i**) or two weak vowels: **ei, au, ui**.

**exclamation:** A word used to express emotion: *How* strong! *What* beauty!

**gender:** A distinction of nouns, pronouns, and adjectives, based on whether they are masculine or feminine.

**indefinite article:** A word used before a noun that refers to an indefinite person or object: *A* child. *An* apple.

**infinitive:** The form of the verb generally preceded in English by the word *to* and showing no subject or number: *to do, to bring*.

**interrogative:** A word used in asking a question: *Who? What? Where?*

**main clause:** A group of words that includes a subject and a verb and by itself has complete meaning: *They saw me. I go now.*

**noun:** A word that names a person, place, thing, etc.: *Ann, London, pencil*, etc.

**number:** Number refers to singular and plural: *chair, chairs.*

**object:** Generally a noun or a pronoun that is the receiver of the verb's action. A direct object answers the question "*What?*" or "*Whom?*": We know *her*. Take *it*. An indirect object answers the question "*To whom?*" or "*To what?*": Give *John* the money. Nouns and pronouns can also be objects of prepositions: The letter is *from Rick*. I'm thinking *about you*.

**past participle:** Past forms of a verb: *gone, worked, written*, etc.

**person:** The form of the pronoun and of the verb that shows the person referred to: *I* (first person singular), *you* (second person singular), *she* (third person singular), etc.

**possessive:** A word that denotes ownership or possession: This is *our* house. The book isn't *mine*.

**preposition:** A word that introduces a noun, pronoun, adverb, infinitive, or present participle and indicates its function in the sentence: They were *with* us. She is *from* Nevada.

**pronoun:** A word that is used to replace a noun: *she, them, us,* etc. A **subject pronoun** refers to the person or thing spoken of: *They* work. An **object pronoun** receives the action of the verb: They arrested *us* (direct object pronoun). She spoke to *him* (indirect object pronoun). A pronoun can also be the object of a preposition: The children stayed with *us*.

**reflexive pronoun:** A pronoun that refers back to the subject: *myself, yourself, himself, herself, itself, ourselves*, etc.

**subject:** The person, place, or thing spoken of: *Robert* works. *Our car* is new.

**subordinate clause:** A clause that has no complete meaning by itself but depends on a main clause: They knew *that I was here*.

**tense:** The group of forms in a verb that show the time in which the action of the verb takes place: *I go* (present indicative), *I'm going* (present progressive), *I went* (past), *I was going* (past progressive), *I will go* (future), *I would go* (conditional), *I have gone* (present perfect), *I had gone* (past perfect), *that I may go* (present subjunctive), etc.

**verb:** A word that expresses an action or a state: We *sleep*. The baby *is* sick.

# Appendix D: Careers and Occupations

accountant **contador**
actor **actor**
actress **actriz**
administrator **administrador**
agent **agente**
architect **arquitecto**
baker **panadero**
bank officer **empleado bancario**
bank teller **cajero**
banker **banquero**
barber **barbero**
bartender **barman, cantinero**
bill collector **cobrador**
bookkeeper **tenedor de libros**
brickmason (bricklayer) **albañil**
buyer **comprador**
cameraman **camarógrafo**
carpenter **carpintero**
cashier **cajero**
chiropractor **quiropráctico**
clerk **dependiente**
computer operator **computista**
contractor **contratista**
construction worker **obrero de la construcción**
constructor **constructor**
cook **cocinero**
copilot **copiloto**
counselor **consejero**
craftsman **artesano**
dancer **bailarín**
decorator **decorador**
dental hygienist **higienista dental**
dentist **dentista**
designer **diseñador**
detective **detective**
dietician **especialista en dietética**
diplomat **diplomático**

dockworker **obrero portuario**
doctor **doctor**
draftsman **dibujante**
dressmaker **modista**
driver **conductor**
economist **economista**
editor **editor**
electrician **electricista**
engineer **ingeniero**
engineering technician **ingeniero técnico**
farmer **agricultor**
fashion designer **diseñador de alta costura, modisto**
fireman **bombero**
fisherman **pescador**
flight attendant **azafata, sobrecargo**
foreman **capataz, encargado**
funeral director **empresario de pompas fúnebres**
garbage collector **basurero**
gardener **jardinero**
guard **guardia**
hairdresser **peluquero**
home economist **economista doméstico**
housekeeper **ama de llaves**
inspector **inspector**
insurance agent **agente de seguros**
interior designer **diseñador de interiores**
interpreter **intérprete**
investigator **investigador**
janitor **conserje**
jeweler **joyero**
journalist **periodista**
judge **juez**
lawyer **abogado**

librarian **bibliotecario**
machinist **maquinista**
maid **criada**
mail carrier **cartero**
manager **gerente**
meat cutter **carnicero**
mechanic **mecánico**
midwife **comadrona, partera**
military **militar**
miner **minero**
model **modelo**
musician **músico**
night watchman **sereno, guardián**
nurse **enfermero**
optician **óptico**
optometrist **optometrista**
painter **pintor**
pharmacist **farmacéutico**
photographer **fotógrafo**
physical therapist **terapista física**
physician **médico**
pilot **piloto, aviador**
plumber **plomero**
policeman **policía**
printer **impresor**
psychologist **psicólogo**
public relations agent **agente de relaciones públicas**
real estate agent **agente de bienes raíces**
receptionist **recepcionista**
reporter **reportero, periodista**
sailor **marinero**
salesman **vendedor**
scientist **científico**
seamstress **costurera, modista**

secretary **secretario**
social worker **trabajador social**
sociologist **sociólogo**
stenographer **estenógrafo**
stewardess **azafata**
stockbroker **bolsista**
supervisor **supervisor**
surgeon **cirujano**
systems analyst **analista de sistemas**
tailor **sastre**
taxi driver **chofer de taxi, conductor**
teacher **maestro** (*elem. school*), **profesor** (*high school and college*)
technician **técnico**
telephone operator **telefonista**
therapist **terapista**
television and radio technician **técnico de radio y televisión**
television and radio announcer **locutor**
teller **cajero**
travel agent **agente de viajes**
traveling salesman **viajante de comercio**
truck driver **camionero**
typist **mecanógrafa, dactilógrafa**
undertaker **director de pompas fúnebres**
veterinarian **veterinario**
waiter **mozo, camarero**
waitress **camarera**
watchmaker **relojero**
watchman **sereno, guardián**
worker **obrero**

# Appendix E: Answer Key to Self-Testing Sections

## Lesson 1

A. 1. nosotros  2. ellos  3. ustedes  4. ellas  5. nosotras

B. 1. Yo hablo español.  2. Nosotros hablamos español.
3. Nosotros hablamos inglés.  4. Tú hablas inglés.  5. Tú
trabajas en Lima.  6. Ellos trabajan en Lima.  7. Usted trabaja
en Lima.  8. Usted estudia en Lima.  9. Yo estudio en Lima.
10. Yo necesito dinero.  11. Él necesita dinero.  12. Nosotros
necesitamos dinero.

C. *Interrogative:*  1. ¿Trabaja Elena en Buenos Aires?
2. ¿Hablan ustedes inglés?  3. ¿Necesitas dinero tú?
4. ¿Juan y María estudian español?  5. ¿Trabaja usted en Los
Ángeles?

   *Negative:*  1. Elena no trabaja en Buenos Aires.  2. Ustedes
no hablan inglés.  3. Tú no necesitas dinero.  4. Juan y María
no estudian español.  5. Ud. no trabaja en Los Ángeles.

D. *Masculine:*  1. programa  2. telegrama  3. señor  4. teléfono
5. libro  6. día  7. sistema  8. dinero  9. problema
10. idioma  11. número  12. tema

   *Feminine:*  1. televisión  2. señora  3. banana  4. mano
5. silla  6. casa  7. mesa  8. libertad  9. lección
10. ciudad  11. calle  12. nacionalidad

E. 1. sesenta y seis  2. trece  3. noventa y uno  4. setenta y
tres  5. diez y nueve  6. ciento cincuenta

## Lesson 2

A. 1. las casas verdes  2. los lápices negros  3. los profesores
inteligentes  4. las sillas grandes  5. los libros blancos  6. las
señoritas felices

B. 1. ¿Dónde vive usted, Sra. Vera?  2. Ellos beben café. Yo
bebo té.  3. Nosotros leemos las lecciones.  4. Él decide

estudiar inglés.   5. ¿Comprendes?   6. Ustedes comen
temprano.   7. Ella escribe en español.   8. Nosotros abrimos
los libros.   9. Yo aprendo español.   10. Ellos no reciben el
dinero.

C.   1. ___   2. a   3. ___   4. a   5. a

# Lesson 3

A.   1. Nosotros recibimos el dinero de Carlos.   2. Ella lee la
lección de la profesora.   3. Los estudiantes visitan a la esposa
de Enrique.   4. ¿Tú esperas a la profesora de Teresa?   5. Ud.
no necesita la silla de María.

B.   1. tu   2. sus   de ella   3. nuestro   4. su   de usted   5. mis
6. tus   7. nuestras   8. su   de él

C.   1. un   2. una   3. unas   4. un   5. una   6. unos   7. unas
8. un   9. un   10. una

D.   1. Sí, yo soy alto(a).   2. Sí, yo soy de California.   3. Sí, somos
felices.   4. Sí, usted es (el)/(la) profesor(a).   5. Sí, mi lección
de español es difícil.   6. Sí, ellos son de México.

E.   1. Ellos dan su número de teléfono. Nosotros damos nuestro
número de teléfono. Tú das tu número de teléfono. Uds. dan su
número de teléfono. Ella da su número de teléfono.
2. Yo estoy en mi casa. Ellos están en su casa. Nosotros
estamos en nuestra casa. Ella está en su casa. Tú estás en tu
casa. Uds. están en su casa.
3. Nosotros vamos a nuestras clases. Ud. va a sus clases. Tú vas
a tus clases. Yo voy a mis clases. Ellos van a sus clases.

# Lesson 4

A.   1. La botella es de plástico.   2. La señorita López está
enferma.   3. Las casas son de Jorge.   4. Los estudiantes son
mexicanos.   5. El profesor está en el hospital.   6. Yo soy de
Arizona.   7. Nosotros estamos bien.   8. María es alta.
9. Gustavo y yo somos casados.   10. Mañana es sábado.
11. Yo estoy en la calle Universidad.   12. El hijo de la señora
Nieto es ingeniero.

B.   1. Esperamos al señor Peña.   2. Ella visita al señor Linares y a la señora Viera.   3. El dinero es del señor Díaz.   4. Él va al hospital.   5. Necesitamos el número de teléfono del doctor Mena.

C.   1. No, yo no soy tan alto(a) como el profesor (la profesora). 2. No, el profesor no llega más tarde que los estudiantes. 3. No, yo no soy el (la) estudiante menos inteligente de la clase.   4. No, yo no soy la persona más feliz de la clase. 5. No, yo no soy el (la) peor estudiante.   6. No, nosotros no somos mayores que nuestros amigos.   7. No, usted no es el (la) mejor de la clase.   8. No, la casa de mi amigo no es más grande que mi casa.

D.   1. Nosotros venimos con nuestro hijo. Tú vienes con tu hijo. Ellos vienen con su hijo. Ud. viene con su hijo. Uds. vienen con su hijo. Él viene con su hijo. 2. Yo tengo mis libros. Ella tiene sus libros. Tú tienes tus libros. Uds. tienen sus libros. Ud. tiene sus libros.

E.   1. quinientos   2. mil   3. quinientos cincuenta   4. doscientos 5. novecientos   6. cuatrocientos cincuenta

# Lesson 5

A.   1. Carlos tiene miedo.   2. Él tiene frío.   3. Yo tengo prisa. 4. Ellas tienen calor.   5. Ud. tiene sueño.   6. Tú tienes sed. 7. Nélida tiene cuatro años.

B.   (*Possibilities*):   1. Mi clase de español es a las ocho de la mañana.   2. Nosotros comemos a las doce.   3. Yo voy a la universidad a las siete de la mañana.   4. Yo estudio por la noche.   5. El profesor llega a clase a las ocho menos cinco.

C.   (*Possibilities*):   1. Nosotros preferimos estudiar francés. 2. No, no quiero ir al cine hoy.   3. La clase de español empieza a las once de la mañana.   4. Sí, nosotros entendemos las lecciones.   5. No, nosotros no perdemos mucho dinero en Las Vegas.   6. Cierran la biblioteca a las diez de la noche. 7. Mi programa de televisión favorito comienza a las ocho de la noche.

D.   1. vamos a comer   2. va a comprar   3. va a empezar   4. vas a visitar   5. va a llegar   6. voy a venir   7. vamos a necesitar 8. van a ir

E.   1. ¿Cuántos estudiantes hay?   2. No hay dinero.   3. Hay dos vuelos para Lima.   4. Hay una reunión hoy.   5. ¿Cuántas sillas hay?

## Lesson 6

A.   1. Hoy es miércoles.   2. Las mujeres quieren igualdad con los hombres.   3. La libertad es importante.   4. Nosotros vamos a estudiar la semana próxima.   5. Yo no tengo clases los viernes.

B.   (*Possibilities*):   1. Yo vuelvo a mi casa a las cinco y media. 2. Cuando nosotros vamos a México, volamos.   3. Sí, nosotros recordamos los verbos irregulares.   4. Yo duermo ocho horas. 5. No, nosotros no podemos ir al cine hoy.

C.   1. Ellos recuerdan algo.   2. Hay alguien en el cine.   3. Yo quiero volar también.   4. Recibimos algunos regalos. 5. Siempre tiene éxito.

D.   cinco: quinto   ocho: octavo   diez: décimo   uno: primero   tres: tercero   nueve: noveno   dos: segundo   seis: sexto   cuatro: cuarto   siete: séptimo

E.   1. Para tener éxito, hay que trabajar.   2. Ud. tiene que volver la semana próxima, señor Vega.   3. Ella tiene que trabajar mañana.   4. Hay que comenzar temprano.   5. ¿Tenemos que empezar a los ocho?

## Lesson 7

A.   (*Possibilities*):   1. Nosotros servimos sopa.   2. Yo pido Coca-Cola para beber.   3. No, yo no digo mi edad.   4. Sí, yo sigo en la clase de español.   5. Sí, nosotros siempre pedimos postre.

B.   1. conduzco   2. salgo   3. pongo   4. traduzco   5. conozco 6. quepo   7. hago   8. veo   9. sé   10. traigo

C.   1. Yo conozco a su hijo.   2. Él no sabe francés.   3. ¿Sabe usted nadar, señorita Vera?   4. ¿Conoce usted al embajador? 5. ¿Conocen los estudiantes las novelas de Cervantes?

D. 1. Yo las conozco. 2. Uds. van a comprarlo. 3. Nosotros no queremos verte. 4. Ella la sirve. 5. ¿Ud. no me conoce? 6. Él los escribe. 7. Carlos va a traernos. 8. Nosotros no lo vemos.

E. 1. felizmente 2. especialmente 3. rápidamente 4. fácilmente 5. lenta y cuidadosamente

## Lesson 8

A. 1. Necesito estas revistas y aquéllas. 2. ¿Quiere usted este cuaderno o ése? 3. Yo prefiero estos periódicos, no aquéllos. 4. ¿Quiere usted comprar esta corbata o ésa? 5. No quiero comer en este restaurante. Prefiero aquél. 6. Yo no entiendo eso.

B. 1. está estudiando 2. está comiendo 3. estamos leyendo 4. estás diciendo 5. estoy comprando

C. 1. Me va a comprar los pasajes. 2. Le doy las revistas. 3. Nos habla en español. 4. Les voy a decir la verdad. 5. Les pregunto la dirección de la oficina. 6. Le estamos escribiendo a nuestro profesor. 7. Le escribo los lunes. 8. Le doy la información al señor Vera. 9. Te hablo en inglés. 10. No me compran nada.

D. 1. ¿El dinero? Se lo doy mañana, señor Peña. 2. Ya sé que necesitas un diccionario, Anita, pero no puedo prestártelo. 3. Necesito mi abrigo. ¿Puede traérmelo, señorita López? 4. ¿Las plumas? Ella nos las trae. 5. Cuando yo necesito zapatos nuevos, mi mamá me los compra.

E. 1. Voy a preguntarle dónde vive. 2. Yo siempre le pido dinero a mi esposo. 3. Ella siempre pregunta cómo está usted, señora Nieto. 4. Me van a pedir los libros de química. 5. No vamos a preguntarle nada, señor.

## Lesson 9

A. 1. No, no son mías. 2. No, no son de ella. 3. No, no es mío. 4. No, no es nuestra. 5. No, no es de ellos. 6. No, no son míos. 7. No, no es nuestro. 8. No, no es de ustedes.

B. 1. Yo me levanto a las siete, me baño, me visto y salgo a las siete y media. 2. ¿A qué hora se despiertan los niños? 3. Ella no quiere sentarse. 4. Ud. siempre se preocupa por su hijo, señora Cruz. 5. ¿Te acuerdas de tus maestros, Carlitos? 6. Siempre se están quejando. 7. Primero ella acuesta a los niños. Ella se acuesta a las diez. 8. ¿Quiere probarse este abrigo, señorita? 9. ¿Dónde ponen ustedes el dinero, señoras? 10. Los estudiantes siempre se duermen en esta clase.

C. 1. Abra 2. Hablen 3. Traiga 4. Vengan 5. Cierre 6. Doblen 7. Siga 8. Den 9. Estén 10. Sean 11. Vaya 12. Vuelva 13. Sirva 14. Pongan 15. Escriban

D. 1. Dígales que sí, señor Mena. 2. ¿El postre? No me lo traiga ahora, señorita Ruiz. 3. No se lo diga a Ana, por favor. 4. Traigan las sillas, señores. Tráiganlas a la terraza. 5. No se levante, señora Miño. 6. ¿El té? Tráigaselo a las cuatro de la tarde, señor Vargas.

# Lesson 10

A. 1. Ayer ella entró en la cafetería y comió una ensalada. 2. Ayer María le escribió a Pedro. 3. Anoche ella me prestó su bicicleta. 4. El año pasado ellos fueron los mejores estudiantes. 5. El sábado pasado ellos te esperaron cerca del cine. 6. El verano pasado mis hermanos fueron a Buenos Aires. 7. Ayer le di el dinero. 8. El lunes pasado nosotros decidimos comprar la bicicleta. 9. Anoche le pregunté la hora. 10. Ayer tú no entendiste la lección. 11. El jueves pasado fuimos los primeros. 12. Ayer me dieron muchos problemas. 13. Anoche Marta no bebió café. 14. El miércoles pasado yo no fui a la clase. 15. Ayer por la mañana te dimos té.

B. 1. Sí, acabamos de comer. 2. Sí, acaba de levantarse. 3. Sí, acabo de hablar con ella. 4. Sí, acaban de comprarla. 5. Sí, acabo de bañarme. 6. Sí, acaban de llegar.

C. 1. ¡Ah, sí! Es altísimo. 2. ¡Ah, sí! Estamos ocupadísimas. 3. ¡Ah, sí! Son lentísimos. 4. ¡Ah, sí! Es buenísima. 5. ¡Ah, sí! Es dificilísima. 6. ¡Ah, sí! Es bellísima. 7. ¡Ah, sí! Es facilísimo. 8. ¡Ah, sí! Estoy ocupadísimo.

D. 1. Hace mucho frío. 2. Hace viento. 3. Llueve. 4. Hace mucho calor. 5. Nieva. 6. Hace sol.

## Lesson 11

A. 1. (a) ¿Cuánto tiempo hace que trabaja en Lima? (b) ¿Cuánto tiempo lleva trabajando en Lima? 2. (a) Hace cinco años que trabajamos en Lima. (b) Llevamos cinco años trabajando en Lima. 3. (a) ¿Cuánto tiempo hace que esperan? (b) ¿Cuánto tiempo llevan esperando? 4. (a) Hace tres horas que esperan. (b) Llevan tres horas esperando. 5. (a) ¿Cuánto tiempo hace que estudia español? (b) ¿Cuánto tiempo lleva estudiando español? 6. (a) Hace dos años que ella estudia español. (b) Ella lleva dos años estudiando español.

B. 1. Ayer María estuvo muy ocupada. 2. Anoche no pudieron venir. 3. La semana pasada puse el dinero en el banco. 4. El domingo pasado no hiciste nada. 5. Ayer ella vino con Juan. 6. La semana pasada no quisimos venir a clase. 7. Anoche yo no dije nada. 8. Ayer trajimos la máquina de escribir. 9. Anoche yo conduje mi coche. 10. Ayer ellos tradujeron las lecciones.

C. 1. ¿De quién es ese paraguas? 2. ¿De quiénes son esos revólveres? 3. ¿De quién son estos zapatos? 4. ¿De quién es este dinero? 5. ¿De quién es aquella silla?

D. 1. Vivíamos en Alaska. 2. Hablaba inglés. 3. Veía a mi abuela. 4. Depositábamos el dinero en el Banco de América. 5. Se acostaban a las nueve. 6. Iba al cine. 7. Compraba café. 8. Gastábamos nuestro dinero en libros.

## Lesson 12

A. 1. estábamos comiendo 2. estaban haciendo 3. estaba escribiendo 4. estaba hablando 5. estabas pensando 6. estaba leyendo 7. estaban estudiando 8. estaba trabajando

B. 1. Nos acostamos a las once anoche. 2. Ella estaba muy ocupada cuando la vi. 3. Íbamos a Buenos Aires. 4. Eran las diez y media cuando lo llamé. 5. Ella dijo que quería leer.

C. 1. Nosotros llegamos al aeorpuerto a las seis y media. 2. Mi hermana está en casa. 3. Ellos están en la esquina de Unión y Figueroa. 4. El accidente fue a las doce. 5. Yo estuve en la estación de policía ayer.

D.  1. conocía   conocí   2. sabíamos   supimos   3. podía
    4. pudieron   5. quiso (pudo)   6. quería   supe

# Lesson 13

A.  1. Ayer él sintió mucho calor.   2. Anoche Marta no durmió
    bien.   3. Ayer no le pedí nada.   4. La semana pasada ella te
    mintió.   5. El sábado pasado ellos sirvieron los refrescos.
    6. Ayer no lo repetí.   7. Anoche ella siguió estudiando.   8. El
    lunes pasado tú no conseguiste nada.

B.  1. El ladrón entró por la ventana.   2. Ella pasó por mi casa.
    3. No pudo venir por la lluvia.   4. Hay vuelos para México los
    sábados.   5. Vamos por avión.   6. Él necesita la camisa para
    mañana.   7. Iba a noventa millas por hora.   8. ¿Para quién es
    el periódico?   9. Necesito el dinero para pagar la cuenta.
    10. Ella pagó doscientos dólares por ese vestido.

C.  1. me gustan   2. le hace falta   3. le duele   4. nos hace falta
    5. le gusta   6. Me hacen falta   7. Me duele   8. le (te) gusta

D.  1. ¿Puede venir conmigo?   2. ¿Va a trabajar con ellos?   3. ¿A
    quién le dio las toallas? ¿A usted?   4. El regalo no es para mí.
    Es para ella.   5. No, Carlitos. No puedo ir contigo.

# Lesson 14

A.  1. ¿Qué es la libertad?   2. ¿Qué está haciendo usted aquí?
    3. ¿Qué piensa el profesor de él?   4. ¿Cuál es su número de
    teléfono?   5. ¿Cuáles son sus ideas acerca de esto?

B.  1. (a) Hace tres meses que nosotros llegamos a California. (b)
    Nosotros llegamos a California hace tres meses.   2. (a) Hace
    doce horas que Ud. comió. (b) Ud. comió hace doce horas.
    3. (a) Hace dos días que ellos terminaron el trabajo. (b) Ellos
    terminaron el trabajo hace dos días.   4. (a) Hace veinte años
    que ella lo vio. (b) Ella lo vio hace veinte años.   5. (a) Hace
    quince días que tú viniste a esta ciudad. (b) Tú viniste a esta
    ciudad hace quince días.

C.  1. Hacía diez horas que yo no comía.   2. Hacía media hora que
    lo esperábamos.   3. Hacía dos meses que yo estudiaba es-
    pañol.   4. Hacía cuatro años que ella no bebía.   5. Hacía quince
    años que nosotros trabajábamos para el gobierno.

D.  1. Ana está en la escuela.  2. Ella se lava las manos.  3. Tú te quitas el abrigo.  4. Mamá va a la iglesia los domingos. 5. Felipe está en la cárcel.  6. Nosotros visitamos a la señorita García.

E.  2. recibido  3. volver  4. hablado  5. escrito  6. ir 7. aprendido  8. abrir  9. cubierto  10. comido  11. ver 12. hecho  13. sido  14. decir  15. cerrado  16. morir 17. romper  18. dormido  19. estado  20. poner

## Lesson 15

A.  1. he venido  2. han terminado  3. hemos hablado  4. han dicho  5. has escrito  6. hemos hecho  hemos tenido  7. ha abierto  8. ha puesto

B.  1. Yo ya había traído las sábanas.  2. Nosotros le habíamos escrito sobre nuestros experimentos con plantas tropicales. 3. Ellos habían roto los lápices.  4. Él ya había visto al administrador.  5. ¿Había cubierto usted las mesas, señorita Peña?

C.  1. El artículo está escrito.  2. Éstas son las sillas rotas.  3. La puerta está abierta.  4. ¿Están cerrados los libros?  5. El trabajo está terminado.

D.  1. arbolito  2. hermanita  Teresita  3. vestidito  hijita 4. Juancito  5. cochecito

## Lesson 16

A.  1. El tema de la conferencia será "la civilización y la cultura de México."  2. Los análisis estarán listos la semana que viene.  3. Nosotros aprenderemos el español.  4. Iremos a Santiago el verano próximo.  5. Le diremos que sí.  6. No haré nada el domingo.  7. Sabremos el resultado el próximo mes.  8. El señor Reyes abrirá las puertas.  9. María y Carlos podrán venir.  10. Pondré el dinero en el banco. 11. Volveremos de México el sábado próximo.  12. Vendré a la reunión con la señorita Vargas.  13. Tendremos que estudiar para el examen.  14. Le daré las cartas mañana. 15. Saldremos con Raúl y Mario.

B.  1. iríamos  2. venderían  3. habría  4. serviría
5. trabajarías  6. pondría  7. preferirían  8. seguirían  9. te
levantarías  10. nos quejaríamos

C.  1. trabajemos  2. coma  3. escriban  4. vivas  5. diga
6. cierre  7. vengan  8. se levante  9. pida  10. hagan
11. traiga  12. recomiende  13. movamos  14. vaya  15. se
afeite  16. durmamos  17. dé  18. sepan (conozcan)
19. salga  20. tengas

## Lesson 17

A.  1. Ella quiere que yo traiga los paquetes.  2. Prefiero que
vayamos a su oficina, señorita Díaz.  3. ¿A qué hora quiere
que esté aquí mañana, Señor Acevedo?  4. Pídale que la
ayude, señora Portillo.  5. Dígales que no tengan miedo.
6. Que lo haga Roberto.  7. Que pasen (entren).  8. Ella
quiere que yo sea su amiga.  9. ¿Necesita que le den el dinero
hoy, señor Ortiz?  10. No quiero que hagas nada, Juancito.

B.  1. Espero que puedas cortarte el pelo esta tarde, Robertito.
2. Me alegro de que su mamá se sienta mejor, Sr. Gómez.
3. Temo que no podamos reunirnos la semana próxima,
señorita Herrero.  4. Nos alegramos de estar aquí hoy.
5. Ella espera salir mañana por la mañana.  6. Espero que
pueda venir a la reunión, señor Peña.  7. Tememos no poder
terminar el trabajo esta noche.  8. Siento que esté enferma,
señora Treviño.

C.  1. puedan  2. estudiar  3. escribir  4. terminaremos  5. esté
6. hacer  7. llegan  8. firmar

## Lesson 18

A.  1. Ellos pueden venir.  2. Pedro vaya con nosotros.  3. María
esté muy enferma.  4. una casa que quede cerca del centro
5. Sabe escribir a máquina.  6. Quieran hacer traducciones.
7. Él se levanta a las cuatro de la mañana.  8. Tiene seis
cuartos.

B.  1. Ven acá, por favor.  2. Habla con la maestra.  3. Dime tu
dirección.  4. Escribe la carta.  5. Ponte el abrigo.

6. Tráenos agua caliente. 7. Termina el trabajo. 8. Hazme el favor. 9. Apaga la luz. 10. Ve al centro. 11. Sal temprano. 12. Quédate afuera. 13. Ten paciencia. 14. Sé bueno. 15. Cena con nosotros.

C. 1. No se lo digas (a él). 2. No salgas ahora. 3. No te levantes. 4. No hagas las traducciones. 5. No bebas la limonada. 6. No lo rompas. 7. No les hables. 8. No vayas al centro. 9. ¿Ese vestido? ¡No te lo pongas! 10. No hagas eso.

## Lesson 19

A. 1. Le hablaré tan pronto como lo vea. 2. Quédese aquí en caso de que él llame, señorita González. 3. Él me escribió en cuanto llegó. 4. Vamos a esperar hasta que él venga. 5. No puedo ir sin que lo sepan mis padres. 6. Compraremos el coche cuando tengamos el dinero.

B. 1. haya visto 2. hayan hecho 3. hayas aprendido 4. hayan firmado 5. haya arreglado 6. hayamos archivado 7. haya vuelto 8. se haya acostado

C. 1. Ellos sienten que ustedes hayan estado enfermos. 2. Rosa no cree que yo lo haya hecho. 3. Nosotros tememos que él haya muerto. 4. No es verdad que nosotros hayamos escrito esa carta. 5. Ojalá que papá haya podido venir.

## Lesson 20

A. 1. asistiéramos 2. dejaras 3. se lavaran 4. recogiera 5. pudiera 6. trajera 7. devolvieran 8. tuviera

B. 1. Le pedí que viniera en seguida. 2. Me alegro de que pudieras terminarlo anoche. 3. No creí que ella lo hiciera. 4. No es verdad que mi hermano estuviera preso el año pasado. 5. Temíamos que ella no supiera escribir a máquina. 6. Dudo que la conferencia fuera el sábado pasado.

C. (*Possibilities*): 1. tuviera dinero 2. tenemos tiempo 3. estuviera enfermo 4. no llueve 5. pudieran 6. lo vemos 7. tuviera sueño 8. tenemos hambre

# Vocabulary

*Spanish — English*

## A

**a**   at, to
**a la derecha**   to the right
**a la izquierda**   to the left
**a menudo**   often
**¿a quién?**   to whom?
**a tiempo**   on time
**a veces**   sometimes
**abrigo** (*m.*)   coat
**abril**   April
**abrir**   to open
**abuela**   grandmother
**abuelo**   grandfather
**abuelos**   grandparents
**acabar de**   to have just
**accidente** (*m.*)   accident
**aconsejar**   to advise
**acordarse (o:ue)(de)**   to remember
**acostar(se) (o:ue)**   to put to bed, to go to bed
**adentro**   inside
**adiós**   good-bye
**administrador, -a** (*m.f.*)   administrator
**aeropuerto** (*m.*)   airport
**afuera**   outside
**agosto**   August
**agua** (*f.*)   water
**ahora**   now
**ahorrar**   to save (*money*)
**alcohólico, -a**   alcoholic
**alegrarse (de)**   to be glad
**alemán** (*m.*)   German (*language*)
**algo**   something
**alguien**   someone, somebody
**alguno, -a**   any, some
**alquilar**   to rent
**alto, -a**   tall
**allá**   over there
**amigo, -a** (*m.f.*)   friend
**análisis** (*m.*)   test
**anoche**   last night

**antes (de)**   before
**año** (*m.*)   year
**apagar**   to turn off
**apellido** (*m.*)   surname; —— **de soltera**   maiden name
**aprender**   to learn
**aquel(-los), aquella(-s)** (*adj.*)   that, those (*distant*)
**aquél(-los), aquélla(-s)** (*pron.*)   that (one), those (*distant*)
**aquello** (*neuter pron.*)   that
**aquí**   here
**árbol** (*m.*)   tree
**archivar**   to file
**archivo** (*m.*)   file
**argentino, -a** (*m.f.*)   Argentinian
**artículo** (*m.*)   article
**arreglar**   to fix, to repair
**arroz** (*m.*)   rice; —— **con pollo**   chicken and rice
**asamblea** (*f.*)   assembly
**asistir**   to attend
**aspirina** (*f.*)   aspirin
**atención** (*f.*)   attention
**auto** (*m.*)   auto, automobile
**autobús** (*m.*)   autobus, bus
**autopista** (*f.*)   freeway
**avenida** (*f.*)   avenue
**avión** (*m.*)   plane
**ayer**   yesterday
**ayudante** (*m.f.*)   assistant
**ayudar**   to help

## B

**banana** (*f.*)   banana
**banco** (*m.*)   bank
**bañar(se)**   to bathe
**barbero** (*m.*)   barber
**beber**   to drink
**bello, -a**   pretty
**biblioteca** (*f.*)   library

bicicleta (f.)  bicycle
bien  well, fine
blanco, -a  white
blusa (f.)  blouse
bonito, -a  pretty
botella (f.)  bottle
brazo (m.)  arm
buenas noches  good evening, good night
buenas tardes  good afternoon
bueno, -a  good, kind, nice
buenos días  good morning, good day
buscar  to look for

## C

caber  to fit
cabeza (f.)  head
caer  to fall
café (m.)  coffee
cafetería (f.)  cafeteria
caliente  hot
calle (f.)  street
cama (f.)  bed
caminar  to walk
camisa (f.)  shirt
cansado, -a  tired
cara (f.)  face
cárcel (f.)  jail
carne (f.)  meat
carro (m.)  car
carta (f.)  letter
casa (f.)  house
casado, -a  married
casi nunca  hardly ever
cenar  to have supper, to dine
centro (m.)  downtown (area)
cerca (de)  near, next to
cerrar (e:ie)  to close
cine (m.)  movie theater
ciudad (f.)  city
civilización (f.)  civilization
clase (f.)  class, kind, type
cliente (m.f.)  customer
coctel (m.)  cocktail
coche (m.)  car
comenzar (e:ie)  to begin
comer  to eat
comida (f.)  dinner, meal

¿cómo?  how?
comprar  to buy
comprender  to understand
con  with
¿con quien?  with whom?
concierto (m.)  concert
conducir  to drive
conferencia (f.)  lecture
conocer  to know, to be acquainted with
conseguir (e:i)  to obtain, to get
consulado (m.)  consulate
contador, -a (m.f.)  accountant
contrato (m.)  contract
conviene  it is advisable
copia (f.)  copy
corbata (f.)  tie
cortar  to cut
creer  to believe
cuaderno (m.)  notebook
¿cuál?  which?, what?
¿cuándo?  when?
¿cuántos?, -as  how many?
cuarto (m.)  room
cuarto, -a  fourth
cubrir  to cover
cuenta (f.)  bill
cuidadoso, -a  careful
cultura (f.)  culture

## CH

cheque (m.)  check
chica  girl
chico, -a (adj.)  little, small
chocar  to collide, to run into

## D

dar  to give
de  of, from
de nada  you're welcome
¿de quién?  whose?
deber  must
decidir  to decide
décimo, -a  tenth
decir (e:i)  to say, to tell
dejar  to leave (behind)
dentista (m.f.)  dentist
depositar  to deposit

desear  to wish, to want
despertar(se) (e:ie)  to wake up
después  afterwards, later
desvestir(se) (e:i)  to get undressed
devolver (o:ue)  to return
día (m.)  day
diccionario (m.)  dictionary
diciembre  December
difícil  difficult, unlikely
dinero (m.)  money
dirección (f.)  address
director, -a (m.f.)  director
divorciado, -a  divorced
doblar  to turn
doctor, -a (m.f.)  doctor
documento (m.)  document
dólar (m.)  dollar
doler (o:ue)  to hurt, to ache
dolor (m.)  pain
domicilio (m.)  address
domingo  Sunday
¿dónde?  where?
dormir(se) (o:ue)  to sleep, to fall
  asleep
dormitorio (m.)  bedroom
dudar  to doubt

E

economía (f.)  economics
echar al correo  to mail
edad (f.)  age
edificio (m.)  building
él  he
ella  she
ellas (f.)  they
ellos (m.)  they
embajador, -a  ambassador
empezar (e:ie)  to begin
empleado, -a (m.f.)  employee
empleo (m.)  job
en  in, at, on
en casa  at home
en seguida  right away
encontrar (o:ue)  to find
enero  January
enfermero, -a (m.f.)  nurse
enfermo, -a  sick
ensalada (f.)  salad
entender (e:ie)  to understand

entrar  to enter
escribir  to write; —— a máquina
  to type
escritorio (m.)  desk
escuela (f.)  school
ese (-os), esa (-as) (adj.)  that, those
  (nearby)
ése (-os), ésa (-as) (pron.)  that (one),
  those (nearby)
eso (neuter pron.)  that
español, -a (m.f.)  Spanish also adj;
español (m.)  Spanish (language)
especial  special
esperar  to wait, to hope, to wait for
esquina (f.)  corner
estación (f.)  station; —— de servicio (f.)  service station
estado civil  marital status
estar  to be; —— listo, -a  to be
  ready; —— preso, -a  to be in jail
este (-os), esta (-as) (adj.)  this, these
éste (-os), ésta (-as) (pron.)  this
  (one), these, the latter
esto (neuter pron.)  this
estómago (m.)  stomach
estudiante (m.f.)  student
estudiar  to study
examen (m.)  exam
experimento (m.)  experiment

F

fácil  easy
fantástico, -a  fantastic
favor (m.)  favor
favorito, -a  favorite
febrero  February
fecha (f.)  date; —— de nacimiento
  date of birth
feliz  happy
femenino, -a  feminine
fichero (m.)  file
fiesta (f.)  party
firmar  to sign
físico, -a  physical
francés (m.)  French (language)

G

gastar  to spend (money)
generoso, -a  generous

**geografía** (*f.*)   geography
**gerente** (*m.f.*)   manager
**gobierno** (*m.*)   government
**gracias**   thanks
**grande**   big, large
**gustar**   to please, to be pleasing

### H

**hablar**   to speak
**hacer**   to do, to make; —— **calor**   to be hot; —— **falta**   to need; —— **frío**   to be cold; —— **sol**   to be sunny; —— **viento**   to be windy
**hasta**   until
**hasta luego**   I'll see you later
**hasta mañana**   see you tomorrow
**hay que . . .**   one must . . .
**hermana**   sister
**hermano**   brother
**hija**   daughter
**hijo**   son
**historia** (*f.*)   history
**hombre**   man
**horrible**   horrible
**hospital** (*m.*)   hospital
**hotel** (*m.*)   hotel
**hoy**   today

### I

**idea** (*f.*)   idea
**idioma** (*m.*)   language
**iglesia** (*f.*)   church
**impaciente**   impatient
**impermeable** (*m.*)   raincoat
**importante**   important
**inflación** (*f.*)   inflation
**información** (*f.*)   information
**informe** (*m.*)   report
**ingeniero** (*m.*)   engineer
**inglés** (*m.*)   English (*language*)
**inspector, -a** (*m.f.*)   inspector
**instructor, -a** (*m.f.*)   instructor
**instrumento** (*m.*)   instrument
**inteligente**   intelligent
**invierno** (*m.*)   winter
**ir**   to go
**irse**   to leave, to go away

### J

**jabón** (*m.*)   soap
**jamás**   never
**jefe, -a** (*m.f.*)   boss, chief
**jueves**   Thursday
**jugar**   to play (*a game*)
**julio**   July
**junio**   June
**juntos, -as**   together

### L

**la** (*pl.* **las**)   the (*f.*)
**la** (*dir. obj. pron.*)   her, it (*f.*), you (*formal f.*)
**laboratorio** (*m.*)   laboratory
**ladrón, -ona** (*m.f.*)   thief
**lápiz** (*m.*)   pencil
**las** (*dir. obj. pron.*)   them (*f.*), you (*formal f.*)
**lavar(se)**   to wash (oneself)
**le** (*ind. obj. pron.*)   to him, her, it, you (*formal m.f.*)
**lección** (*f.*)   lesson
**leer**   to read
**lento, -a**   slow
**les** (*ind. obj. pron.*)   to them, you (*formal, pl. m.f.*)
**levantar(se)**   to lift, to raise, to get up
**libertad** (*f.*)   liberty
**libro** (*m.*)   book
**licencia** (*f.*)   license
**límite** (*m.*)   limit
**limonada** (*f.*)   lemonade
**lo** (*dir. obj. pron.*)   him, it, (*m.*), you (*formal m.*)
**lo siento**   I'm sorry
**los** (*dir. obj. pron.*)   them, you (*m. pl.*)
**lugar** (*m.*)   place
**lunes**   Monday
**luz** (*f.*)   light

### LL

**llamar**   to call
**llegar**   to arrive
**llevar**   to take, to carry
**llover (o:ue)**   to rain
**lluvia** (*f.*)   rain

## M

**madre**  mother
**maestro, -a**  teacher
**mal**  badly
**maleta** (*f.*)  suitcase
**malo, -a**  bad
**mano** (*f.*)  hand
**mañana** (*f.*)  morning
**mañana**  tomorrow
**máquina de escribir** (*f.*)  typewriter
**martes**  Tuesday
**marzo**  March
**más**  more, most
**matar**  to kill
**matemáticas** (*f.*)  mathematics
**matrícula** (*f.*)  registration
**mayo**  May
**mayor**  older, oldest
**me** (*obj. pron.*)  me, to me, (to) myself
**mecánico** (*m.f.*)  mechanic
**media hora**  half an hour
**medianoche** (*f.*)  midnight
**medicina** (*f.*)  medicine
**médico** (*m.f.*)  medical doctor
**medir** (e:i)  to measure, to be . . . tall
**mejor**  better, best
**mejorar**  to improve
**menor**  younger, youngest
**menos**  less, least, fewer
**mentir** (e:ie)  to lie
**mes** (*m.*)  month
**mesa** (*f.*)  table
**mi** (*adj.*)  my
**mí** (*obj. of prep.*)  me
**miércoles**  Wednesday
**milla** (*f.*)  mile
**millón** (*m.*)  million
**mineral** (*m.*)  mineral
**mío, -a** (*adj.*)  my, of mine
**mío, -a** (*pron.*)  mine
**modelo** (*m.*)  model
**momento** (*m.*)  moment
**morir** (o:ue)  to die
**mover** (o:ue)  to move
**muchacha**  girl, young woman
**muchacho**  boy, young man
**muchas gracias**  thank you very much

**mucho, -a** (**-os, -as**)  much (many); very
**mucho** (*adv.*)  (very) much, a great deal, a lot
**mucho gusto**  how do you do, much pleasure
**muebles** (*m.*)  furniture
**muela** (*f.*)  tooth, molar
**mujer** (*f.*)  woman
**museo** (*m.*)  museum
**muy**  very

## N

**nacimiento** (*m.*)  birth
**nacionalidad** (*f.*)  nationality
**nada**  nothing
**nadar**  to swim
**nadie**  nobody, no one
**necesitar**  to need
**negocios** (*m.*)  business
**negro, -a**  black
**nevar** (e:ie)  to snow
**ni**  neither, nor
**ninguno, -a**  no, none, not any
**niña**  girl, child
**niño**  boy, child
**no**  no, not
**noche** (*f.*)  evening, night
**nombre** (*m.*)  name
**norteamericano, -a**  North American
**nos** (*obj. pron.*)  us, to us, (to) ourselves
**nosotros, -as**  we, us
**novela** (*f.*)  novel
**noveno, -a**  ninth
**novia**  girl friend, bride
**noviembre**  November
**nuestro(-s), nuestra(-s)** (*adj.*)  our
**nuestro(-s), nuestra(-a)** (*pron.*)  ours
**número** (*m.*)  number
**nunca**  never

## O

**o**  or, either
**octavo, -a**  eight
**octubre**  October
**ocupación** (*f.*)  occupation
**ocupado, -a**  busy

oficina (f.)  office
oficina de correos (f.)  post office
ómnibus (m.)  omnibus
otoño (m.)  fall
otra vez  again

### P

paciencia (f.)  patience
paciente (m.f.)  patient
padres (m.)  parents
pagar  to pay
pantalones (m.)  trousers
paquete (m.)  package
para  to, for, by, in order
paraguas (m.)  umbrella
pariente (m.f.)  relative
parque (m.)  park
pasado, -a  last
pasaje (m.)  ticket
pasajero, -a (m.f.)  passenger
pasaporte (m.)  passport
pasar  to go by, to pass, to spend
  (time), to come in
pedir (e:i)  to ask for, to request, to
  order
pelo (m.)  hair
pensar (e:ie)  to think
peor  worse, worst
pequeño, -a  small, little
perder (e:ie)  to lose
perfume (m.)  perfume
periódico (m.)  newspaper
pero  but
perseguir (e:i)  persecute
personal (m.)  personnel
pescado (m.)  fish
piano (m.)  piano
pierna (f.)  leg
piso (m.)  floor, story
planta (f.)  plant
plástico, -a  plastic
playa (f.)  beach
plomero (m.)  plumber
pluma (f.)  pen
poco, -a  little (quantity)
pocos, -as  few
poder (o:ue)  to be able to
policía (f.)  police (organization)

policía (m.f.)  policeman, policewoman
pollo (m.)  chicken
poner(se)  to put, to put on
por  around, along, by, for, through
por favor  please
¿por qué?  why?
porque  because
posible  possible
postre (m.)  dessert
precio (m.)  price
preferir (e:ie)  to prefer
preguntar  to ask (a question)
preocupar(se)  to worry
presidente, -a (m.f.)  president
prestar  to lend
primavera (f.)  spring
primero, -a (m.f.)  first
primo, -a (m.f.)  cousin
probar(se) (o:ue)  to try, to taste, to
  try on
problema (m.)  problem
profesión (f.)  profession
profesor, -a (m.f.)  professor
programa (m.)  program
pronto  soon
próximo, -a  next
puerta (f.)  door
pues  well, then
puesto (m.)  position, job

### Q

¿qué?  what?
quedar(se)  to be located, to stay, to
  remain
quejarse  to complain
querer (e:ie)  to want, to wish
querido, -a  dear
¿quién?  who?, whom?
química (f.)  chemistry
quinto, -a  fifth

### R

radio (f.)  radio
rápido, -a  fast
recibir  to receive
reciente  recent
recoger  to pick up
recomendar (e:ie)  to recommend

recordar (o:ue)  to remember
refresco (m.)  soda
refrigerador (m.)  refrigerator
regalo (m.)  present, gift
restaurante (m.)  restaurant
resultado (m.)  result
reunión (f.)  meeting
revisar  to check
revista (f.)  magazine
revólver (m.)  revolver
rojo, -a  red
romper  to break

S

sábado  Saturday
sábana (f.)  sheet
saber  to know, to know how
sacar  to take out; —— copia  to photocopy
salir  to go out
se (reflex.)  (to) himself, herself, etc.
secretario, -a (m.f.)  secretary
seguir (e:i)  to follow, to continue; —— derecho  to continue straight ahead
segundo, -a  second
seguro, -a  sure, certain
seguro social (m.)  social security
semana (f.)  week
sentar(se) (e:ie)  to sit, to sit down
sentir (e:ie)  to regret
sentir(se) (e:ie)  to feel
señor (abr. Sr.)  Mister, sir, gentleman
señora (abr. Sra.)  Mrs., Madam, lady
señorita (abr. Srta.)  Miss, young lady
separado, -a  separated
septiembre  September
séptimo, -a  seventh
ser  to be
servir (e:i)  to serve
sí  yes
siempre  always
silla (f.)  chair
sin falta  without fail
sistema (m.)  system
sexo (m.)  sex

sexto, -a  sixth
sobrevivir  to survive
sobrina  niece
sobrino  nephew
sofá (m.)  sofa
solicitud (f.)  application
solo, -a  alone
soltero, -a  single
sopa (f.)  soup
su  his, her, its, your (formal), their
suegra  mother-in-law
suegro  father-in-law
suéter (m.)  sweater
suicidarse  to commit suicide
suyo(-s), suya(-s) (pron.)  yours (formal) his, hers, theirs

T

talonario de cheques (m.)  checkbook
también  also, too
tampoco  neither
tan  so
tarde (f.)  afternoon
tarde  late
tarea (f.)  homework
te (pron.)  you (fam.), to you, (to) yourself
té (m.)  tea
teatro (m.)  theater
teléfono (m.)  telephone
telegrama (m.)  telegram
televisión (f.)  television
tema (m.)  theme
temer  to fear
temperatura (f.)  temperature
tener  to have
tener . . . años  to be . . . years old; —— calor  to be warm; —— frío  to be cold; —— hambre  to be hungry; —— miedo  to be afraid; —— prisa  to be in a hurry; —— razón  to be right; —— sed  to be thirsty; —— sueño  to be sleepy
tener éxito  to succeed
tener que  to have to
tercero, -a  third

terminar  to finish
termómetro (m.)  thermometer
terraza (f.)  terrace
testamento (m.)  testament, will
tía  aunt
tienda (f.)  store
tintorería (f.)  cleaner
tío  uncle
toalla (f.)  towel
todavía  yet
todo, -a  all
tomar  to take, to drink
trabajar  to work
trabajo (m.)  work, job
traducción (f.)  translation
traducir  to translate
traer  to bring
traje (m.)  suit
tropical  tropical
tu  your (inf.)
tú  you (inf.)
tuyo(-s), tuya(-s) (adj.)  your (inf.) of
  yours
tuyo(-s), tuya(-s) (pron.)  yours (inf.
  sing.)

## U

universidad (f.)  university
usar  to use, to wear
usted (abr. Ud.)  you (form.)
ustedes (abr. Uds.)  you (pl.)

## V

vacaciones (f.)  vacation
vecino, -a (m.f.)  neighbor
velocidad (f.)  speed
vender  to sell
venir  to come
ventana (f.)  window
ver  to see
verano (m.)  summer
verdad (f.)  truth
verde  green
vestido (m.)  dress
vestir(se) (e:i)  to dress, to get
  dressed
vez (f.)  time
viajero, -a (m.f.)  traveller
vidrio (m.)  glass
viernes  Friday
visitar  to visit
viuda  widow
viudo  widower
vivir  to live
volar (o:ue)  to fly
volver (o:ue)  to come (go) back
vuelo (m.)  flight

## Y

y  and
yo  I

## Z

zapato (m.)  shoe

## English — Spanish

### A

**a** un(a)
**accident** accidente (*m.*)
**accountant** contador, -a (*m.f.*)
**ache** doler (o:ue)
**address** domicilio (*m.*)
**administrator** administrador, -a (*m.f.*)
**advise** aconsejar
**afternoon** tarde (*f.*)
**afterwards** después
**again** otra vez
**age** edad (*f.*)
**airport** aeropuerto (*m.*)
**alcoholic** alcohólico, -a (*m.f.*)
**all** todos, -as
**alone** solo, -a
**also** también
**always** siempre
**ambassador** embajador, -a (*m.f.*)
**and** y
**any** alguno, -a; cualquier, -a
**anyone** alguien
**application** solicitud (*f.*)
**April** abril
**Argentinian** argentino, -a
**arm** brazo (*m.*)
**around** alrededor (de), por
**arrange** arreglar
**arrive** llegar
**article** artículo (*m.*)
**ask (a question)** preguntar; —— **for** pedir (e:i)
**aspirin** aspirina (*f.*)
**assembly** asamblea (*f.*)
**assistant** ayudante (*m.f.*)
**at** en; a
**at home** en casa
**attend** asistir
**attention** atención (*f.*)
**August** agosto
**aunt** tía
**auto; automobile** auto (*m.*); automobile (*m.*); coche (*m.*), carro (*m.*)
**autobus** autobús (*m.*)
**avenue** avenida (*f.*)

### B

**bad(ly)** malo, -a (*adj.*); mal (*adv.*)
**banana** banana (*f.*)
**bank** banco (*m.*)
**barber** barbero, -a (*m.f.*)
**bathe** bañarse
**be** ser, estar; —— **able** poder (o:ue); —— **acquainted with** conocer; —— **advisable** convenir (e:ie); —— **glad** alegrarse (de); —— **ready** estar listo, -a; —— **cold** (*weather*) hacer frío; —— **hot** (*weather*) hacer calor; —— **windy** hacer viento; —— **sunny** hacer sol; —— **cold** tener frío; —— **thirsty** tener sed; —— **hungry** tener hambre; —— **hot** tener calor; —— **sleepy** tener sueño; —— **in a hurry** tener prisa; —— **afraid** tener miedo; —— **right** tener razón; —— **. . . years old** tener (cumplir) . . . años
**beach** playa (*f.*)
**because** porque
**bed** cama (*f.*)
**bedroom** dormitorio (*m.*)
**before** antes de
**begin** comenzar (e:ie); empezar (e:ie)
**believe** creer
**best** (el, la) mejor
**better** mejor
**bicycle** bicicleta (*f.*)
**big** grande
**bigger** más grande
**bill** cuenta (*f.*)
**birth** nacimiento (*m.*)
**black** negro, -a
**blouse** blusa (*f.*)
**book** libro (*m.*)
**boss** jefe, -a (*m.f.*)
**bottle** botella (*f.*)
**boy** niño, chico, muchacho
**break** romper
**bring** traer
**brother** hermano

**building** edificio (*m.*)
**bus** autobús (*m.*)
**business** negocios (*m.*)
**busy** ocupado, -a
**but** pero
**buy** comprar
**by** por; para

## C

**cafeteria** cafetería (*f.*)
**call** llamar
**car** carro (*m.*); coche (*m.*)
**careful** cuidadoso, -a
**certain** seguro, -a
**chair** silla (*f.*)
**check** cheque (*m.*)
**check** revisar (*verb*)
**checkbook** talonario de cheques (*m.*)
**chemistry** química (*f.*)
**chicken** pollo (*m.*)
**chicken and rice** arroz con pollo
**chief** jefe, -a (*m.f.*)
**child** niño, -a (*m.f.*)
**church** iglesia (*f.*)
**city** ciudad (*f.*)
**civilization** civilización (*f.*)
**class** clase (*f.*)
**cleaner** tintorería (*f.*)
**close** cerrar (e:ie)
**coat** abrigo (*m.*)
**cocktail** coctel (*m.*)
**coffee** café (*m.*)
**collide** chocar
**come** venir; —— **back** volver (o:ue); —— **in** entrar
**commit suicide** suicidarse
**complain** quejarse (de)
**concentration** concentración (*f.*)
**concert** concierto (*m.*)
**consulate** consulado (*m.*)
**continue** seguir (e:i); —— **straight ahead** seguir derecho
**contract** contrato (*m.*)
**copy** copia (*f.*)
**corner** esquina (*f.*)
**cousin** primo, -a (*m.f.*)
**cover** cubrir
**culture** cultura (*f.*)

**customer** cliente (*m.f.*)
**cut** cortar

## D

**date** fecha (*f.*)
**daughter** hija
**day** día (*m.*)
**dear** querido, -a
**December** diciembre
**decide** decidir
**dentist** dentista (*m.f.*)
**deposit** depositar
**desk** escritorio (*m.*)
**dessert** postre (*m.*)
**dictionary** diccionario (*m.*)
**die** morir (o:ue)
**difficult** difícil
**dine** cenar
**dinner** cena (*f.*)
**director** director, -a (*m.f.*)
**divorced** divorciado, -a
**do** hacer
**doctor** doctor, -a (*m.f.*)
**document** documento (*m.*)
**dollar** dólar (*m.*)
**door** puerta (*f.*)
**downtown** (*area*) centro (*m.*)
**dress** vestido (*m.*)
**dress** (*oneself*) vestir(se) (e:i)
**drink** tomar; beber
**drive** conducir

## E

**early** temprano
**easy** fácil
**eat** comer
**economics** economía (*f.*)
**eighth** octavo, -a
**either . . . or** o . . . o
**employee** empleado, -a (*m.f.*)
**end** terminar
**engineer** ingeniero, -a (*m.f.*)
**English** (*language*) inglés (*m.*)
**enter** entrar
**evening** noche (*f.*)
**exam** examen (*m.*)
**experiment** experimento (*m.*)

## F

**face**   cara (*f.*)
**fall**   otoño (*m.*)
**fall**   caer (*verb*)
**fall asleep**   dormirse (o:ue)
**fantastic**   fantástico, -a
**fast**   rápido, -a
**father**   padre
**father-in-law**   suegro
**favor**   favor (*m.*)
**favorite**   favorito, -a
**fear**   temer
**February**   febrero
**feel**   sentir(se) (e:ie)
**feminine**   femenino, -a
**few**   pocos, -as
**fewer**   menos
**file**   archivo (*m.*); fichero (*m.*)
**file**   archivar (*verb*)
**fifth**   quinto, -a
**find**   encontrar (o:ue)
**fine**   bien
**finish**   terminar
**first**   primero, -a
**fish**   pescado (*m.*)
**fit**   caber
**fix**   arreglar
**flight**   vuelo (*m.*)
**floor** (*story*)   piso (*m.*)
**fly**   volar (o:ue)
**follow**   seguir (e:i)
**for**   por; para
**for whom?**   ¿para quién?
**fourth**   cuarto, -a
**freeway**   autopista (*f.*)
**French** (*language*)   francés (*m.*)
**Friday**   viernes
**friend**   amigo, -a
**furniture** (*pieces of*)   muebles (*m.*)

## G

**generous**   generoso, -a
**geography**   geografía (*f.*)
**German** (*language*)   alemán (*m.*)
**get**   obtener; conseguir (e:i); —— **dressed**   vestirse (e:i); —— **un-dressed**   desvestirse (e:i); —— **up**   levantarse

**gift**   regalo (*m.*)
**girl**   niña, chica, muchacha
**girl friend**   novia
**give**   dar
**glass**   vidrio (*m.*)
**go**   ir; —— **to bed**   acostarse (o:ue); —— **away**   irse; —— **by**   pasar; —— **out**   salir
**good**   bueno, -a
**good afternoon**   buenas tardes
**good-bye**   adiós
**good day**   buenos días
**good evening**   buenas noches
**good morning**   buenos días
**good night**   buenas noches
**government**   gobierno (*m.*)
**grandfather**   abuelo
**grandmother**   abuela
**grandparents**   abuelos
**green**   verde

## H

**hair**   pelo (*m.*)
**half**   medio, -a
**hand**   mano (*f.*)
**happy**   feliz
**hardly ever**   casi nunca
**have**   tener; —— **just**   acabar de; —— **supper**   cenar; —— **to**   tener que
**he**   él
**head**   cabeza (*f.*)
**her**   su(s) (*adj.*); la (*dir. obj.*); le (*ind. obj.*)
**here**   aquí
**hers**   suyo, -a, suyos, -as; (el, la, los, las) de ella
**herself**   se
**help**   ayudar
**him**   lo (*dir. obj.*); le (*ind. obj.*)
**himself**   se
**his**   suyo, -a, suyos, -as; (el, la, los, las) de él
**his**   su(s) (*adj.*)
**history**   historia (*f.*)
**homework**   tarea (*f.*)
**hope**   esperar
**horrible**   horrible
**hospital**   hospital (*m.*)

hot   caliente
hotel   hotel (*m.*)
house   casa (*f.*)
how?   ¿cómo?
how do you do   mucho gusto
how many?   ¿cuántos?, -as
hurt   doler (o:ue)

### I

I   yo
idea   idea (*f.*)
impatient   impaciente
important   importante
improve   mejorar
in   en
information   información (*f.*)
inflation   inflación (*f.*)
inside   adentro
inspector   inspector, -a (*m.f.*)
instructor   instructor, -a (*m.f.*)
instrument   instrumento (*m.*)
intelligent   inteligente
it   lo (*m.*); la (*f.*)
its   su(s) (*adj.*)
itself   se

### J

jail   cárcel (*f.*)
January   enero
job   empleo (*m.*); puesto (*m.*)
July   julio
June   junio

### K

kill   matar
kind   clase (*f.*)
kind   bueno, -a (*adj.*)
know   conocer; saber

### L

laboratory   laboratorio (*m.*)
language   idioma (*m.*)
large   grande
last   pasado, -a
last night   anoche
late   tarde
later   después

learn   aprender
least   menos
leave   irse; dejar
lecture   conferencia (*f.*)
leg   pierna (*f.*)
lemonade   limonada (*f.*)
lend   prestar
less   menos
lesson   lección (*f.*)
letter   carta (*f.*)
liberty   libertad (*f.*)
library   biblioteca (*f.*)
license   licencia (*f.*)
lie   mentir (e:ie)
lift   levantar
light   luz (*f.*)
limit   límite (*m.*)
little   chico, -a (*size*); poco, -a (*quantity*)
live   vivir
look for   buscar
lose   perder (e:ie)

### M

magazine   revista (*f.*)
maiden name   apellido de soltera (*m.*)
mail   echar al correo
make   hacer
man   hombre
manager   gerente (*m.f.*)
many   muchos, -as
March   marzo
marital status   estado civil (*m.*)
married   casado, -a
masculine   masculino, -a (*m.f.*)
mathematics   matemáticas (*f.*)
May   mayo
me   me (*dir. and indir. obj.*)
meal   comida (*f.*)
measure   medir (e:i)
meat   carne (*f.*)
mechanic   mecánico (*m.f.*)
medical doctor   médico (*m.f.*)
medicine   medicina (*f.*)
meeting   reunión (*f.*)
midnight   medianoche (*f.*)
mile   milla (*f.*)
million   millón (*m.*)

**mine**   mío, -a, míos, -as (*pron.*)
**mineral**   mineral (*m.*)
**Miss; young lady**   señorita
**model**   modelo (*m.*)
**moment**   momento (*m.*)
**Monday**   lunes
**money**   dinero (*m.*)
**month**   mes (*m.*)
**more**   más
**morning**   mañana (*f.*)
**most**   más
**move**   mover (o:ue)
**movie** (*theater*)   cine (*m.*)
**mother**   madre
**mother-in-law**   suegra
**Mr., sir, gentleman**   señor
**Mrs., madam, lady**   señora
**much**   mucho, -a, muchos, -as, (*adj.*);
    mucho (*adv.*)
**museum**   museo (*m.*)
**must**   deber
**my**   mi(s) (*adj.*)
**myself**   me

### N

**name**   nombre (*m.*)
**nationality**   nacionalidad (*f.*)
**near**   cerca de
**need**   necesitar; hacerle falta a uno
**neighbor**   vecino, -a (*m.f.*)
**neither**   tampoco
**neither . . . nor**   ni . . . ni
**nephew**   sobrino
**never**   nunca; jamás
**newspaper**   periódico (*m.*)
**next**   próximo, -a
**next to**   cerca de
**nice**   bueno, -a
**niece**   sobrina
**night**   noche (*f.*)
**ninth**   noveno, -a
**no; not**   no
**no one**   nadie
**nobody**   nadie
**none**   ningún, ninguno, -a
**North American**   norteamericano, -a
**not any**   ningún, ninguno, -a
**notebook**   cuaderno (*m.*)
**nothing**   nada

**novel**   novela (*f.*)
**November**   noviembre
**now**   ahora
**number**   número (*m.*)
**nurse**   enfermero, -a (*m.f.*)

### O

**obtain**   conseguir (e:i)
**occupation**   ocupación (*f.*)
**October**   octubre
**of**   de
**office**   oficina (*f.*)
**often**   a menudo
**older**   mayor
**oldest**   (el, la) mayor
**omnibus**   ómnibus (*m.*)
**on**   en
**on time**   a tiempo
**open**   abrir
**or**   o
**order**   pedir (e:i)
**our**   nuestro, -a, nuestros, -as (*adj.*)
**ours**   nuestro, -a, nuestros, -as
    (*pron.*)
**ourselves**   nos
**outside**   afuera
**over there**   allá

### P

**package**   paquete (*m.*)
**pain**   dolor (*m.*)
**parents**   padres (*m.*)
**park**   parque (*m.*)
**party**   fiesta (*f.*)
**pass**   pasar
**passenger**   pasajero, -a (*m.f.*)
**passport**   pasaporte (*m.*)
**patience**   paciencia (*f.*)
**patient**   paciente (*m.f.*)
**pay**   pagar
**pen**   pluma (*f.*)
**pencil**   lápiz (*m.*)
**per**   por
**perfume**   perfume (*m.*)
**persecute**   perseguir (e:i)
**personnel**   personal (*m.*)
**photocopy**   sacar copia
**physical**   físico, -a

**piano**   piano (*m.*)
**pick up**   recoger
**place**   lugar (*m.*)
**place**   poner (*verb*)
**plane**   avión (*m.*)
**plant**   planta (*f.*)
**plastic**   plástico, -a
**play** (*a game*)   jugar
**please**   por favor
**plumber**   plomero, -a (*m.f.*)
**police** (*organization*)   policía (*f.*)
**policeman**   policía (*m.*)
**policewoman**   policía (*f.*)
**position**   puesto (*m.*)
**possible**   posible
**post office**   oficina de correos (*f.*)
**prefer**   preferir (e:ie)
**present**   regalo (*m.*)
**president**   presidente, -a (*m.f.*)
**pretty**   bello, -a; bonito, -a
**price**   precio (*m.*)
**problem**   problema (*m.*)
**program**   programa (*m.*)
**profession**   profesión (*f.*)
**professor**   profesor, -a (*m.f.*)
**put** (**on**)   poner; ponerse; —— **to
bed**   acostar (o:ue)

R

**radio**   radio (*f.*)
**rain**   llover (o:ue)
**rain**   lluvia (*f.*)
**raincoat**   impermeable (*m.*)
**raise**   levantar
**read**   leer
**receive**   recibir
**recent**   reciente
**recommend**   recomendar (e:ie)
**red**   rojo, -a
**refrigerator**   refrigerador (*m.*)
**registration**   matrícula (*f.*)
**regret**   sentir (e:ie)
**relative**   pariente (*m.f.*)
**remain**   quedarse
**remember**   acordarse (de) (o:ue);
recordar (o:ue)
**rent**   alquilar
**repair**   arreglar
**report**   informe (*m.*)

**request**   pedir (e:i)
**restaurant**   restaurante (*m.*)
**result**   resultado (*m.*)
**revolver**   revólver (*m.*)
**rice**   arroz (*m.*)
**right away**   en seguida
**room**   cuarto (*m.*)
**run into**   chocar

S

**salad**   ensalada (*f.*)
**Saturday**   sábado
**save** (*money*)   ahorrar
**say**   decir (e:i)
**school**   escuela (*f.*)
**second**   segundo, -a
**secretary**   secretario, -a (*m.f.*)
**see**   ver
**sell**   vender
**separated**   separado, -a
**September**   septiembre
**serve**   servir (e:i)
**service station**   estación de servicio
(*f.*)
**seventh**   séptimo, -a
**sex**   sexo (*m.*)
**she**   ella
**sheet**   sábana (*f.*)
**shirt**   camisa (*f.*)
**shoes**   zapatos (*m.*)
**sick**   enfermo, -a
**sign**   firmar
**single**   soltero, -a
**sister**   hermana
**sit**   sentarse (e:ie)
**sixth**   sexto, -a
**sleep**   dormir (o:ue)
**slow**   lento, -a
**small**   pequeño, -a; **smaller**   más
pequeño
**snow**   nevar (e:ie)
**so**   tan
**soap**   jabón (*m.*)
**social security**   seguro social (*m.*)
**soda**   refresco (*m.*)
**sofa**   sofá (*m.*)
**some**   algún, alguno, -a, algunos, -as
**someone**   alguien
**something**   algo

**sometimes**  a veces
**son**  hijo
**soon**  pronto
**sorry**  lo siento
**soup**  sopa (*f.*)
**Spanish** (*language*)  español (*m.*)
**Spanish** (*nationality*)  español, -a
**speak**  hablar
**special**  especial
**speed**  velocidad (*f.*)
**spend** (*time*) pasar; —— (*money*) gastar
**spring**  primavera (*f.*)
**station**  estación (*f.*)
**stay**  quedarse
**stomach**  estómago (*m.*)
**store**  tienda (*f.*)
**street**  calle (*f.*)
**student**  estudiante (*m.f.*)
**study**  estudiar
**succeed**  tener éxito
**suit**  traje (*m.*)
**suitcase**  maleta (*f.*)
**summer**  verano (*m.*)
**Sunday**  domingo
**sure**  seguro, -a
**surname**  apellido (*m.*)
**survive**  sobrevivir
**sweater**  suéter (*m.*)
**swim**  nadar
**system**  sistema (*m.*)


### T

**table**  mesa (*f.*)
**take**  tomar; llevar
**take out**  sacar
**tall**  alto, -a
**taste**  probar
**tea**  té (*m.*)
**teacher** (*elementary school*)  maestro, -a
**telegram**  telegrama (*m.*)
**telephone**  teléfono (*m.*)
**television**  televisión (*f.*)
**tell**  decir (e:i)
**temperature**  temperatura (*f.*)
**tenth**  décimo, -a
**terrace**  terraza (*f.*)

**test**  análisis (*m.*)
**testament**  testamento (*m.*)
**thanks**  gracias
**that** (*adj.*) (*near person addressed*) ese, esa (-os, -as); (*distant*) aquel, aquella (-os, -as); (*pron.*) ése, ésa (-os, -as), aquél, aquélla (-os, -as); (*neuter*) eso, aquello; (*relative pron.*) que, quien
**theater**  teatro (*m.*)
**their**  su(s) (*adj.*)
**theirs**  suyo, -a, suyos, -as (el, la, los, las), de ellos, de ellas
**them**  los, las (*dir. obj.*); les (*ind. obj.*)
**theme**  tema (*m.*)
**themselves**  se
**thermometer**  termómetro (*m.*)
**these** (*adj.*) estos, -as; (*pron.*) éstos, -as
**they**  ellos; ellas
**thief**  ladrón, -ona (*m.f.*)
**think**  pensar (e:ie)
**third**  tercero, -a
**this** (*adj.*) este, esta; (*pron.*) éste, ésta; (*neuter*) esto
**those** (*adj.*) (*near person addressed*) esos, esas; (*distant*) aquellos, aquellas; (*pron.*) ésos, -as, aquéllos, -as
**Thursday**  jueves
**ticket**  pasaje (*m.*)
**tie**  corbata (*f.*)
**time**  hora (*f.*); tiempo (*m.*); vez (*f.*)
**tired**  cansado, -a
**to**  para; a
**today**  hoy
**together**  juntos, -as
**tomorrow**  mañana
**too**  también
**tooth**  diente (*m.*); muela (*f.*)
**towel**  toalla (*f.*)
**translate**  traducir
**translation**  traducción (*f.*)
**traveller**  viajero, -a (*m.f.*)
**tree**  árbol (*m.*)
**tropical**  tropical
**trousers**  pantalones (*m.*)
**truth**  verdad (*f.*)
**try; try on**  probar(se) (o:ue)

**Tuesday**  martes
**turn**  doblar
**turn off**  apagar
**twenty**  veinte
**type**  clase (*f.*); tipo (*m.*)
**type**  escribir a máquina
**typewriter**  máquina de escribir (*f.*)

## U

**umbrella**  paraguas (*m.*)
**uncle**  tío (*m.*)
**understand**  comprender; entender (e:ie)
**university**  universidad (*f.*)
**unlikely**  difícil
**until**  hasta
**us**  nos (*dir. and ind. obj.*)
**use**  usar

## V

**vacation**  vacaciones (*f.*)
**very**  muy
**visit**  visitar

## W

**wait**  esperar
**wake up**  despertarse (e:ie)
**walk**  caminar
**want**  querer (e:ie)
**wash** (*oneself*)  lavar(se)
**water**  agua (*f.*)
**we**  nosotros, -as
**Wednesday**  miércoles
**week**  semana (*f.*)
**well**  bien, pues
**what?**  ¿qué?; ¿cuál?
**when?**  ¿cuándo?
**where?**  ¿dónde?
**which?**  ¿cuál?

**white**  blanco, -a
**who?**  ¿quién?; ¿quiénes?
**whom?**  ¿quién?; ¿a quién?
**whose?**  ¿de quién?
**widow**  viuda
**widower**  viudo
**window**  ventana (*f.*)
**winter**  invierno (*m.*)
**wish**  desear
**with**  con
**without**  sin
**without fail**  sin falta
**woman**  mujer
**work**  trabajo (*m.*)
**work**  trabajar (*verb*)
**worry**  preocupar(se)
**worse**  peor
**worst**  peor
**write**  escribir

## Y

**year**  año (*m.*)
**yes**  sí
**yesterday**  ayer
**yet**  todavía
**you**  (*fam. sing.*) tú; (*dir. and indir. obj.*) te
**you**  (*polite*) (*subj. pron.*) usted (Ud.), ustedes (Uds.); (*dir. obj.*) le, la, los, las; (*indir. obj.*) les, se
**younger**  menor
**youngest**  menor
**your**  (*adj.*) (*fam.*) tu(s); (*formal*) su(s), de Ud., de Uds.
**yours**  (*pron.*) (*fam.*) (el) tuyo, (la) tuya, (los) tuyos, (las) tuyas; (*formal*) (el) suyo, (la) suya, (los) suyos, (las) suyas; (el, la, los, las) de Ud., de Uds.
**yourself**  (*fam.*) te; (*formal*) se
**yourselves**  se

# INDEX

(References are to page numbers.)

**a:** + **el**, 33; for *at*, 122-123; personal, 21
**acabar de**, 100
adjectives: absolute superlative, 100-101; agreement of, 20; comparison of, 34-36; demonstrative, 76; forms of, 19; past participles used as, 144; position of, 19; possessive, 26
adverbs: comparison of, 34-36; formation of, 72
affirmative and negative expressions, 60-61
article, definite: agreement, 18, 20; contractions with **el**, 33; forms of, 18; uses of, 58, 138-139
article, indefinite: forms of, 27

cardinal numbers, 15, 38
cognates, study of, 15, 22, 30, 38, 47, 63, 73, 83, 94, 102, 117, 124, 133, 140, 145, 163, 170, 178, 183, 189
commands: direct, **Ud.** and **Uds.** forms, 90-91; familiar (**tú** form), 175-176; indirect or implied, 166; negative familiar, 176; object pronouns with, 92-93
comparison: of adjectives and adverbs, 34-36
conditional: forms of, 158; irregular forms, 159
**conocer**, uses of, 71
contractions: **a** + **el**, 33; **de** + **el**, 33
**cuál** for *what*, 136

**de:** + **el**, 33; possession with, 26
**¿de quién (es)** . . .? for *whose?*, 114
definite article, *see* article, definite
demonstrative: adjectives, 76; pronouns, 77
diminutives, 144-145
direct objects, *see* pronouns
**doler**, 131

**en** for *at*, 122
**estar:** present indicative of, 29; uses of, 32; with progressive tenses, 78, 120

future: irregular forms, 157; tense, 156

gender of nouns, 14
**gustar**, 130-131

**hacer:** in time expressions, 112, 137-138; meaning *ago*, 137
**hacer falta**, 131
**hay:** uses of, 46; hay que, 62

imperative, *see* commands
imperfect: contrasted with preterit, 120-122; indicative forms, 115; irregular forms, 116-117; subjunctive, 186-187; verbs with special meanings in, 123-124
indefinite article, *see* article, indefinite
indirect object, *see* pronouns
interrogative sentences, 12
**ir: a** + infinitive, 45

negation: double negatives, 61; simple, 13
nouns: agreement, 18, 20; gender of, 14; plural of, 18
numerals: cardinal, 15, 38; ordinal, 61-62

ordinal numbers, 61-62

**para,** uses of, 129–130
past participle: forms of, 139; in perfect tenses, 142-143; irregular forms, 139; used as adjectives, 144
**pedir**, use of, 82-83
personal **a**, 21
pluperfect: indicative, 143
plural: of adjectives, 20; of nouns, 18
**por**, uses of, 129
possession, 26
possessive adjectives, 26
possessive pronouns, 86-87
**preguntar**, use of, 82-83
present tense: indicative of regular verbs, 11, 20; indicative of stem-

changing verbs, 44, 59, 66; indicative of verbs irregular in first person singular, 67; perfect indicative, 142; perfect subjunctive, 181-182; subjunctive, 160-162

preterit: contrasted with imperfect, 120-122; irregular forms, 113-114, 128; of **ser, ir** and **dar**, 99; regular forms, 98; verbs with special meanings in, 123-124

progressive forms of tenses: 78, 120

pronouns: demonstrative, 77; direct object, 69-70; direct and indirect used together, 81; indirect object, 79-80; possessive pronouns, 86, 87; reflexive, 88; subject, 10; used as objects of prepositions, 132

reflexive constructions, 88, 89

reflexive pronouns, 88

**saber:** uses of, 71

**se**, impersonal, 68

**ser:** present indicative of, 28; uses of, 32

stem-changing verbs, 44, 59, 66, 128, 162

subject pronouns: omission of, 11; uses of, 10

subjunctive: after conjunctions that imply uncertainty or unfulfillment, 180, 181; after **sin que**, and **a menos que**, 181; forms in the present, 160-162; imperfect, 186-187; in formal commands, 90-91; in *if* clauses, 188; in indirect or implied commands, 166; omission of main clause, 166-167; present perfect, 181-182; to express doubt and unreality, 172-173; to express emotion, 167-168; to refer to someone or something that is indefinite, unspecified or non-existant, 173-174; with impersonal expressions, 168-169

superlative: absolute, 100-101; comparative, 35

**tener:** expressions with, 42

**tener que,** uses of, 62

tenses, *see* present, etc.

time: how to tell, 43

verbs: see each separately and tables in Appendix; stem-changing, 44, 59, 66, 128, 162; with irregular first person singular, 67; with special meanings in the preterit and the imperfect, 123-124; with special meanings in the reflexive, 89

weather expressions, 101-102